*IF YOU COULD ~~~~~~~~~~~
RE~~~~~~~ OF ANYTH~~~~
YOU WANTED, WHAT WOULD YOU CHAN~
OR IMPROVE?*

What would be different?
Are there dreams or hopes that have never found
their way into reality?

The central thesis of our work is this: to ensure a sense of intimacy and meaningful connection through life, cultivate the relationship that has been with you through life: your brother- or sisterhood. For while there is much that may have been ignored, or taken for granted, there is far more to be remembered, and much to be fulfilled as grown siblings. Reawakening this original support group, especially helpful as we age and experience multiple transitions in life, helps us access the kind of closeness we once took for granted in childhood . . . and provides a unique template for all other relationships of support. . . .

Sibling Revelry

*8 Steps to Successful
Adult Sibling Relationships*

Jo Ann Levitt, R.N., M.A.,
Marjory Levitt, Ph.D.,
and Joel Levitt

DTP
Trade Paperbacks

A DELL TRADE PAPERBACK

Published by
Dell Publishing
a division of
Random House, Inc.
1540 Broadway
New York, New York 10036

Library of Congress Cataloging-in-Publication Data
Levitt, Jo Ann.
    Sibling revelry : 8 steps to successful adult sibling relationships /
  Jo Ann Levitt, Marjory Levitt, and Joel Levitt.
        p.   cm.
    Includes bibliographical references.
    ISBN 0-440-50896-7
      1. Brothers and sisters. 2. Adulthood—Psychological aspects.
    I. Levitt, Marjory. II. Levitt, Joel. III. Title.
BF723.S43 L48 2001
306.875—dc21   00-065606

Printed in the United States of America
Published simultaneously in Canada

Book design by Joseph Rutt

July 2001

FFG 10 9 8 7 6 5 4 3 2 1

Acknowledgments

We would like to thank the following people, organizations, and communities for the light they have brought into our lives, for the inspiration and instruction they've provided, and for the faith they have had in us. This list is not complete because our work and our communities continue expanding and because lists of gratitude and appreciation by their nature are a work in progress.

- Our parents, Sophie and Semond Levitt

- Our grandparents and extended family

- Barbara and her family and the kids, Andrew, Leo, and Michael

- Our friends (who allow us to claim them as honorary siblings)

- Mariah and Ron Gladis and the Gestalt family

- Jenny Bent, our agent, who planted the seed for this work and inspired us to carry it through

- Danielle Perez, our editor, who helped distill the essence of our message, imparting to us a sense of our audience and of ourselves as teachers

- Esther and Jerry Hicks and the family of Abraham

- Kripalu Center and members of the Kripalu community

- The Landmark Education Corporation leaders and the Philadelphia and Boston Center communities

- The staff of Canyon Ranch in the Berkshires

- Lynne and Jerry DiCaprio, and the therapists and staff of D.C.P.S.

- Dr. V. Michael Vaccaro, faculty and students at Hahnemann and Temple universities

- The Miquon School family

- Those whose pioneering work in sibling relationships provided background, vision, and direction

- The Web site mydocsonline.com, which provided an electronic forum to help us coordinate our work

We would also like to acknowledge those readers of the first draft who provided insight, anecdotes, and "ahas," especially Charles Hirsch, Jonathan Harmon, Jim Peightel, M.D., Jenny Bent, Gloria Rodgers, Barbara Levitt, M.D., and Sophie Levitt. We thank them for their time and invaluable comments.

Finally, we wish to thank our students and workshop participants who graciously offered time and energy to this project and who willingly submitted to the various dialogues, explorations, and experiments that have provided the foundation for our work. In many cases the stories presented in this book are an amalgam of two or more people whom we interviewed or worked with. We have disguised all workshop participants, patients, and volunteers to protect their anonymity.

Jo Ann, Marjory, and Joel Levitt

Contents

Sibling Revelry

Preface

Of all our relationships, the sibling relationship is often the most invisible, or the most taken for granted. Unless we're the oldest children, our siblings were "present" from the beginning. Why should we take notice? We've forgotten they matter to us or that we matter to them. In some cases we've suffered harm at one another's hands. If we take our siblings so much for granted, then we hardly recognize who they are or the potential they hold to be our true lifelong companions. Finally, as adults, many of us avoid picking up the sibling relationship where we left off and developing it, saying, "I didn't choose her. She's not my 'significant other.'"

But increasingly that's not true. The sibling connection is, in fact, our longest-lived relationship. It outlasts the relationships we have with our parents, spouses, and children, and is now viewed as one of the core experiences from which our life relationships unfold. This relationship, which was present from the beginning, in a sense is waiting to be "chosen" by each of us as important and worthy of further development. It can't be escaped. Whether we work out deep-seated issues arising from the family of origin with the original members of the cast or with stand-ins from our families of choice, we've got to finish the unfinished business. Research by clinical psychologist Walter Toman in such works as *Family Constellation* indicates that we approach new relationships outside the family of origin according to expectations we developed at home with our sisters and brothers.

There are powerful demographic trends fueling the growing interest in siblings. As a nation we are graying quickly—nearly 34.5 million people are seniors as of 2000. In sheer numbers, baby boomers crossing the midcentury mark tip the scales; this same group is supporting, mourning, and otherwise letting go of parents and stepping into the family lead. At the same time, family structures have shifted; with one of two marriages ending in divorce, families quickly acquire new children (read: new brothers and sisters for their original offspring). As the sibling relationship becomes the family focal point, it's sisters and brothers who decide where family dinners or holidays will be celebrated. More and more, it's sisters and brothers who provide lifelong continuity and an anchor for the sense of family.

Siblings, especially females, are often involved in caretaking of aging parents or in organizing new family structures to handle the dependents in their lives, both children and parents. Intrinsically, then, developing sibling ties means not only investing in the future but building dividends that, for obvious reasons, pay off in the present. Additionally, more and more evidence indicates that strengthening your relationship with your sibling can lead to enriched bonds with others in your life—your spouse, your children, even your friends and co-workers. Even, paradoxically, with your parents!

Finally, the increasing number of people living alone highlights the need for alternative support systems such as those provided by our siblings. According to the 1996 Population Report published by the United States Bureau of the Census, the number of middle-aged people living alone has more than doubled, from 5.7 percent in 1970 to 11.9 percent in 1996, and the trend is increasing. As people age, the statistics become staggering. Among adults 75 and older, 53 percent of women and 21 percent of men live alone. An antidote to alienation lies in strengthening relationships that have a built-in history.

Returning to our sisters and brothers provides opportunities to experience meaningful connection. Understanding and putting the power of the sibling relationship to work will provide us with important support systems as we age. Thus, more people than ever are entering into middle and presumably old age without partners. Those who have never married or had children now have expanded choices as to where and with whom they will spend the rest of their lives. Increasingly, people are finding themselves linked by choice in a network that has a sister, a brother, or both at the center.

Siblings Come of Age

In the years since we began formally teaching and researching the sibling relationship, we have noticed more essays, books, and research materials appearing on the topic than ever before. There's a growing momentum in this area of interest and investigation. The popular media, including newspapers, magazines, movies, and TV, seem to examine sibling relationships with endless fascination. We can't help ourselves. The relationship is as complex as any we will encounter in our lives, whatever its quality in this moment. Of interest to us is the prevalence of sibling stories in the popular media—from Donny and Marie Osmond on the cover of *TV Guide* (May 21–27, 2000) to heart-wrenching portrayals of the lives of Jacqueline and Hilary du Pré in the film *Hilary and Jackie*. As a nation, we seem fascinated with the lives of siblings, from the sublime to the horrible.

A quick perusal of the self-help section of your local bookstore or Amazon.com reveals many volumes guiding parents in reducing sibling rivalry, a handful of titles dealing with twins, and another handful of picture books, anecdotes, and homilies extolling the bonds between sisters and brothers.

Many authors have attempted to fill this gap in the last ten years or so, and their additions to the literature have provided the spark people need to begin the work of transformation of this fundamental relationship. We discovered the landmark works on adult sibling relationships: *The Cain and*

Abel Syndrome by Randy Carlson; *Mixed Feelings* by Francine Klagsbrun; *The Accidental Bond: How Sibling Connections Influence Adult Sibling Relationships* by Susan Scarf Merrell; *Original Kin: The Search for Connection Among Adult Sisters and Brothers* by Marian Sandmaier; and the reissues of Stephen Bank and Michael Kahn's *The Sibling Bond* and Elizabeth Fishel's *Sisters: Shared Histories, Lifelong Ties.* There are many more.

Biologists and geneticists have had an interest in siblings insofar as they help to prove or disprove hypotheses relating to nature versus nurture, or heritability of traits. Medical science has a deep and abiding interest in siblings, especially twins, for the clues they provide in the battle against disease. There are probably more heroic tales of sibling valor from the annals of medicine than from anywhere else. It is almost commonplace to read of a sibling donating bone marrow or an organ to another sibling.

A New Era for Siblings

Just as we are formed in the crucible of our parents' making, so do our sisters and brothers influence us. As we have observed, times change and bring with them a different focus. We strongly suspect we're entering the era of the sibling. We're not alone in this imagining. On the negative side is Robert Bly's *The Sibling Society*, with his horrific vision of a culture that looks to its peers for wisdom rather than its elders. Lost among video games, that sibling society has no one in charge. Though the generation born after World War II has preferred listening to its own voice, on the positive side this cohort is growing wise based on its own years of experience. The growing ascendancy of parallel and peer relationships can be seen as an augury of a time that is marked by greater equality, cooperation, and compassion.

We have the heartwarming, real-life stories of the Delany sisters, Sarah and Elizabeth, who lived together until the death of Elizabeth at 105. Fictional accounts of sibling relationships, from Louisa May Alcott's *Little Women* to Wally Lamb's *I Know This Much Is True*, and Joshua Hammer's best-selling *Chosen By God*, have long been a mainstay of leisure-time reading. Francine Klagsbrun, writer, editor, and lecturer, reminds us in her book *Mixed Feelings* that the Bible, fairy tales, myths, and legends often focus on siblings. Romulus and Remus, twin brothers, were the mythic founders of Rome. The Greek Pantheon comprised brothers and sisters. In the popular sphere we see recent publications such as "Siblings," a photographic essay by Nick Kelsh and Anna Quindlen, and the book *Sisters* by Carol Saline and Sharon Wohlmuth.

Siblings As the Next Frontier

At any given time in history there are dominant themes. In the twentieth century we witnessed the early pioneer and self-starter give way to the family and company man of the fifties. From the advent of the liberated woman of the seventies, we saw couples entering into dialogue and individuals seeking recovery, and finally children working to free themselves from the dysfunction of their families of origin. We believe that research and a national dialogue on siblings is the next frontier of investigation. This relationship has come of age. It is taking over center stage as the relationship we turn to increasingly as our source of strength and sustenance through the beginning of the third millennium.

Why the growing interest in siblings? Over the last twenty years, in therapy, group settings, and self-improvement seminars we've conducted, we've found that after people work on their issues with parents, the work naturally turns to the sibling group. For others, the sibling provides a less threatening access to parental psychological material. They see elements of their parents in their siblings and begin the work there.

Those who have made some peace with their parents are

now eager and ready to take on the work of healing with their brothers and sisters. In fact, readiness to deal with the present sibling bond may be enhanced by the greater clarity an individual attains after working through issues of the parent-child relationship.

Strengthening the sibling bond thus has a threefold benefit: First, siblings gain emotional riches by reclaiming that childhood closeness; second, they can enrich other relationships by resolving unspoken issues in their sibling relationships; and finally, they can benefit from the support system that the sibling relationship offers.

Finding Our Way Back to One Another

The story of Chris and Jimmy shows us the value of reestablishing this connection. Chris and Jimmy are from Portsmouth, New Hampshire. Before attending a Sibling Revelry Workshop with her brother, Chris, now 39, came upon a diary entry she had written of her brother Jimmy in December 1968:

> Well, he's been pretty nice to me. And he sneaks cookies into my lunch box . . . I think I'd be very lonely without Jimmy. The other kids in my class ignore me or make fun of my glasses. I like it when he comes and waits for me, at the gate after school. Don't really know what I would do without my brother Jimmy.

Thirty years later, the story was very different. Chris traded in her glasses for contacts. She married her high school sweetheart, who later left her. She raised twins by herself. Working a full-time job, she got her monthly support about once a quarter and could barely make ends meet. Chris felt alone and overwhelmed by the size of her tasks and hopeless to dig out of the hole she felt she was in.

Her brother, Jimmy, got into trouble as he grew up but

straightened out when he joined the navy on his eighteenth birthday. He stayed single and had seen Chris only a few times over the years. Until the Sibling Revelry workshop he had never even met his only nieces. Jimmy described his life as a voyage by ship in high seas without any navigational instruments or destination. He said he was just trying to keep the bow pointed into the wind.

In a scene that held our group spellbound, Chris and Jimmy spoke about these concerns for the first time. Suddenly, Chris realized she wasn't alone. Not only was Jimmy there for her, he had always been there, in a certain sense. She hadn't been able to realize it, or acknowledge his contribution, in effect pushing him away. For his part, Jimmy realized that he had a home port where he was loved, and where people knew him. He didn't have to be the loner. His training then allowed him to look up at the stars, visualize the direction of Chris's house, and find his way home.

The key has to do with generosity of spirit, or creating an environment where love and acceptance can more easily enter the picture. Or as Amanda, one of our workshop participants, said, "What I want most is for my brother and sister to accept me as I am, whether I'm angry, happy, or silly. I want to be comfortable being wholly myself."

We hope our book will provide the "where to begin" and the "what to do next" that will help you create that experience of acceptance.

Introduction

One of the most frequently asked questions in our Sibling Revelry Workshops is: "When are you going to write a book?" When we decided to write, we returned to the wisdom of our workshop participants who had provided us with a list of their dreams and expectations in relation to their siblings. Combining all their responses, we discovered recurrent themes and used them to guide us in our work. Here are the most commonly cited wishes and desires:

To develop more trust
To have more contact
To be willing to take risks
To discover that past hurts are really past
To feel safe enough to have a heart-opening experience
To know my siblings respect and accept me as I am
To be more supportive of one another
To allow feelings of nurturance and care for one another
To be more comfortable expressing negative feelings
To leave room for forgiveness
To give up expectations of how my brother/sister should be
To move into a more equal, caring relationship
To let go of needing to control
To relax and enjoy ourselves
To be comfortable just being myself
To find new ways to express love to each other
To laugh more often

When working with individuals to resolve parent-child issues, we found similar wish lists. If we conducted a course for married couples, we would likely find the same requests on their lists. It seems that we want the same things from our siblings as we do from all our intimate connections. And often we spend hundreds of hours in therapy, thousands of dollars, and many sleepless nights trying to capture it for ourselves. Notice the simplicity of these wishes. Then consider for a moment: What are yours?

If you could have your sibling relationship be anything you wanted, what would you change or improve? What would be different? Are there dreams or hopes that have never found their way into reality? This is a good time for you to contemplate a new way to experience your sister or brother.

The Central Thesis of Our Work

The central thesis of our work is this: In order to ensure a sense of intimacy and meaningful connection through life, cultivate the relationship that has been with you through life—that with your brothers and sisters. For while there is much that may have been ignored or taken for granted, there is far more to be remembered and much to be fulfilled as grown siblings. Reawakening this original support group, especially as we age and experience multiple transitions in life, helps us access the kind of closeness we had in childhood and provides a unique template for all other relationships.

Research supports this hypothesis from all directions. The original and most influential in-depth psychologists—Adler, Freud, Jung, and Sullivan—assume that an individual's most elementary and enduring experiences are those that take place in the family of origin, among parents and siblings. These relationships form the template, or master, for all subsequent relationships. The example set by our parents and reinforced through relationships with siblings informs our choices from the playground to the boardroom. Walter Toman, a professor of clinical psychology, has made a career of exploring the impact of birth order and sibling position in such works as *Family Constellation* and *Family Therapy and Sibling Position*. He acknowledges that these initial experiences will also inform our choice of mate *and* the likely success of our long-term partnerships.

New Structures for Relating

Compare the creation of a new relationship with your siblings to choosing between building or remodeling your house. Before we can decide to build or remodel a house large enough to accommodate our adult selves, we've got to evaluate the present structure. It may be that the old house simply needs remodeling and expanding—a fresh coat of paint and a few new windows added to an otherwise sound foundation. No one can say what relationships we should have or how they can best unfold, but sooner or later each of us must make a determination. Is this sibling relationship the way I want it? Can we say we really are in a relationship? Are we getting and giving all we can? Or are we biding our time, afraid to make waves, or cynical about the possibility of expecting and receiving more from our siblings? As we address these questions, we discover the necessary tasks to refresh, renew, and, in some cases, resurrect our relationships with our sisters and brothers.

The entire range of sibling experience, from dysfunctional to merely functional to fully loving and supportive, occurs in that small society known as our family. And it's primarily our relationship to siblings that provides us our first experience of society. We learn many aspects of "citizenship," including how to share, how to fight, how to negotiate, how to represent our own interests, how to come together, and how to go our separate ways. And for most of us, though it shifts and changes through a lifetime, there are aspects that get firmly rooted as our way of relating, our identity, in all of our relationships. If we want to change our relationships, then, we must look to these underlying structures that hold them in place.

There are other relationships that can be looked at as mimicking sibling relationships. Janet, a psychologist friend of ours, has shared a house with Mel, an interior designer, for more than six years. They consider themselves sister and brother. More and more people we know are deliberately cultivating siblinglike friendships. This idea opens up intriguing possibilities. Are they building a structure that replicates the closeness of the sibling bond, or is this meant as practice to fix or make up for what went wrong in the past? Whatever the source, these friendships can also be enhanced by applying the techniques of this book.

The Power of Change

Change, even for the better, can be painful. The Japanese have a successful model of change used in business organizations that we could apply to families. For them, change is a process as delicate as transplanting a fragile plant. For the plant to thrive, the soil must be carefully prepared. Thus, in Japan much time is spent preparing the organization for change. In the same way, we want to help you prepare the ground for the kinds of changes you anticipate bringing to your siblings and your family. Exercises and explorations are carefully created with this end in mind.

In order to make changes, we must understand what lies at the heart of our problem. We all have habits that bind us to a way of being. That much seems to be part of the wiring of the human animal. What is essential to understand is that no matter what we do, no matter how we develop ourselves, habit patterns determine the outcome of our lives. So our key questions must be: Which habits will we reinforce, and which will we extinguish? Translated to the sibling domain, we then ask ourselves: What kind of habits and behaviors will support the sibling relationship we say we want to have?

For example, you may have a half-century habit of being sarcastic and putting down your younger brother. That habit itself will confer certain qualities to the relationship independent of your professed love and closeness. Changing that one habit could bring about significant changes not only with him but with all of your close connections. So we come to the important question: What needs changing? What specific behaviors, responses, or activities do *not* enhance your relationship? These could be as simple as relating to your brother only when you take him out drinking, or avoiding your sister because of her sermons on proper conduct. We ask you to closely examine these relationships. It's possible you'll find a new perspective on why things are the way they are. Or you may unearth unexpected sources of strength and support from your siblings.

You may say, "That's all well and good, but my siblings are not my support group. I can't really count on them." Or, "I have a good relationship with my sister. What's all the fuss?" Or, "Why rock the boat? And besides, you don't know my brother. He's crazy [or irresponsible, or evil, or etc.]."

There's nothing wrong with any of these conclusions. Many people find their relationships tolerable though perhaps not acceptable. What we want to offer you, however, is the opportunity to make your sibling relationships extraordinary. By going back, discovering, and reworking the roots of those connections, we now have access to a whole new way of being, not only with siblings, but with our friends, coworkers, and families as well. We also have the practical skills to transmit to our children, so that they may have a foothold on creating harmonious lifelong relationships with their sisters and brothers. That is what we reveal to you throughout these chapters.

From the Authors

Although we have worked on our relationship for many years and consider it a work in progress, we have no fear or question about the outcome. As two sisters and a brother, we have grown up with different configurations and ways of relating. What Marjory shares in many ways summarizes our process:

My sister and I have always been very close, though we had plenty to sort out. Most of this was early sibling stuff—turf wars, little sister/big sister power struggles, and that kind of thing. By adolescence, we were simply tight and close, and we've been that way ever since. My relationship with my brother was almost the opposite. I hardly remember him when we were little. But as adults, I used to fear that if I said what I really wanted to say to my brother, he would forever cast me out of his life. Naturally, this fear put a bit of a damper on my ability and willingness to communicate with him. I always felt like I was (or had to) tiptoe around him. I don't anymore. I can't exactly remember when my fear left me, even though I spent years in therapy and otherwise "working" on this issue. One day I understood that our connection wasn't fragile or conditional, and that was that.

To further introduce ourselves: In birth order we're Jo Ann (we had a brother Michael who came first, but he died shortly after birth), Marjory, and Joel. Jo Ann has designed and directed personal-growth programs at Kripalu Center in Lenox, Massachusetts, works at Canyon Ranch, also in Lenox, as an RN, has written cookbooks, and serves as intuitive counselor and coach for people in healing crisis or for those wanting to awaken their creativity. Marjory, the middle child and first Ph.D. in the family, is a psychologist who teaches at

Temple University, mentors masters and doctoral level students, runs therapy groups, and has a private practice. She's also a consultant to educators and industry on issues of diversity and racial-identity development. Joel, the youngest, is a management consultant who on any particular day may be found training executives or consulting for companies in Labrador, Singapore, or Los Angeles and has written books about the Internet and management. He and his wife, Barbara, raise three sons in Philadelphia.

Through our lives we have weathered many family and personal storms. Our three-way relationship is the springboard for this work. Since all three of us teach and train, it was not difficult to conceive a course emphasizing our particular "specialty": relationship-building as siblings. The upshot was a weekend workshop titled Sibling Revelry, which we have taught at Kripalu Center in Lenox from 1996 to the present. From watching brothers and sisters relate to one another in new ways and with newfound freedom, we experienced a critical turning point, understanding perhaps for the first time the power and potential that the sibling bond could provide universally.

Besides our weekend workshops, we also offer afternoon and evening sessions at Kripalu Center, at Temple University, and at other retreat centers around the country. In our workshops, approximately 25 percent of our sibling participants come on their own; the rest bring one or more of their siblings. While greater change happens immediately when all siblings are present, we have also received feedback from solitary members that although they anticipated certain changes or improvements taking months, once they had been through the process, the changes happened in a matter of days. The key is that *they* were open to change, as workshop participants. In so many instances, only we ourselves stand in the way of our progress.

A Primer for Siblings

In this book, we share with you the key ingredients that help siblings draw closer, presented in a workable eight-step format. We like to think of this work as an upgrade and improvement on a built-in design of human dynamics—that is, the inborn tendency to grow closer as we age.

The eight steps are laid out in simple order based on a progression we have found most effective. Three keys lie at the heart of the eight steps: first, find what is not working in the relationship and begin the process of acceptance and release; second, accentuate what does work; third, embark on something new and altogether different, which we refer to in the image-making process. By following the eight steps you will naturally move back and forth among these key processes and build their strengths into your relationship. Although the steps are organized in a linear fashion, they often emerge simultaneously: For example, as soon as you make room for the quirkiness of your sister or your brother's habit of distance, you have energy freed up to engage in new and different behaviors with either of them.

Our work offers you a host of skills. Relax and understand that you are not alone in your difficulties. Hopefully, you'll feel encouraged knowing there are tools and tasks here that you can easily master. Above all, realize that whatever work you initiate has far-reaching effects, not only for you and your siblings, but for their families as well.

When you have completed the eight steps, combined with a series of stories, interviews, teachings, assignments, and explorations, undoubtedly you and your siblings will experience some or all of the following:

- A deeper understanding and ability to listen to one another.

- Increased openness toward one another's differences.

- An enhanced capacity to problem-solve the inevitable difficulties.

- An appreciation of one another that will help support the growth and unfolding of family life in the future.

- Positive change in the quality of relationships outside the sibling bond.

Besides the parental influence, the sibling relationship is one of the templates we use to form relationships. Insofar as the sibling relation is a healthy, effective, and vital template, it can be translated to other siblinglike relationships in our lives. Unresolved conflict, miscommunication, and lack of connection with siblings can impact all of our relationships. Taking chances, reawakening, and improving our sibling relationships, however, will also have a powerful effect on all our other relationships.

In *Family Constellation* (1976) Walter Toman has observed that parents tend to utilize and even replicate their sibling experiences in raising their own children. Thus, we have not been overly surprised to hear from workshop participants that relationships within their families of origin have also improved.

The Need for Patience and Persistence

Sometimes a miscommunication can sour an otherwise solid relationship. Two brothers, Harvey and Michael, who run a highly successful textile firm, joined us for an afternoon workshop. They could not have articulated more divergent points of view about their lives and their relationships. If one said "good," the other said "bad." This opposition was automatic. When we suggested that they attempt to express a little of their anger with each other more directly, they both looked at us in utter disbelief. Harvey, the younger brother, said, "I'm feeling really protective of Michael. He's allowed to say whatever he wants to me. I know we're on exactly the same wavelength, and I'm not angry!" Michael agreed he wasn't angry either. This shocked Harvey. "I thought you were always mad at me, and thought I was a loser and a pain." Michael looked genuinely hurt and surprised at the same time. He said with obvious affection, "Are you crazy? Anybody tries to hurt you, I'll break them in half. I think you're a great guy. I wouldn't have any other brother!"

Harvey, the younger brother, was so afraid of losing Michael's approval that he adopted a mask of cynicism and resignation, while continuing to play the one-upmanship game. Michael had taken on the bullying and teasing role, all the while assuming that Harvey understood his real feelings. These brothers are like millions of other siblings who function in the presence of undeclared yet deeply rooted assumptions that go back to childhood. These views are frequently frozen in time at a young age. It takes patience and persistence to uncover the nature of their messages and the roles they have played in squelching authentic communications. When the underlying assumption is defined and uprooted, the miscommunication goes away and love is present.

Working from a Vision

To clear the record, we do not operate from the assumption that your sibling relationship needs to be fixed, nor do we assume that something's wrong. We work more from a vision—from a sense of the hidden potential for even more closeness in sibling relationships. Here is the possibility for an extraordinary relationship; here are fun times; here is closeness and sharing. These possibilities enhance our lives and make our sibling bonds all the more durable. So rather than ask what's wrong, we'd rather pose this question: What more do you want to share with each other? What more do you want to enjoy? In the many hours of interviews, workshops, and experimental sessions that refine these exercises, we've found that even among siblings at war, there's almost always a seed or a kernel of love. There is some element of goodness to be enhanced and expanded.

The Workshop Format

Below is an outline of the format of our three-day Sibling Revelry Workshop. In our shorter-length workshops, we may focus only on steps 1, 2, or 3 to get the ball rolling.

Day One—Sib Stories in the Round
    Group Intentions for the Weekend
    Ground Rules
    Step 1: Define your relationship (as part of game, song, story, or mime).
    Homework: Either alone or with sibs, discuss the following: How was sibling rivalry expressed/suppressed/acted upon within your family of origin? Make notes in journal to bring next day.

Day Two—Group Explores Sibling Rivalry and Begins
    Healing Process
    Step 2: Discern major elements of sibling rivalry/compare notes within group.
    Birth-order conversation in three separate groups: olders, middles, and youngest children. Acknowledge de-identification process.
    Step 3: Walking meditation followed by creation of a new vision.
    In small groups, compare notes on vision, firm up.
    Step 4: Homework: Make lists of types of sibling contact: describe as is and how you want it to be. Share with siblings participating in course.
    OR: make one or two phone calls to MAKE contact with siblings not in course.

Step 5: (Afternoon): Journey of healing: guided meditation/visualization/letter writing.

(Dinner hour): Brothers meet only with brothers and sisters only with sisters for informal gab, comparing notes.

(Evening): Talent show/building a bridge together/artwork/stories.

Day Three—Groups of Three Explore Family Legends
Step 6: Writing process: revamp legend; compare notes with others.

Steps 7 and 8: How we're alike; how we're different; create lists for each sibling. Then add to lists the talents, strengths, and contributions each sibling has made in your life.

Share with siblings present in room *or*: call one or more siblings to let them know what you feel their strengths and gifts are in your life.

Group Sharing/closing song/meditation.

As in this book, our workshop format includes the recounting of sibling memories and important moments in family history; enjoying games, parodies, and skits; exploring rivalry or wounding; restating family legends in a more positive vein; creating new images for the future. Thus, the eight-step format presented here parallels the work of the weekend workshops with added material for home study.

Preparing for the Journey
A new journey begins. Riding alongside us is the baggage we pack from the past. The sibling journey is no different from any journey of transformation; however, the stakes are greater. After all, this is your family. You may find yourself

reclaiming an important piece of your identity or reviving hitherto unused energy and power to invest in a new level of relating with them and with others. You may even find that conflicts and stresses in other significant relationships diminish as you gain greater clarity in this primary relationship.

For the authors, this book, like any relationship, is a work in progress. We appreciate receiving your feedback to add to our stock of transformational anecdotes. Please e-mail us c/o Joel Levitt: jdl@maintrainer.com.

How to Use This Book

There is no one correct way to read this book. It closely parallels the progress of our sibling workshops, with the eight steps to relationship building summarized in the first eight chapters. We've designed the explorations and text to build progressively toward greater self-awareness, as well as greater utility and application in your relationship. Musings and anecdotes provide real-life illustrations of the possibilities available for change. If you follow the book as written, you'll notice a gradual, incremental change in your relationships. However, if you prefer to skip around and dip into the explorations and text according to your interests, please do so. We know there is benefit in doing things your way.

Throughout the book we will ask you to carry out various explorations, experiments, and homework. These are set up so you can explore each of the topics in greater depth and develop your own ideas and intentions. Whether you do the work on your own or with your brothers and sisters, it will have considerable impact. A sibling does not have to be in your life (absent through estrangement or death) for you to benefit from the exercises. And you may choose to include your honorary or extended sisters and brothers, if you have them.

We will also note explorations you can use for holidays or family gatherings. There will be exercises that we ask you first to complete on your own, then share with siblings. Let yourself be the judge of how, when, and with whom to conduct these experiments. We're your champions; however, we will invite you to stretch and exercise new muscles in completing these explorations. Most important—have fun!

In conducting preliminary research for this book all three of us interviewed many sibling groups and individuals about their relationships with sisters and brothers. Along the way, we accumulated inspiring, humorous, and useful examples of working sibling relationships. No doubt you have unique stories that bring you together with your sisters and brothers. This is a good place to remember them. As an aside, all those who so generously offered their stories in this work have had their names and identifying characteristics altered to assure anonymity.

Approaching the Eight Steps

The eight steps are summarized here so that you can begin sensing the organization and focus of the work. Read through these steps, gathering ideas of what is expected at each level and assembling what you need. We strongly suggest involving your siblings whenever possible. If they're not available, involve friends, relatives, or co-workers. Having a group will feed into the synergy and strength of the process, much like the work of the original sibling workshops. No matter how you choose to approach these steps, however, we are certain that you will learn a great deal, release whatever is no longer useful, and, in many instances, approach your siblings with greater interest, support, and willingness to reconcile.

Step 1: Define Your Relationship

Do you find it difficult to pin down the qualities of your sibling relationships? In any journey it is important to figure out what is "so," what is real. In this step you grapple with pivotal questions such as: Who are your siblings? What role do they play in your life? What role have you played in theirs? For some sibling groups, the act of asking the question in itself solves fundamental problems, such as the issue of how important we are to one another. For others, dissonance can creep in between the assumptions of the historical sibling relationship and the experience of the present one. For example, Agnes, a 43-year-old woman who was in one of our workshops, realized that her family myth of closeness had no basis in reality. She rarely talked to her siblings. In fact, her brother got married and "forgot" to invite her to the wedding. Agnes realized that being close requires more than harboring stories of closeness from the past, and at present she is evaluating what she intends to do about this.

Chapter 1 confronts one of the biggest areas of confusion for sisters and brothers: our sense of a shared past. It dispels the illusion that there were events in the past that everyone remembers in the same way. Usually siblings remember events differently and assign different meanings to what they do remember. Although you shared your childhood with this person, what you discover through this process is that you actually inhabited two different worlds.

Memories and conversations emerge. Now you sense who they are to you and you to them in more concrete terms. There is certainly work to do but you've begun the process. We don't suggest massive changes at this point, just keen observation and note taking. Before painting an old house, for example, a contractor or homeowner will walk around and look closely to see what's there. That's how this process begins. See what you have to work with before you slap a new coat of paint on the old house.

Step 2: Witness the Effects of Old Rivalries

This step takes on the tough issue of rivalry. Anyone who has raised children, especially children close in age, has seen rivalry in action. And many of us can still call up memories of our early childhood battles. Initially, rivalry is a powerful narcissistic force. At that stage, parental intervention, the complex interaction of sibling temperaments, and the natural opportunities for socialization help to tame this primitive force. When the sibling relationship matures and grows past childhood, rivalry transforms to a powerful force to bond us. However, some adult sibling relationships are frozen in conflicted childhood relationship patterns, often unwittingly encouraged by parents, and the rivalry has not had a chance to transform.

Step 2 provides you with an opportunity to evaluate your sibling relationships in the light of past conflicts and differences. Explorations are designed to unearth the roots of conflict and nudge you toward authentic adult contact with your siblings.

We all have concerns, complaints, and issues about our siblings. Some of these concerns get in the way of our being with one another. Siblings may be very different (as we three are) but have much in common. In this step you identify the issues or concerns that get in the way of a smooth connection with your brothers or sisters.

Step 3: Envision a New Future

An underlying tenet of this book is that each of us has the ability to change. If we consider the outcome of things that originally seemed permanent or unchanging, such as the former Soviet Union or the Berlin Wall, we realize that change can occur in every moment. And it may come in any possible form. What is needed and helpful, however, is a blueprint for what we want. We must first imagine the possibility before we can experience it as reality.

Often we fail to focus on what we want from our sibling relationships to avoid the disappointment of not getting it. We get caught in the trap of our negative predictions. Chapter 1 presents an added explanation: Our society and our culture idealize the sibling relationship. When we compare our flesh-and-blood relationship with the idealized version, we often come up short.

So, we visit Memory Lane. Start by imagining your best

moments with your siblings. You may have to visit your storehouse of memories in order to convert less powerful images from the past into alternative and more appealing ones that include fun, closeness, or a new type of connection as part of your future. You can even return to the cultural icons of sisterhood and brotherhood and include aspects of the ideal in your real relationships. Allow your sibling journal to function as a bankbook of ideas for a more desirable future.

Step 4: Explore New Modes of Contact

We are connected to our brothers and sisters through a variety of interactions that often have their origins in the past. For many of us, what that means is that our sibling relationships may be based in habit patterns that have outlived their usefulness. For example, you could have a habit of screaming at your older sister whenever she gives you advice. On the other hand, your older sister could have a habit of shamelessly correcting your grammar. To a large extent, these often-unconscious habits determine the nature of the relationship. Once we realize that possibility, we can explore new modes of contact or new habits.

As we discover in step 4, all relationships are held in place through long periods of time by certain patterns and practices. These patterns are difficult to see because they have surrounded the relationship for decades, back to childhood. Some of these patterns and practices may have been inherited from prior generations. The trickiest thing about them is that these patterns *appear* to be reality. Yet they are really our interpretations, based on early experiences we may have had as an angry, scared, or needy young child. Thus, they become templates, which remold the relationship each time in keeping with the old pattern. One way to recognize the presence of an old pattern is to examine the degree to which you feel alive and connected in a given situation. The less engaged you are, the more likely you're on automatic, repeating a practice or pattern.

Explorations in this chapter help you look at some of the ways in which you're connected. How often do you gather in person? Speak on the phone? E-mail? We call this a structural inventory. Exploring the underlying structures through which you relate helps you to see what works in light of the future you want to create. For example, some families discuss everything and others share nothing of importance. With the latter, siblings may have no idea what is really important to the others. Their views of one another may have been frozen twenty or thirty years ago. By completing this process, some sisters and brothers are awed to discover how little there is of truly contemporary content in their relationships.

Once you've looked in detail at the quantity and quality of your contact, now you can think about what you would like to have with each sibling. Imagine this experience based in present-day reality but extending toward a more open, supportive, and fun-filled future. A few small adjustments can then have vast repercussions in terms of how you relate.

Step 5: Heal Past Wounds and Misunderstandings

Life hurts. Sometimes your siblings unwittingly inflicted pain on you, or you may feel guilty about pain you inflicted on them. In either case, there comes a time when you recognize that these wounds are still affecting you and need to be healed. Explorations in chapter 5 help you remember and resolve conflicts, sorting through issues of fear, anger, guilt, and hurt.

By now, many of you have resolved differences that plagued your sibling relationships for years. There are many ways to heal these wounds. Some heal spontaneously, others in the presence of a religious revelation or rebirth. There are also psychological and cognitive methods to promote healing. We honor your courage and willingness to stay in the ring, duking it out with these demons.

Step 6: Invent New Family Legends

In every culture, legends have a powerful influence on people's lives. In the United States, we live surrounded by myths about rugged individualism. In Japan, many subscribe to the myth of the samurai warrior serving his master. In 1919 Russia, the myth of creating an egalitarian society for the workers toppled the czarist government. These myths and legends have far-reaching effects, influencing how we work, play, and relate to one another.

One problem with family legends is that some of them are so ingrained that they become invisible. They become so much part of the fabric of day-to-day life that they cannot be distinguished from any other aspect of life. Through dialogue and introspection, you have an opportunity to uncover legends that have been in the background of your life.

The process of uncovering family legends can be done alone or with relatives or lifelong friends. Many times legends can be unearthed through conversations with your siblings, parents, and grandparents. When you discover how the legends came to life, you can then identify the prevailing ones that shaped your sibling relationships.

In step 6 you are invited to create powerful legends of your own. Here you are empowered to take a more active stance in creating the family life you envision. Myths and legends are your building blocks. With energy and perseverance, you can create them in alignment with the vision for your future.

Step 7: Make Room for Differences

The stage is set. All your plans and dreams are in place. You've opened yourself to a new level of relationship, and your siblings are now engaged directly or indirectly in this new future. Trial and error has sobered you to the challenges of the process. The presence of healing between you and your siblings, or new modes of contact and communication, has brought a light to the end of the tunnel.

Keeping the envisioned relationship in place requires new habits and patterns of thinking, as well as patience, courage, and a good sense of humor. In step 7, you explore ways to look at your sibling relationships that expand and deepen your commitment. Particularly important is the ability to make room for and accept the differences that show up between you and your siblings.

Step 8: Honor Your Strengths

In the final step, you list the gifts you've received from one another and take time to acknowledge one another. You begin to build from the strengths each one brings to the relationship. Acknowledgment and appreciation are practices that can bring you into the presence of your love for your siblings, and can facilitate making the choice, again and again, to live in this model of closeness with them.

Completion

Now you have completed the eight steps. All along you've been working from the model from our workshops, fine-tuning the steps to your personal needs. In the end, you can reflect on your progress, see what inroads you've made, and continue to build a network of support and strength that will carry your sibling relationships into the future. At any time during this process you may choose to go back to previous chapters and redo any parts that were left incomplete. If you did explorations alone, you may want to include your siblings in this round. If you included your siblings, you may want to initiate a review of the material together, which helps you move to a new level with them. Often, the passage of time and immersion in these activities can help you identify beliefs and habit patterns in need of refining, or "growing up." This recapitulation then serves to consolidate your thoughts and feelings, and accelerates your growth in all areas.

The Explorations

To make it easier to engage in the explorations, we have broken them down into different sections and categories. We map these out for you below.

Each exploration begins with a section called "setting the stage." In this section we give you the necessary background or context for the exploration. At the top of the exploration we give you a list of materials and the amount of time needed. We encourage you to set aside time when you won't be disturbed.

On the left side of the page are the actual steps to be followed. Many steps are preceded by a category that asks you to carry out a specific action. For example:

Change characters:	React as if you were someone else.
Imaginary lives:	Make up something.
Lights, Camera, Action:	Something active follows.
Lists and landmarks:	Make a list.
Mapping the territory:	Draw a map of the territory.
Memory Lane:	Remember the past.
Motion:	Move around.
Pow-wow:	Get into contact with your siblings.
Reflections:	Think about the topics presented.
Rescripting the play:	Rewrite what is happening to suit you better.
Stop, look, and listen:	Pay attention to this.
Witness:	Pay attention to what is happening without reacting.

On the right side of the page are prompts, examples, and additional help with each step. Following each exploration is a section called "what happened." This section explains what was supposed to happen, why you are doing this, or other pertinent information. Some explorations have short follow-ups called "encores."

In most cases, writing materials will be needed. We strongly recommend creating a sibling journal. It's a crucial medium for documenting your transformation. When other elements are needed or new designs are brought into play, we'll describe what you'll need. Above all, we urge you to adapt these explorations to suit your specific circumstances.

Importance of Setting the Context

Preparation is an important facet of these explorations. Taking care of yourself and any tenderness or vulnerability you may encounter will depend on how well you've set a context in which to do the work.

We recommend that you begin each exercise or exploration with a period of relaxation. There are several varieties described in the text and in the appendix. If you're not already familiar and comfortable with a particular relaxation/meditative practice, try experimenting with the varieties we describe. Each of us has learned to relax in a different way. Some find the best method is deep breathing, muscle contraction, and release. Others find movement or physical exercise the best way to bring about relaxation. Still others find maximal relaxation through prayer, song, or mantra. Alicia, one of our volunteer participants, prepared herself by making bread. As the dough was rising, she completed her responses to the explorations.

Whatever type of meditation you choose, just know that being centered and calm is the result you're striving for. Setting aside a special place will help. If it's not possible to have a dedicated private space, try to carve out a corner of a bedroom. If that is not possible, at least have a private place to keep your sibling journal.

Workshop participants and volunteers who worked with us during the many stages of this book have told us that the work they do on their sibling relationships has had a beneficial impact on all their intimate relationships. This is a bonus, and also an invitation. We invite you to explore and do the work regardless of your current situation with your siblings. If, for example, your siblings are unavailable, explore these topics with your chosen family, friends, or extended family. Not only will you move closer to them, you may find it suddenly easier to approach that formerly unapproachable sibling.

One caveat to this process: Although we are firm believers in the power of change and transformation, we understand that occasionally a difficult sibling relationship cannot be made right. In such extreme cases, we consider the need for prayer and surrendering to the workings of spirit. With or without your sisters and brothers, however, through this work you can develop greater comfort, satisfaction, and completion in your own experience of the sibling connection.

With regard to reluctant siblings, approach them tenderly, gingerly. We've seen life-altering change occur between warring siblings as a result of one simple gesture. On the other hand, there are some relationships that are too damaged or toxic to transform. If you find yourself in this category, allow yourself to carry on alone, to complete the inner work that you need in order to be free and to be able to accept the reality of your relationship.

In all exploration, there is the possibility that you may feel psychologically or emotionally overwhelmed at one time or another. Should you find this to be true, we recommend that you seek professional counseling, and use that relationship to support you through the rough spots. Sometimes, all that is needed to restore balance is to slow down or take your time with the material. We invite you to join us in the paradox of doing and not doing—there's nothing you *have* to do, and there's a great deal you *can* do . . . if you want to.

Most of all—have fun! This work of building sibling relationships is an important contribution not just to the cohesiveness of your family but to the family of humanity at large. We appreciate the work you do on behalf of us all.

CHAPTER 1

Define Your Relationship

Our work is to stay present, available to the universe
and vulnerable to the truth. When we are wholeheart-
edly present, exploring the conditioned mind, who we
really are sees who we really aren't.

> Stephen and Ondrea
> Levine, *Embracing the
> Beloved: Relationship As a
> Path of Awakening*

Sell your cleverness and buy bewilderment.

> Rumi, quoted in *The
> Essential Rumi*

The first step in the eight-step process is to define your relationship. Until you know what you're working with and
how you actually view your sibling connection, there's no
point in attempting change. Besides, it is difficult to transform a relationship that is ill-defined, amorphous, or unex-
amined. So this is the point where you settle in to have a
good look and see how you represent this all-important relationship to yourself and to others. Defining your relationship
will thus entail identifying differences and traits you have in
common, as well as the roles you play in one another's lives,
and how all that has shifted through time.

"I would say that my sister and I are getting to know
each other all over again," Jeremy, one of our workshop participants, explained. A 38-year-old Silicon Valley computer

expert, he went on to describe what he saw developing in their relationship:

> Jenny is the wild one in the family. She's into photography and sports, has run eight marathons, and loves to kayak on the rapids. If you searched the far corners of the earth, you couldn't find two people more opposite than we are. With my business ventures foremost in my mind, it's rare I even venture out unless I have my cell phone or Palm Pilot with me. For years Jenny and I took our differences for granted and never bothered to get to know one another. But when she developed breast cancer last year it shocked the living daylights out of me. I realized my amazing athletic sister might not live forever and I could conceivably lose her. Suddenly getting to know her became paramount in my mind. What I've been discovering as I do these exercises is that we do share characteristics in common. We both have tremendous passion and love for life and a great sense of humor. We both want big families. And we both think sibling relationships are important to nurture. It's been a blessing to get to know her. . . .

If someone asked you to describe your relationship with your brother or sister, what would you say? Notice the first things that come to your mind. Would you say close, distant, estranged, or best friends? Then consider how you would define its chief characteristics. What role do you play in each other's lives? Is it the same or has it changed through the varying storms and seasons of life? Every journey begins where we are, and that is the starting point for our exploration. First we take a look and notice what's present in our experience. As we share our recollections, discernible patterns begin to emerge, which provide a foundation for expanding our awareness. Awareness is the keynote in our journey; you might even call it a bridge to cross from the past to the future. So our first efforts have to do with broadening awareness. As we unearth our memories, take a few moments to ponder the nature of your sibling connection.

We All Grew Up in Different Families

The magical, almost surreal quality of early childhood images and experiences shape us at the core. Examples abound in every popular medium. In the screen adaptation of Neil Simon's play *Brighton Beach Memoirs,* two brothers grow up in a poor Jewish home in Brooklyn during the 1930s. Stanley, the older brother, works hard but can't scrape together enough money to support his ailing father, as is expected of him. If we were to ask Stanley about his sibling relationship, he might say, "Oh, he's my kid brother. My job is to teach him about the world and make sure he gets to college. I'm like his second father." If we were to ask Eugene about his relationship, he might say, "My brother is the light of my world. He brings order and logic with him. He makes everything bearable. He teaches me about right and wrong and how to take care of myself. I couldn't live without him."

In the movie, Eugene gets to test that hypothesis when Stanley runs away from home. Having gambled his weekly salary of seventeen dollars (trying to make extra money to bring home), Stanley is so ashamed that he takes off that night, vowing to join the army. Eugene tries to persuade him to stay home, but Stanley is resolute. Reflecting on his brother's departure, in effect Eugene sees his own childhood ended, and the prospect of growing up alone a difficult venture.

Obviously, Stanley would have a different experience to relate about Eugene. Hearing them both describe their history, you might think they grew up in two separate families. That, in fact, is true.

In this chapter we initiate the journey by exploring two

related points of departure. First is the realization that although we may have grown up in the same house with the same parents, most siblings actually grew up in different families. Any memories we hold in common are random and unrelated and invariably spring up as the result of telling and retelling stories from our past rather than jointly remembering in common. In later chapters we discuss the formation of family legends, which arise out of this process of retelling family stories. The second focus of this chapter enters your home turf. There we begin the process of mapping and describing your present sibling relationships through a series of exploratory exercises. This mapping involves reporting where you are today without judgment, inference, or added meaning. Good luck on the journey.

In our family, Joel, the youngest, lived in a world dominated by two older sisters. There was never a time when he was without them . . . no memory or experience that did not include adjusting to or accommodating their presence in his life. The same holds true for Marjory with regard to Jo Ann. There is no *is* without the big sister in the picture. Apart from these sibling constellations, different groupings occurred in the family. Joel and his father formed a masculine unit within the larger family unit. Marjory and Jo Ann stuck with Mom.

Although siblings share similar genetic characteristics and much of the same history, nevertheless the family each child grows up in is actually quite different. So many details affect our experience of life, from the age, education, and affluence of our parents when we are born to the presence or absence of siblings and others in our households. This is a major stumbling block in the systematic study of sibling relationships. In the language of research, it is difficult to control for the variables (factors you are not studying that might impact the results) since so many affect sibling development. The same holds true for research into the effects of birth order.

Clearly, when you are born, and in what family constellation, has an enormous impact on your experience of life.

A patient of Marjory's describes his family:

My sister Laura is the oldest and she's the perfect one. She was my dad's favorite, whereas I never got anything from him but criticism and abuse. She could do no wrong. I'm two years younger than Laura and we had a brother two years younger than me but he died when he was only a few weeks old. No one ever talked about him; to this day I think I'm the only one who remembers him, even though I never met him. Seven years later my little brother Anthony was born. I hardly knew him. I wasn't that interested in him once he got past the cute baby stage. When he started first grade, I was starting high school. I never had much in common with him. Laura says she grew up in a perfect world. I think I grew up around a miserable sadist in a world where I couldn't do anything right. Anthony says he grew up all alone, nobody even knew where he was most of the time. It's hard to believe we all come from the same family.

The dilemma of being brought up in different families becomes even more pronounced in abusive families. Some of the differences among siblings come about as a result of memories that are repressed. In effect, there are large gaps in the recall and experience of what family life was about. The experience of Al and Nathan bears this out. Al was a 58-year-old manager at a major hospital in the south. He started his story: "I've been sober for over twelve years."

Al had done a tremendous amount of work getting his life together. Originally a shoe salesman from Philadelphia, he had built a stable and loving second marriage, returned to school to earn a master's degree in health-care administration, and learned to relate well to his adult kids and his grandchildren. Examining his childhood as part of his quest for emotional health and recovery from addiction, he said:

My father was an alcoholic. He would come home drunk, beat the three of us up, and pass out on the couch. It didn't seem unique at the time, since all my friends had similar stories. However, I hated him most for what he did to Mom and the humiliation I felt when we had to get him out of one jam after another. When he awakened he was usually hung over and remorseful for what he had done. I remember these incidents clearly as if they happened yesterday. For a long time I denied the problems in my family just like I denied my own alcoholism. However, as I accepted my disease I started to remember my childhood. To me it seemed as if our family history was a known and accepted fact by everyone. But I found out that wasn't true.

Five years ago, about the time I was trying to make sense of my childhood, my wife and I went back to Cleveland, to my brother Nathan's house for Christmas dinner. Since he was drinking heavily, there was not much I could say. While mentioning some of the work I had been doing, trying to get him interested in attending an AA meeting, I told him I had begun to remember Dad's beatings and other stuff from childhood. Nathan's face screwed up and he started yelling at me. He said we had a great childhood and how dare I darken the memory of our father. I couldn't believe it! He went on to call me a worthless slimeball wanting to blame others for my problems and sputtered that all the stories were a pack of lies. He was so angry we almost came to blows. Minnie and I left. We've seen him since but I haven't raised the topic again. I'm so afraid of his reaction that I don't discuss anything personal anymore.

The experience of Al and Nathan points to the difficulty of reconstructing a common history and trustworthy relationships in a climate marred by alcoholism and abuse. Whose memory is reliable in this instance? If healing and recovery are not the objectives for all family members, then the outcome for any member trying to heal the past may be one of isolation and ostracism. Yet, as mentioned earlier, we never assume that any family is a closed system, or that one's personal transformation cannot in some way affect the family at its deepest level.

Although we address mainly full siblings—brothers and sisters with the same biological parents—we also include half, step, adoptive, fictive, or other extended sibling relationships in our work. Our research has demonstrated that these relationships benefit from a mature and thoughtful reappraisal. Whatever your original family constellation, you can apply the techniques and principles laid out in the coming chapters. As adult siblings, we are working with the voluntary re-creation of a biological and historical relationship. For shared history alone does not guarantee a mature peer relationship; just as growing up in a "full" sibling relationship does not intrinsically imply common experience.

We Each Have Our Version of the Sibling Relationship

For all intents and purposes, Eugene and Stanley in *Brighton Beach Memoirs*, like the three of us, and you and your siblings, grew up in different families. In reviewing our own history, we concluded that there was little possibility of reconstructing a common past. Therefore, we came up with three independent and overlapping versions of our experience. Lest we appear to be too perfect for words, you should know that we arrived at this stroke of genius after months of belligerently trying to prove that each of our *own* versions was the *true* version of events. Jo Ann even went so far as to interview our mother to reconstruct her version of events.

Since Mom didn't remember a lot of things, however, it didn't work that well. In some cases she verified Joel's version, or Marjory's version. Once that backfired, we had to invent a more autonomous and mature way to describe our shared but uncommon past.

We each have our own version of the sibling relationship. Thus, in our family of three, there are six relationship combinations: the one I have with my sister, the one she has with me; the one I have with my brother, the one he has with me; and so on. In the book *The Sibling*, Brian Sutton-Smith and B. G. Rosenberg developed a system to describe the complexity of sibling relationships. As an amusing aside, the two authors dedicated the book to their older siblings "who will undoubtedly regard this as just another form of harassment." According to their theory, birth order *and* gender influence every child, so that the oldest sister of four sisters will have, obviously, an entirely different life experience than an older sister of three brothers. No wonder we're all confused about this brother and sister business!

Defining Your Relationship: The First Step

We go back to our first impressions, which help constitute our definition of the relationship. Distinguishing the nature of her relationship to her sister, Esther, a 42-year-old English teacher, realizes that she is not very close nor does she feel that she even has a sister.

I grew up in New Haven, Connecticut. My sister Elaine is four years older. Always the goody-goody; she did everything by the rules. I really don't have too many early childhood memories of her. In fact it feels to me that I didn't have a sister at all. I spent most of the time by myself in my room, and Elaine spent most of the time with her friends.

Although we rarely did things together, I do remember Elaine being very bossy and pushing me around. I went along with her, so as not to make waves. But I felt so different from her that it accentuated my feeling of always being alone and alienated. There were things I could never share. I know that in recovery programs they talk about the invisible child. For me, sisterhood was more like the invisible relationship. At any rate, it all seemed to unravel when I was fourteen and Elaine eighteen—she had gone steady with a guy named Tony, and they married right out of high school. After that, we truly lived in different worlds.

To describe and define our relationships with our siblings is actually the first step in the journey of transformation. It is the first time we turn our attention toward ourselves and create a point of focus within the sibling relationship. The simple act of focusing turns out to have an effect all its own, and that effect mimics the Heisenberg uncertainty principle. This law of physics states that the observer always has an impact on the system being observed. You can't study an atom without changing it. In interpersonal observations as well, the Heisenberg principle applies.

Whenever you begin studying some aspect of your life, your whole system responds. That is why we introduced the importance of enhanced awareness: Your life changes in the act of observing it. Observing and defining the specifics of your relationship will start to have an effect not only on you and your siblings but on other aspects of your life. Once you initiate the process, there is no way to know how it will turn out. However, the very act of looking closer invariably alters the terrain in some way.

Setting the Stage

These first few explorations are important because they provide a reference point. Rereading them in a few weeks will show you any changes you have made. When you do the explorations, try to capture the picture of each sibling relationship at this point in time, as if you were taking a snapshot. Then collate them together in your journal, much like a photo album in words. At a later date you can review these exercises and see what progress was made. Often you'll notice that you've left behind some baggage or that things have subtly shifted. In the final analysis, these explorations help you realize how much more satisfying your sibling relationship has become. Good luck.

Exploration 1-1   Basic Centering Exercise

What you will need:

- Find a time and place in which you can relax and remain undisturbed. Use this centering exercise whenever you need help to relax or focus your mind.
- Your sibling journal is useful but not necessary.
- You will need a full ten minutes to complete this exercise.

Witness: Begin by scanning your mind for distractions. Is there something urgent that needs attention before you begin? Best to take care of it, if you can. Otherwise, make a note and set it aside for the time being. Examples include: remembering a phone call you forgot to return, a load of laundry that needs doing, etc. Make sure you have removed all distractions, phone, fax, or unnecessary interruptions.

Motion: Take a few moments to stretch your body, releasing any tension that may have accumulated in your lower back, neck, or shoulders. Bring your shoulders up to your ears, hold them in place, squeeze tight, and then release them. Repeat this several times. Keep your journal handy and write any thoughts that come up so you don't have to keep thinking about them.

Move your jaw from side to side and up and down, releasing any tension that may have accumulated.	Often the muscles of the jaw retain more tension than any other muscle in the body.
Begin taking deep breaths while keeping your eyes closed.	Since the breath is linked to emotional states, prolonging and deepening each inhalation and exhalation will naturally help calm your mind.
Continue this slow, rhythmic breathing process for 3–5 minutes.	If you find yourself becoming light-headed, focus on the exhale, and shorten the inhale.
Now sit and relax. If thoughts arise in your mind, simply watch them come and go.	

This centering process, or one similar to it, precedes most exercises, so remember this—you'll hear it and use it again. Appendix A has variations and additional exercises for centering.

What Happened

Notice how agendas and activities begin to take a backseat to your relaxation. Return to deep breathing if necessary. Then fully acknowledge and take in the experience of being centered and calm. By following these steps without rushing, you create an opening through which inspiration and new thoughts can emerge.

If you don't have a full ten minutes for relaxation, we suggest the following short version, which takes only two to three minutes and still produces good results.

Exploration 1-2   Short Version Centering Exercise
What you will need:

- Find a time and place in which you can relax and remain undisturbed. Use this centering exercise whenever you need help to relax or focus your mind.
- You will need only 2 to 3 minutes to complete this exercise.

Motion: Raise your shoulders up to your ears, taking in a full breath of air.

If you get distracted, just stop and make a note.

Slowly release the air, lowering your chin to your chest, and smile to yourself with eyes closed.

Repeat for two minutes, then stop to take in the effects of relaxation.

Setting the Stage

All of these exercises may be done alone. If you have the kind of connection that allows for the honesty and intimacy necessary in sharing the results of these exercises, invite your sibling to join you, or simply share the insights you've gained as a starting point for your real life sibling conversation. You can also share your thoughts and experiences with others close to you—a spouse, a partner, or an especially close friend.

Exploration 1-3 Siblings Present Tense

What you will need:

Sibling journal; 15 minutes

Lists and landmarks: Write the names of your brothers and sisters.

Think about each name as you write it.

Use your imagination to envision the connection you now have to each of them.

Think of how often you do things together. Think of the last conversation you had.

Mapping the territory: Next to each name, write a brief description or a list of words that relate how you experience your relationship now.

Some examples from Al's relationship to his brother Nathan: very distant, feelings of sadness, some anger and frustration. Afraid of his addiction.

For each sibling, answer the following questions:
- When was the last time you saw this sister or brother?
- What were the circumstances?
- How often do you see them, talk to them, e-mail, write, call, etc.?
- Who generally initiates contact?
- Are your contacts characterized by mostly positive or mostly negative feelings?
- Do you find that it takes time for you to "recover" from visits and get-togethers?
- How difficult would it be for you to choose a gift that he or she would really love?
- What would the gift be?

These are concrete questions. Try to answer them without thinking about your opinion about the answer. Just think about and answer the questions. Add any other questions of this type and answer them, too.

What Happened

It is important to see what the relationship looks like objectively. For example, Lucy, one of our group members, insisted that she was close to her sister. Her answers to the above questions, however, did not reflect closeness. In fact, she observed the opposite—that in reality they hardly had contact. Whatever the present level and quality of contact you have with your sibling is okay. This is the beginning of a road map.

Intermission

Many people naturally think in terms of metaphors. They see relationships as natural phenomena. In this exploration, think about your sibling relationship in metaphorical terms. Any metaphor is fine; we enjoy song or movie titles.

Exploration 1-4   Siblings Present Tense: Find the Metaphor

What you will need:

Sibling journal; 10 minutes

Mapping the territory: On a new page, begin meditating, doodling, and playing with the material from exploration 1-3.

For some people a song or movie title captures the essence of their relationship. See if you can invent or recall the name of a novel, a movie, or a favorite song that depicts your relationship.

Some examples might be: *War and Peace*, "The Wind Beneath My Wings," "Purple People Eater," or *Hannah and Her Sisters*. Or you may choose to write lyrics as they occur to you.

Take some time to reflect in silence. You may want to reread your notes and responses. Notice any contrast or pattern in your feelings and/or expression.

After you've written some examples, describe anything more that occurs to you about the nature of your present sibling relationship.

Witness: If you have more than one sibling, notice your comfort and preferences as you move, in thought, from one to another.

Do you feel open and relaxed about one sibling and confused or contracted about another? Notice too if you feel more hopeful when describing one relationship than another. Is there anything else that interests you that you want to acknowledge at this time?

See if you can come up with a few sentences, song titles, or lyrics that summarize and capture the quality of your relationship with each of your siblings.

Samples: "So far away . . ." "Thank you for letting me be myself . . ." "There were never such devoted sisters." "He ain't heavy; he's my brother."

What Happened

The movie title that came to Joel's mind for our childhood and adolescence is *The Good, the Bad, and the Ugly*. "Jo Ann was the Good (she was totally good until she reached college, when she had a few years of being moderately bad). Marjory was the Bad (she was so bad that she wore black for most of her teen years), and I was the Ugly (I clearly didn't fit in, I must have been an ugly one). That says it all!"

Esther, mentioned earlier, summarizes her relationship with her older sister:

We had so little in common. Elaine was into clothes and shoes, and going out on dates. She loved to read movie magazines and flirt with the guys on the football team. This was a difficult realization for me, but early on I discovered I didn't give a hoot about guys. I would go up to my room and have fantasies about kissing the girls in my class. It took a long time for me to realize that I was a lesbian, and of course there was no reference point at that time in our neighborhood, no model for that experience in my world. Which is one reason why I kept to myself.

I didn't feel I had an ally in Elaine; she was much too absorbed in looking pretty and going out with boys. I don't even remember when or how I told her I was gay, but it seemed not to make much of an impression on her. I think she always had me pegged as an oddball, and this was just one more item on her list of things that separated us. She basically carried on with her life, and I with mine. If I had to characterize how she was to me in those early years, I think it would probably have to be *Gone with the Wind*.

How We Got to This Point

To understand your present relationships with your siblings, you must delve into your history. Whatever position you occupy in the birth order, you arrived on the family scene with some of the patterns already in place that would produce your distinctive sibling relationships. Hundreds of invisible habits, routines, behaviors, and practices anchor and define sibling relationships. Individually the habits are weak threads, but taken together, they form an unbreakable rope that keeps us in our place. In sibling relationships the individual threads are invisible, plentiful, and intertwined, and these combined attributes make them very powerful. Part of our intention with this book and the explorations and exercises is to clarify these individual threads and untangle them where needed, while at the same time remembering the strength of that unbreakable rope that sustains us in our relationships.

Because our sibling relationships are forged in the dreamy, absurd, or dislocated experiences of childhood, it helps to remember the initial memories. Such memories and stories form an unconscious matrix or web out of which we continue to live and define ourselves. You might call the behavior and attitudes that emerge from this matrix a "conversation" we repeat to ourselves over and over unconsciously, which then informs the actions, attitudes, and experiences we continue to have in relation to our siblings. In some ways these stories become embedded like computer programs that provide instructions for how we relate to one another.

Togetherness/Separateness

Delores and Nicole are middle-aged, African-American sisters born and raised in a family of fifteen children. They grew up in Chicago. Both attended a weekend workshop at Kripalu Center for Yoga and Health, where they met Jo Ann. They gladly consented to an interview and recounted their family history. As they spoke, the overriding theme that characterized their childhood was "togetherness."

Delores, now 53, and fourth oldest in the family, shares her perspective:

> Our father was a minister, our mom a housewife. She went out to work one day and came back that same evening saying, "Never again." Her work was at home with us. There were ten girls and five boys; one brother died at the age of two but the fourteen of us lived together. We may not always have had enough to eat but we had so much love, it didn't seem to make a difference.
>
> We were raised very strictly because my father was a minister. In church we took up a pew of our own and were always picture perfect. But when we got home there'd be a ruckus in the back bedroom. Dad was strict but good-hearted; he'd come home from church and it wasn't unusual to see six of us toppling around on the floor with him, trying to find candy in his pockets.

Nicole, fifth from the youngest, shares her perspective as well:

> I remember Delores used to bribe me with a quarter to get me to massage her back. That's my oldest memory. All of us kids doubled and tripled up in our bedrooms. But no one wanted to sleep with me 'cause of my asthma. I used to snore and wheeze all night long. Delores was kind enough to take me on. She always looked out for me. However, the thing that stands out in my memory was how closely bonded we all were. We were like a secret society; in fact to this day it shocks me when my friends share something with me that they don't feel free to mention to their own sisters or brothers. There isn't anything I wouldn't share with my siblings.

The Arctic During War

Jake, one of our workshop participants, tells a very different story. Describing his childhood growing up in a white, middle-class Protestant household near Roanoke, Virginia, what comes to mind for him is "separateness." Jake's image is one of constantly reaching out to his brothers Edward and Christopher and having great difficulty overcoming the gap, or distance, between them.

> My older brother Edward's pattern of separation and distance seems to summarize how things were growing up. Whenever there was conflict Edward would disappear. There were plenty of opportunities because our parents were always fighting or disappointed in one another. Home was like the arctic during a war: cold with bursts of fighting. I remember these fights with sadness; I used to be the only one who would try to come between them. Often they escalated into pushing matches

between both parents. I'd get hysterical, scream, and try to pull them apart, and in turn my mother would yell at my father, "See what you've done! You've made Jake upset and angry!"

Christopher, the youngest, would try to calm everyone down and be the kind, nurturing presence. He still does that; only now it's with his wife, his own two daughters, and his job working for the family court. Edward, currently a top film editor, would always leave and go sulk in his room. Now he stays away from us and relates more to his movie-production chums.

As for me, I went into business as a wood broker selling to Far Eastern furniture manufacturers. When I get home I still carry the role of go-between. I'm the only one who sees my parents regularly. And I still act as referee when they get into squabbles. They live in the same house but on two separate floors, and they seem to have made peace with a relationship that is more like housemates than husband and wife. At any rate, this same quality of distance marks the pattern for my brothers and me; we're estranged and separate, but not completely divorced from each other's lives. At times I notice the distance and feel sad. However, I don't feel there's much interest in growing closer on any of our parts, which makes me even sadder.

In these examples, patterns for interacting are set in motion early in life. The environment children grow up in has a built-in set of expectations for how to interact, based on the parents' model. Thus, the past continues to impinge upon the present. Although you've begun by identifying the current state of your sibling relationships, in the next exploration you'll have a chance to dip into and explore images of early life growing up with your siblings.

Setting the Stage

First, let us begin with centering. Follow the steps in Exploration 1-1, or find a different means of relaxation. This time you may want to take a walk or soak in the bathtub for a while. Take a long enough time-out to reduce stress or worry and bring yourself into a state of relaxation and alert focus.

Again, these experiments are designed to be effective completely on your own. Or you can choose to complete them with your brothers or sisters. In some cases you may want to complete certain exercises with surrogate or honorary siblings.

This exercise can be made into a party game for some families. The goal is to remember events that concerned other members of the family. Everyone will have different recollections about events (and even trivial things like colors of dresses, stuffed animal names, etc.).

Deposits in the Sibling Memory Bank
Exploration 1-5: Siblings Past Tense

What you will need:

Sibling journal; about 15 minutes

Memory Lane: Go back to the earliest moment you can remember one of your siblings.

Before you pick up your pen, take a moment to reflect on your past.

Now attempt to reconstruct that event or image with as much detail as possible.
• Where were you at the time you remember your brother or sister?
• What were you wearing?
• What was he or she wearing?
• Looking down, can you see your shoes?

If you have more than one sibling, repeat this process for each one.

- Looking up, is there a sky or a ceiling overhead?
- Look around you—are you standing or sitting?
- Is anyone else with you?
- Was there action or was it a quiet scene?
- Was anyone talking?
- Think back and see if you can uncover any particular feelings.
- Do you remember any of the thoughts you were thinking?

Begin to fill in the details of that memory, bringing alive your experience.

With a few lines, sum up your reaction to this memory. Then, see if you can detect or recall any conclusion you might have made as a child, any family myth or conversation resulting from this early memory.

Read over your notes and catch the predominant feeling or tone: Is this a warm, sunny scene? Or is it scary, sad, or neutral? (For example: After getting beat up by an older sister, you conclude that you are weak, or that "I can't trust my brother"; or, "My mom now expects me to take care of my sister," etc.) These may be clues to some of the dominant relationship issues and/or styles that are prominent right now.

If you have worked on this exercise without a sibling, or with a surrogate sibling or friend, read your notes aloud, and notice whatever feelings arise. Notice too if other memories are stimulated by this exercise. Write down anything that interests you as you observe your feelings and memories.

Often, workshop participants and volunteers report that childhood memories begin to flood back to them as they start the process of recall. This may happen for you, too.

What Happened

Some people we've worked with reported that they had a difficult time remembering anything in detail. If this is the case for you, see if you can get copies of family photographs from your childhood. Sometimes, looking through these can reawaken memories.

If none of these options works for you, and you have a living parent or parents, ask what they observed and remember. Interview other relatives or close family friends, too. Finally, if you're still uncertain, make something up! What do you imagine your response to the birth of your sibling would have been? (Or his or her response to you?)

Encore

Exploration 1-6 Extra Credit Siblings Past Tense

What you will need:

60 minutes

For those siblings who bring their brothers and sisters into this exercise, add these two steps.

Pow-wow: If one or more of your siblings is interested in exploring your connection, ask them to duplicate this exercise and recall their own sibling memories, write them down, and meet together later to share notes.

Once you've been together, take time to reflect on what you've heard and enter your reactions in your journal, along with the notes about your early memories. What you've written folds into a living commentary about yourselves and your relationships.

What Happened

Lydia, a buyer for Macy's, recounts this early impression of her older brother James:

> I'm sitting in the den coloring. It's a rainy day, and I don't know where my twin sister Linda is. Then James comes in the room. James is eight; Linda and I are six. I tend to keep away from him. But James came over and wanted some of my crayons. I don't know why; he never liked coloring. But he started pushing me. He would push me or kick me and still be very quiet, like he didn't want anyone to hear. All he said was, "Lydia, you can't keep all the crayons to yourself." Then he pushed me around some more. He would never want Linda to know this because she'd come running in the room and fight him off. I guess I wasn't as strong as Linda. Anyway, I had had a feeling that James was jealous of us. We both had a little secret; we were friends, and even though he was older and got more things he wanted from my parents, he could never have what we had. To this day James lives off by himself, a little out of the mainstream.

Lydia often wondered if his aloofness to society as a whole could be traced back to the triangle between the three of them.

Robert recounts the feeling of joy and awe seeing his new baby brother Mark, some five years younger than he:

> They put my little brother on the bed after his diaper was changed. I'm just looking at him. His hands and feet are so little. I think maybe he's a windup doll, but no, he's laughing and cooing and turning from side to side. He's a happy baby. I feel like something important, maybe even a treasure has come into our family. I

see my mom smiling more, and for some reason that makes me happy. Or at least it takes me off the hook.

Once you've noted some of your early memories, don't be surprised if others pop to the surface in the days following. Sharing these aloud can often spark a series of more remote or forgotten themes. If this is the case for you, take the time to jot them down, preferably in your sibling journal. It may be that these exercises stimulate dreams of childhood, too. For some, recalling early childhood may stimulate emotional discomfort, particularly if the memories include violence or abuse. At any time, you may slow down. Stop doing the exercises and put the book aside for a time. Some may want to consult a mental-health professional and continue to work on the issues that have emerged.

Setting the Stage

In our next exploration, you will be visiting not only childhood memories but the place in which you grew up. This is a great party exercise. You can play it during holiday or family gatherings with all or some of your siblings and your parents present. Pass out paper and crayons with the assignment below. If you have children of your own, this exercise is also fun for them. They can draw their own house, and you can draw yours. One workshop participant told us that she did this with her children, ages 11 and 9. The children were so curious about the house and street she grew up on that they made a field trip back to her old neighborhood. A woman who participated in one of our afternoon workshops told us that she'd taken this exercise to her whole family by bringing a roll of butcher paper and a bucket of Magic Markers to her family's traditional Thanksgiving celebration. She tacked the paper to one long wall and the whole family took turns drawing the old neighborhood. Use your imagination and enjoy this exploration.

As with all of our explorations, you may share this with a sibling, or not, as you choose. We've noticed that this seems to be an exercise that most sibling groups have fun doing together. We've even had workshop participants spontaneously pass their drawings around and the next siblings in line add a touch or two. We've had siblings literally rolling on the floor laughing at the memories offered by a sister or brother. Of course, we've also had siblings in tears at a particularly poignant scene drawn and offered. Experiment. Add your own unique flourish to the exercise.

Centering Exercise

Before you begin this exercise, take a good stretch in the middle of the room. Clasp your hands behind your back and pull back gently to ease tension in your shoulders. Then, with your hands still clasped together, see if you can bend forward, lowering your head toward your knees. When you have come back to a standing position, try one of the balancing poses that are often used in yoga practice. With the "tree" or the "stick" you have to balance on one leg for a brief while. You'll find the same benefits as with other centering exercises (1-1 or 1-2). Your breath slows down and becomes more rhythmic. Your vision becomes still as you focus on a point in front of you to help maintain balance. And inwardly, a sense of peace and serenity flows through you.

Exploration 1-7 The title of your work can be:
Growing Up on (your address) Street
What you will need:

- 30 minutes or more
- Paper and crayons (or, if you like to play with art supplies and a variety of visual effects, use pastels, paint, and Magic Markers).
- Large paper, poster board, or Styrofoam board.
- Magazine photos, captions, and titles for collage effects.

Witness: Allow yourself to drift for a little while. Maybe you have your eyes closed. Be sure you are comfortable. Take your time, and allow memories from childhood to emerge.

Use your visual memory, if you can. *See* scenes from as far back as you can.

Memory Lane: Summon a mental picture of the first home you remember.

Lights, Camera, Action: When you feel, see, or sense this image, begin to draw. Or you may use paint and pastels or cut out pictures that represent your street, your house, and your neighborhood. Spend a little time looking at your drawing and add any details you want to add.

If you have negative feelings about drawing, use your nondominant hand, or simply allow yourself to tolerate the discomfort.

If you need some assistance, try answering the following questions in picture form:

- Where did you play?
- Can you see your kitchen? Your bedroom?
- What was across the street?
- What did the front of your house look like?
- Who is with you?
- Were there pets, flowers, or gardens nearby?

When you are complete, have another look. Did you forget anything? Now is the time to add any descriptive words or finishing touches.

Witness: What is the story you have told? Notice who is with you and who isn't. Notice if you have any feelings about this. Do you have feelings about the process of going back?

You may want to make notes in your journal of the feelings, thoughts, images, and awarenesses you had during this process.

What Happened

Children live passionate lives. Your early days were filled with everything from boredom, to terror, hate, love, and expectation. Looking back at incidents from the past is invariably interesting, frequently uproariously funny, and occasionally poignant or painful. Looking back will help orient you to the present and may unveil a passion for life you had that has been submerged or stifled. Your siblings may be the only ones who remember the passionate, spontaneous, joyous person you once were.

Summary
Step 1: Define Your Sibling Relationship

- We begin by defining the sibling relationship and considering what roles we've played in one another's lives. How we describe and define the relationship is actually the first step in the journey of transformation.
- As siblings we share the same history and genetic characteristics and yet the family each of us grows up in is different. This factor is intensified in abusive or dysfunctional families.
- We each have our own version of the sibling relationship.

- Despite our shared history, what we aspire to now is a *voluntary re-creation* of this biological and historical relationship; we want it to develop into something stable and mature.
- The simple act of observing our relationships can lead to change, as we've learned from extending the Heisenberg principle.
- Our family shaped us; we arrived on the scene with patterns already in place that would contribute to the formation of our distinct sibling relationships.
- Recalling early memories, events, and shared experiences helps us reconstruct the underlying pattern or "conversation" through which we continue to reinvent our sibling relationships.

Seeds of Change

Review the following list of statements and see which apply to you, once you've completed the work of this chapter. You may want to acknowledge that changes are already in the works. If not, use these affirmations to guide your continued efforts. Whatever the outcome, note your progress and take courage from it.

❑ I have been willing to take a closer look at my relationships with my siblings.

❑ Out of my observations, I have stumbled upon some of the key characteristics of our relationships.

❑ Observing how my siblings and I view our different interactions and involvement, I am beginning to see that we really do have distinct versions of who we are as siblings.

Grains of Hope, Pearls of Wisdom

Allow these statements to provide hope and faith in your process. You may wish to add to this list and keep a running copy in your sibling journal.

- ✓ I am interested in exploring more deeply and understanding the underlying patterns or conversations that hold my sibling relationships in place.

- ✓ Focusing on my sibling connections is a fruitful avenue of discovery. I am certain that good will come from it, although I am not yet sure how the process will unfold.

CHAPTER 2

Witness the Effects of Old Rivalries

Many people suffer from relationship senility. The mind has become fatigued from trying. Self-protection and an unwillingness to go further have left us confused, insisting we understand.

> Stephen and Ondrea Levine, *Embracing the Beloved: Relationship As a Path of Awakening*

I was watching those rocks. Then I felt a hard jerk.
A very fresh green-headed Quilligan Quail
Sneaked up from *in back* and went after my tail!
And I learned there are troubles of more than one kind.
Some come from ahead
And some come from behind.
So I said to myself, "Now I'll just have to start
To be twice as careful and be twice as smart.
I'll watch out for trouble in front and back sections
By aiming my eyeballs in different directions."

> Dr. Seuss, *I Had Trouble in Getting to Solla Sollew*

Let's face it: People do things that get on their loved ones' nerves. For siblings these patterns are likely to be rooted in the childhood relationship. In this chapter we look directly at the behaviors, habits, and issues that stand in the way of closer relationships among siblings. The chief issue, of course, is sibling rivalry. Before siblings can embrace revelry they have to deal with any remnants of rivalry from the past.

When I think back on family life, what I'm aware of is how competitive things were, especially between me and my older sister Ginny. I always had the feeling that there was only one of everything, the perfect prom dress, the perfect date (of course she wound up getting him, because she was prettier). Later in life, we subscribed to the same idea, but now there was only one successful career (this time I wound up getting it as a market analyst). It's easy to trace the roots of this understanding in the way our parents, coming out of Depression mentality, kept sending out strong messages: don't use it all up, be thrifty, there's not enough to go around. In the last ten years Ginny and I have sorted this out and decided to make room for a universe with greater abundance; however, it's interesting to see the subtle ways I still compete with her. (Meredith, age 52.)

Meredith runs her own PR agency outside of Philadelphia and frequently visits her sister Ginny, an elementary school teacher, in Allentown, Pennsylvania. Close friends now, they laugh at the way Ginny's teenage daughters compete in sports and scholastics. For Meredith it's a relief that some things stay the same, generation after generation. Sibling rivalry, as she observes, is a fairly predictable outcome in raising a family.

Tracing sibling rivalry from childhood through adulthood, we have a chance to understand its origins and free ourselves from its damaging, limiting effects. One thing we come to realize is that sibling rivalry, at the right age, in the right circumstance, and with a supportive environment, is necessary for growth and individuation. Some people are surprised to learn that rivalry is normal and can be the basis of a great adult relationship. The ubiquitous and dreaded sibling rivalry can also help children and adolescents prepare for the interpersonal challenges life will bring us as we establish our independent identities. Some experts believe that rivalry is, in fact, an essential part of the process of socialization, and see only children as disadvantaged. The issue, as with many stages of growth, has to do with getting stuck, failing to fully resolve our differences, and having leftover childhood rivalries stay with us as adults.

Our task, then, is to free up relationships that are stuck. For those of you whose rivalry has already transformed, we will look at utilizing the energy behind the rivalry, or love, to enjoy one another even more. We hope that as a result of this inquiry, sibling rivalry will take its place as a normal aspect of our growth and development, and we'll learn to integrate its positive and energizing effects more fully into our lives.

For as long as we have recorded history, we have myths and stories about competition among siblings. Perhaps the most famous story of sibling rivalry involves Cain and Abel, Adam and Eve's sons. As they grew up Abel was a shepherd and Cain the tiller of the land. Both brothers brought sacrifices to God. "And the Lord had respect unto Abel and to his offerings: but unto Cain and to his offerings He had not respect." (Genesis 4:2–4:26.) In this story we can clearly see the roots of rivalry. Cain was devastated by God's lack of respect (or attention). He took it out on his brother. In modern families one brother might be acknowledged for his achievements and another might not. Disappointment is then transferred onto the favored sibling. Usually, rivalry stops short of murder but murderous impulses sometimes remain lurking just below the surface.

For Esther and Elaine, described in chapter 1, sibling rivalry characterizes the better part of their adult experience. It seems difficult to change or overcome. Esther traces it back to its early roots:

> Come to think of it, an early photo sums up the relationship triangle in our family. We're at the beach; I must be about three years old, and Elaine is seven. Mom is standing and looking at her with a look of total love and adoration. And I'm off to the side scowling and holding my hand over my eyes as if to shield myself from the sun. Elaine definitely "got" Mom, but I was happy because Dad was mine. Dad taught me how to throw a ball, ride a bike, and scavenge on the beach. He was very affectionate, and that made me feel special. In a way it seems as if we won the sibling rivalry game, but not with one another. We each fought and won our own private parent.

According to Freud, what is "normal" for siblings is rivalry. Buried in our unconscious is our rage and misery at being forced to share that scarce resource known as mother/father (i.e., love and nurturing). Now it is well known that Freud himself, as the oldest child in a family of eight, had a difficult relationship with his siblings. Evidence of that difficulty is well documented by his biographers and reflected in his key theories. That's why we see him replicating this rivalry, teaching it to his children, and we then read about the normalcy of rivalry in the writings of his daughter, Anna Freud. Whatever his impact on modern psychosocial theory, however, the net result in the Western World is that sibling rivalry is a force to be reckoned with. It is an expected part of growing up. We are foolish if we ignore the depth and force of these rivalries. We are also foolish if we believe that is the end of sibling relations.

The Twin Aspects of Competition and Cooperation

Rivalry drives aspects of the relationship consciously and unconsciously. Often the rivalry functions as a stumbling block to a solid adult-sibling connection. In that case we must distinguish what is left undone or conflicted from childhood. From our point of view, however, sibling rivalry is one aspect of childhood that, in healthy individuals, is naturally balanced by cooperation. Research by Victor Cicirelli and Gene Brody, in *Sibling Relationships: Their Causes and Consequences,* confirms that by the time children reach late adolescence and early adulthood, they have grown out of the intense, immature version of their rivalry. It may still be in the background (as are all traits grown through) but it does not dominate the relationship. In some successful sibling groups, rivalry is used for fun, competition, and play. Researchers are coming to believe that these twin aspects of competition and cooperation provide an excellent training ground to develop human beings who will have to move out into a larger world and contend with the exact same phenomena—but often without the softening effect of family ties.

Joel muses on his two young sons, Leo, 11, and Michael, 9:

There is no doubt that these two would occasionally like to murder each other. One day I came into their room and Leo was holding Michael down on the floor. Michael was screaming, "Get off me, get off me," and of course Leo just kept holding him down. Then suddenly Michael yelled out, "I hate you!" Shocked, Leo let go of him, and said, "You're not supposed to hate me. You're supposed to love me. We're brothers. Brothers are supposed to love each other!" Michael responded with great fury, "I don't care. I hate you and I always will."

Joel muses further:

At the same time we will often witness acts of caring that you wouldn't expect from children that age. For example, some time ago at the close of bedtime stories, I overheard Leo tell Michael that there was a Band-Aid fairy just like there was a tooth fairy. Naturally Michael believes whatever his older brother tells him. So that night Michael took the Band-Aid off his knee and put it under his pillow. Waiting for the moment when his brother fell asleep, Leo crept down from his bunk and slid a quarter under his pillow. The next day Michael informed us of his good fortune!

Rivalries Contained

In an article in *Good Housekeeping,* therapist Carolyn Hoyt comments on her daughters' rivalry:

I don't mind if my two girls fight . . . but when they grow up, move out, and set up their own lives, I want them to love each other. To cry on each other's shoulders. To meet over mocha lattes and laugh about all the crazy things they did when they were kids.

I usually imagine these scenarios when I'm in the middle of breaking up their latest battle. She took my toy! She knocked down my tower! She's in my room! She's bugging me!

Hoyt goes on to give parents pointers about handling sibling battles, most of which have to do with getting out of the way and de-emphasizing differences. As children we were engaged in these sibling battles and comparisons when we were not yet fully conscious. They were our means of dealing with jealousies and competition and provided a foil for whatever tension or conflict might be present in the household. As we grew, our rivalries, as well as other behaviors such as excessive laughing, noise-making, or roughhousing, were contained, converted, or suppressed, usually due to our parents' efforts.

"Back in the Fold"

Melissa, the older of two siblings who grew up in St. Louis, Missouri, and who works there now as a social worker, describes her relationship with Mitchell, her 41-year-old brother, who is also attending the workshop:

None of my training prepared me for how to deal with this relationship with my brother. Mitchell runs an antique business and has actually become the star of St. Louis. Although we hardly spoke to each other for years, when we were growing up, I was his champion. After Mom died, I became his chief support. We put on plays in our neighborhood, raised money for UNICEF, and threw teenage parties. Mitch outdid everyone with his wild Halloween costumes. But the trouble began when at 23 he finally came out and declared himself gay. I was stunned and ashamed, deep down. How could I face my friends? Several years later, when Dad died of a heart attack, I felt something harden in my heart towards Mitch, almost as if he were responsible. I had been appointed executor of the estate. Little by little I started secreting away favorite dishes, photos, books. I even auctioned some family furniture on my own. Now when I think of it my stomach turns. I don't know what got into me.

As I continued in my therapy, I began to see how I had made Mitch wrong for everything that went bad in our family. Forget about his being gay. If cookies were missing from the cabinet, it was Mitchell's fault. If I didn't make it in the school auditions, it was because

Mitch was the real actor. If I had a headache, Mitch was too noisy. When I finally got this down deep in my gut, I was so ashamed I could hardly speak. Then I began the work of forgiving myself. Gradually the grief and fear began to lift. One Sunday morning, it all came together as I was cooking breakfast for my kids. On the top shelf of the china cabinet was a set of dishes that I hadn't used for years but that had come from Mom and Dad's original wedding set. Carefully packing them up, I delivered them to Mitchell's store with a note attached. Later on I actually sat down and wrote him a letter asking forgiveness. That was two years ago. I can hardly believe I got through it, but even more astonishing was Mitchell's response to me.

In the workshop, Mitch then shared with us briefly:

I cried like a baby. You don't know what a relief it was for me—not so much to get those dishes—but to feel my sister back in my life and to be reconnected with my family history. I had felt disowned, and there was nothing I could do about it. I couldn't change being gay. I couldn't bring Dad back or Mom for that matter. But to feel that Melissa was taking me back in the fold and that I had a family where I belonged—that was worth ten times the estate and all the wealth I'd accumulated in this lifetime.

Sometimes a shock or loss precipitates separation between siblings. It's almost as if the rivalry inherent in the family situation receives reinforcement. Now, the rivalry has a life of its own, a *raison d'être*. When a rift develops out of difficult circumstances, such as with Mitch and Melissa, it often lasts for years. Sometimes the original problem or misunderstanding is so buried in the past that siblings hardly know why they're not talking to each other.

In more fortunate circumstances, however, parents are there to intervene, and the rivalry has a chance to be shaped or transformed. That was the case for us Levitt sisters, now both in our fifties. Although we fought incessantly for many years, we really had no idea what we were fighting about. Perhaps it was the tension between our parents. Perhaps it was the growing edge around adolescence. At any rate, our parents grew so tired of our bickering that Dad finally came up with an ingenious solution: install a private phone in our room as a reward for not fighting. But the catch was—we had to stop fighting for a full thirty days. Once we'd stopped our shrieking and wailing long enough to get the coveted telephone, we'd developed new habits of solving problems with each other.

Although evidence from recent research suggests that teenage sisters in a similar situation would most likely have arrived at a series of peaceable solutions on their own, this was a dramatic and creative intervention, and remarkably successful. When parents fail to intervene, on the other hand, their children often suffer abuse at the hand of a sibling. Current findings in articles such as "Reluctant Referees," by Harriet Barovick, indicate that physical abuse among siblings may be more frequent than spousal abuse and parent-child abuse. These scars may literally and figuratively last for a lifetime, and can effect a permanent rift in sibling groups. Psychologists now urge parents to prevent sibling conflict from escalating beyond a reasonable point. Harriet Barovick points out, "A . . . journalist who was consistently taunted by his older brother says that when he now receives a compliment, he often tends to think the person is lying, because on some level he fears that the disparaging things his brother said about him are true."

The Building Blocks of Sibling Rivalry

In Carl Reiner's 1990 movie *Sibling Rivalry*, quite a few siblings have difficult or compromised relationships. Two main characters, the sisters Marjorie and Janine, exemplify this. Marjorie doubts that her sister's new love affair will last. Janine responds to her: "You always do this. When I'm happy, you put me down. Try to be happy for me just once. . . ."

For her part, Marjorie is ashamed of her sister. Visiting Janine, she finally blurts: "I have spent most of my life pretending that you're retarded. That way I could avoid being with you or thinking we're related." Even though this movie is a parody, it provides important commentary on the way rivalrous patterns are set in motion. These on-screen sisters, just like the rest of us, continue to elaborate patterns of rivalry, without really knowing each other, and without being able to access what they (and we) want from each other.

This movie encapsulates the basic ingredients of sibling rivalry: competition, communication blocks, misunderstandings of long duration, and eventually a complete conflict in values. The above vignette could be used as an illustration of de-identification—where one sibling studiously avoids the territory of the other. Marjorie claims order, stability, and conventionality. Janine is more unconventional, flamboyant, and chaotic. This is not to imply that either sister—or any of us, for that matter—consciously *plans* to de-identify with her sibling. The dynamic is more subtle and primitive than that.

It is hard to describe how or when this sibling competition sets in; however, it invariably affects the nature of our future communications. This is the case with Adele and Joyce.

Adele, a program participant from Charleston, South Carolina, remembers with sadness and guilt how mean she was to her younger sister Joyce. Although they were separated as children and raised by separate aunts and uncles, they still spent weekends with each other and had the usual sibling squabbles. But Adele resented Joyce's beauty and easy popularity with boys.

> Once I met Joyce downtown, and I was shocked to see that she was wearing my new pair of Capezios. She must have been seventeen; I was nineteen. To this day I can't believe what I did: I made her take off those shoes right in the middle of the street and walk home barefoot. There are some things in life you wish you could erase; that one's definitely on the top of my list.

Importance of Birth Order

Although sibling rivalry contributes to our early formation, as we can see by the above examples, it is not the only force affecting our growth and development. Alfred Adler, an early disciple of Freud, considered birth order to be instrumental in the shaping of the personality and the development of social concern. His convictions led to his break with Freud, who considered sibling influence to be secondary, compared with the primacy of parental influence. Other researchers have turned their attention to the enigma of birth-order effect on such things as success, intelligence, and educational achievement, among them William Altus in his work "Birth Order and Its Sequelae," and Selwyn Becker, Melvin J. Lerner, and Jean Carrol in their work "Conformity As a Function of Birth Order and Type of Group Pressure." While we do know that every president of the United States has had at least one sibling, we do not have the data to make other absolute claims about the effects of birth order. Results of a great deal of investigation have been largely inconclusive. The most promising findings have never been replicated, or modern research methods have failed to show the same kinds of trends indicated in earlier research.

Aside from birth order, which has certainly influenced the

quality of relationships in the family in significant ways, rivalry and competition play a key role in setting up the struggle for the family's resources of love, praise, and attention. As family interactions unearth relics of old conflicts, it seems that the energy bound up in rivalry and opposition in some ways still holds to those old patterns. Although we see rivalry at work more subtly as siblings age, once we unravel oppositions and unspoken conflicts, we can in effect "grow" the relationship to a more adult stature.

Evidence of rivalry (along with revelry) is readily apparent between the Anzalone sisters, who jointly own and operate a small luncheonette in Mesa, Arizona. Since Joel frequently stops there on business, he interviewed each of the sisters. Maria, the middle sister, always makes sure he has bagels to take home with him. The whole family inquires about his health. In fact, to his mind, the restaurant presents itself like an extended family experience. Everyone who comes to eat has something to say about what goes on.

Helen, the oldest, describes her relation to her two sisters as very close. "We're an Italian family. We were born to be close. Even though you see us squabble, that doesn't mean a thing. Who else could work so close for so long in this tiny space?" (The restaurant must be no more than four hundred square feet.)

Sofia, the youngest, who lost her husband when she was young, comments further:

There's no one in the world I can rely on like my sisters. When my husband passed away, I went to my sisters for support, not my friends, not the church or anyone else. I knew they would understand. Mom and Dad also work here; everyone does different shifts. Maria gets on my nerves, though, because she's so outgoing. She remembers all her customers by name and is the kind of person who can always find a positive thing to say about anyone.

Maria, the middle sister, pipes in: "Don't take Sofia too seriously. She really cares about everyone more than she lets on. And wait till you see her daughter Anna. She's beautiful."

Sofia: "You see what I mean?"

In the exercises below you have the opportunity to examine your sibling dynamics and explore what kinds of things bring you closer or drive you apart. In what ways do you relate as if your history is still in effect? On the other hand, what elements in your relationship are your strengths? In our family, for example, although we often use humor to deflect sad or somber feelings, our jokes and camaraderie bring us together. It's safe to say that we've come through a tough experience when we've made a joke out of it.

For the Anzalone sisters their obvious strength is the cohesion of the family unit and ability to work together under pressure. There is a sense of all for one and one for all, tempered by humor and the ability to poke fun at one another and their clientele.

Setting the Stage

In this exploration you will create a catalog of experiences, noting which of your sibling dynamics tend to draw you closer and which contribute to the distance between you.

Exercise 2-1   Together/Apart

What you will need:

Sibling journal; 15 minutes

Lists and landmarks: Draw a line down the middle of the page. At the top of the left column write the words, "Keeps us separate/apart." At the top of the right column write, "Helps bring us together."

For each of your siblings, create a separate page with the same notations.

Reflections: Begin reflecting aloud or in writing on the habits or ways of interacting that exists between you and each of your siblings.

Distribute behaviors between the two columns, as appropriate.

Witness: Now sit back and take notice. Are there any patterns to be observed in what you've written?

Are you reminded of anything else? Make notes of these memories.

There is great value in realizing which aspects of your interactions with your siblings are positive and which are negative. The value comes out of making the unconscious conscious. Examining these factors will start the process of transformation.

Lights, Camera, Action:
Review your lists.
Place an asterisk next to patterns you feel are hard to dislodge or change or are particularly distancing.

Circle or underline those patterns that seem to be most nurturing of your relationship.

Being able to see how you act with them and what you do with greater objectivity is essential. Many times the patterns (both positive and negative) are inheritances from the family's way of relating. You didn't make this up, it's been taught to you from the beginning.

Encore

Exploration 2-2 Together/Apart

What you will need:

Same as above, with your sibling

Pow-wow: As in previous exercises, share these insights with your siblings (or your siblings by choice).

See if they have the same barriers and the same attractions.

As an example, Jo Ann's journal has the following entries:

For Joel:
Keeps Us Separate/Apart

Fear of disturbing him when he's with his family. Fear of pissing him off. His frequent travel.

Helps Bring Us Together

His sense of humor and love of the absurd in life. His ability to coach me. A shared work ethic. His incredible children. His acceptance of my ignorance.

For Marjory:

Fear that I'm not doing it right. Fear of her criticism. Her smoking.

Laughing at the same things. Similar view of growth process. Love of walking and talking. Her ability to coach me. Willingness to be silly.

Intermission

For the moment, set your lists aside. Like the preparation of a good stew, these exercises need time to simmer, time for the flavors to mingle, and time for you to draw even more deeply from what you've brought together thus far.

Caution: Try not to fall into the trap that you must do something about your relationship with your siblings *right* *now*. If you were to faithfully complete every exercise in this book, and never actually *do* anything, we guarantee that your connection to your siblings would still shift dramatically. Consider the time and effort you are spending on this to be an investment in your self-awareness.

Encore

Exploration 2-3   Together/Apart
What you will need:

Sibling journal; no extra time required

Witness: Begin to observe the course of your relationships with your siblings from this point on. You don't have to do anything other than watch with as much objectivity as you can muster. Watch and feel. Note the results of your observations in your sibling journal.

Part of our objective is to help you develop the skills of a witness/observer.

Setting the Stage

In the following exercise you have an opportunity first to notice what's missing between you and your brother or sister and then to build a bridge to the future by imagining what it would be like to have it. This exploration provides further opportunity to think out of the box and to consider your sibling relationship as a work in progress, rather than a fait accompli.

Once again, take a moment to center yourself. Then sit back and close your eyes. You can temporarily "vacate" normal consciousness by imagining yourself at the beach or in the mountains, or wherever you would most like to be. Take a walk in your imagination and feel yourself restored by the beauty of the surroundings, whether you are indoors or outdoors. After three or four long, deep breaths, you're ready to embark on this new exploration.

Exploration 2-4 If Only . . .

What you will need:

Sibling journal; 15 minutes

Lists and landmarks: Write ten sentences starting with: "If only . . ." and then fill in the blank with statements about your brother or sister.

For example: "If only Jonathan would call me more often"; "If only I felt free to tell Sally how I really feel about her moving away"; "If only Jamie and I could laugh and party the way we used to when we were in high school."

Mapping the territory: After you've completed each sentence, add in a rejoinder: "If only . . . then I would . . ."

For example: "If only I were willing to disagree more openly with my siblings, then I would feel less defensive and more freewheeling with them."

After your ten sentences about each brother or sister, write one overarching statement: "A possible vision for how things might be different in the future."

Experiment with different thoughts on how you might approach one another.

What Happened

The power in "if only" is that it can start you dreaming of a relationship that better suits you and your siblings. One thing that seems to be extinguished in growing up is the ability to see, even in a daydream, a different relationship with people we've known for a lifetime.

Kenny, a participant in an afternoon workshop at Temple University, created a vision that was simple yet very touching: "My brother doesn't steal from me anymore. No more freeloading. In fact, he brings the pizza and beer when he comes over."

Stephen, a participant at the same workshop, had this vision of his relationship with his two older, and very ambitious, sisters: "Lisa, Cheryl, and I make it a point to gather twice a year: once in my neck of the woods, and once out on the West Coast near them. I can relax about their accomplishments and not feel so embarrassed and lazy. In my vision, we've finally come to understand and accept each other. They even came to like my cabin here in the Vermont woods."

Your vision might, as in the example above, include activities and behaviors that you no longer wish to share. For example, Henry, a young man in another of our groups who is in recovery from alcohol and cocaine abuse, shared his possible vision, which included: "No more drinking buddies, me and Ron go to the gym and he helps me stay clean. He doesn't suggest we meet at McGlinchy's [a neighborhood bar] but suggests we go to a meeting [12-Step] instead and buys me coffee afterward."

Remember, this is exploratory. Nothing in fact need be different. All you're doing is opening your mind to new possibilities, thinking and dreaming out of the box. If you feel comfortable, you might introduce this chapter to your brothers or sisters. Or you may request some of their versions of "if only" in relation to you. Either way, keep these notes in a safe place. Continue exploring and expanding the vision you want for a more enjoyable, fulfilling sibling relationship.

Do We Really Know Our Siblings?

We assume that we know our siblings and that they know us. In the case of Bill and Eric, we can see that much of what we think we know is our own inner story, something we've made up in the absence of real information. This so-called story continues to guide and inform our interactions, often contributing to the built-in barrier between us. Although both from Los Angeles, it seems that these brothers were miles apart in terms of how they experienced their relationship.

His brother Bill lay on the hospital bed. For the hundredth time, Eric cursed his fate. Although Bill was active, had watched his diet, and was only 57, he was dying. This certainly wasn't the death they had talked about at bedtime half a century ago. Instead, they'd imagined dying like heroes, dogfighting the Japanese Zeros to the end. Of course, Eric, the older brother, would die first, as he had done everything first. But things hadn't worked out that way. Turning from the hospital bed, Eric gazed out the window at the twilight. For years they had been so close, but now his brother Bill was a stranger to him.

Two days earlier, during a pain-free moment, Bill complained that no one was ever there for him. Furious, Eric said nothing, though he had taken the week off to be there and had been in daily contact with the hospital prior to that, even to the point of neglecting his own family. How could it be this way? Eric thought to himself. Doesn't Bill know I love him?

In fact, Bill doesn't. When communication in the present is neglected, we rely on the old stories from the past to fill the void and help us relate to the situation. For Bill and Eric, even in the eleventh hour, they have a chance to know each other, to become real people, and to fill the gap with real communication rather than superficial dialogue.

There's More to Us than Sibling Rivalry Alone

In summary, we acknowledge that rivalry is a force to be reckoned with. Any readers who have raised children have seen how intense rivalry can be. On some days it seems the only dynamic at play. On other days, however, the children seem secure in their roles in the family and accepting of their parents' love and attention. They are capable of the most moving and profound love and sensitivity to one another.

These paradoxes—of great fury coupled with great love—exist at the heart of all sibling relationships.

For us, as adults, the jokes and ribbing provide a chance to poke fun at one another and make sure we're not taking anything too seriously. In childhood and into the teen years, we fought like proverbial cats and dogs. Somehow we made it through, though.

This may or may not be true for you and your siblings. It is important to examine and review, to use the powers of recall and naming to begin to sort out what needs attention, care, and healing.

Sibling rivalry may have things to tell us about how we'll turn out in our later years. It may be that the stress and struggle in childhood sibling relationships actually serve to prepare us for the world we will later inhabit as adults. Consider the possibility that strong sibling rivalries have the power to be converted to even stronger bonds of love. That has been the case for us.

Summary
Step 2: Witness the Effects of Old Rivalries

- For as long as there has been recorded history, there are myths and stories about competition among siblings.

- According to Freud, sibling rivalry is normal, based in our unconscious fear and rage at having to share our scarce resources of love and nurturing (i.e., our parents).

- Our view is that rivalry, while a normal aspect of childhood, is naturally balanced by cooperation.

- Chief aspects of sibling rivalry include competition, communication blocks, misunderstandings that may continue over long periods, and eventually a complete conflict in values.

- De-identification is the process by which one sibling studiously avoids the territory of another sibling; it is a means of avoiding sibling rivalry.

- Rivalry often drives aspects of our adult sibling relationships (and peer relationships) both consciously and unconsciously. Often, how we define a particular sibling relationship actually turns out to be based more on our projection than on reality.

- It takes courage and effort to begin to discover who our siblings really are.

- Although we see rivalry at work more subtly as siblings age, by unraveling opposition and unspoken conflicts, we can in effect "grow" the relationship to a much more adult stature.

Seeds of Change

Decide whether these questions are true or false in your experience:

❑ I cannot remember any signs of rivalry or conflict among my siblings and myself.

❑ As I review childhood experiences, I am getting clearer about how sibling rivalry developed and the ways in which it was expressed between my siblings and myself.

❑ I notice the ways sibling rivalry separated or created differences between my siblings and me.

❑ I am becoming more aware of the "turf" each of us carved as our own and the ways we de-identified, or deliberately avoided one another's turf.

Grains of Hope, Pearls of Wisdom

✓ I am interested in discovering the more subtle aspects of sibling rivalry and ways that it has unconsciously driven not only my sibling relationships but other peer relationships.

✓ I feel a sense of hope and excitement as I begin to dive deeper into my sibling experience. Although sometimes uncomfortable in this discovery process, I am learning that it is all right to unearth new information. It is a contribution to my growth and development.

CHAPTER 3

Envision a New Future

Everyone lives according to some vision, whether it is
conscious or not. That vision becomes the hidden force
that energizes our motivations.

> Joan Borysenko, Ph.D.,
> *Pocketful of Miracles*

We are human and our lot is to learn and to be hurled
into inconceivable new worlds. A warrior . . . knows
that there is no end to the new worlds for our vision.

> Carlos Castañeda,
> *The Wheel of Time*

The third step—envision a new future—may appear to be almost magical: creating something out of nothing, or different
from what exists. Yet, we have found that it is much easier
to change long-held patterns of behavior if you first imagine
a new future. Take time to construct a model for your new
sibling relationships. Envision your brothers and sisters being there for one another, helping and loving one another.
Imagine a stress-free, cozy gathering with your whole sibling group present. Dare to picture a distant, even estranged
sibling back in the family fold, and the years of painful separation soothed and healed. As in these examples, the act of
imagining in itself initiates the process of breaking habits
that hold your relationships firmly in place.

The natural movement of growth in the sibling
relationship supports this "magical" process of change.
Michael Kahn and Karen Lewis have collected sibling re-

search from many branches of individual, group, and family therapy in *Siblings in Therapy*. Their research indicates that most sibling relationships follow an "hourglass" pattern. The intimacy and intensity of the early years narrows during late adolescence and through the adult years. In late adulthood, sibling intimacy again increases to reach a comparable stage of intensity.

We have seen this pattern reproduced in our workshops. Many, though not all, of our participants are in their middle years, finished with the bulk of the tasks of raising children, and looking ahead to significant change in their lives. Often, care of aging parents will bring semi-distant siblings together with a renewed desire to be cooperatively connected. Sometimes the empty-nest syndrome, retirement, or diminished energy and/or resources will provide impetus for a renewal of sibling bonds. Victor Cicirelli, developmental psychologist, tells the story of several sibling pairs who enjoyed retirement outings and adventures together after years of somewhat cursory connections. In *Siblings in Therapy*, he recounts the story of a man of 90 who continues his weekly correspondence with his brother in Europe—a brother he has not seen since he was 11 years old!

One of many interesting elements revealed in sibling research is that closeness in the relationship does not depend on physical proximity. Elderly people report feeling as close or closer to deceased siblings and distant siblings as they do to siblings and old friends nearby.

Another end of the developmental spectrum is represented by young adults seeking to create their own lives as they leave their families of origin. Many workshop participants fall into this category. It can be painful to fly solo; to feel as though you must leave your precious childhood companions behind in order to fulfill your own dreams. We have worked with siblings at this end of the spectrum as well, to assist them in creating enough distance for individual growth without abandonment and/or rejection of the nurturing aspects of their sibling bonds.

With this in mind, we invite you—wherever you are in the developmental spectrum, as we have invited participants in our workshops—to imagine a bright, rosy future for you and your brothers and/or sisters. Time, experience, and statistics are on your side, supporting your success.

The Next Logical Step in the Process

I'm holding a mental picture of my baby sister feeling good about herself, doing well in college, now that she's studying interior design in Rhode Island. Instead of turning to drugs or all-night partying, she's calling me on the phone to talk about her problems. The old sense that I'm there for her has returned; she feels at ease and familiar, and I in turn am relaxed, inquiring about Cara's life and being her pal like I used to be.

Ron, who's nine years older than his sister Cara, has always been her champion and support. Ron, introspective and quiet, is a high-tech engineer working near Boston. He was happy when his sister chose a school not far from him. Ron never married, and his relationship with Cara, though strained at times, is one of his few enduring personal ties. Her previous choices had greatly pained him, although he didn't mention the depth of his discomfort to her.

Now I can resume the relationship that's been on the back burner these past five years. Even though I did have my reaction to Cara's lifestyle and her new set of friends, I can see that was just my way of being big-brotherly, looking out for my little sister. I've always been a kind of surrogate father for her, probably because of our age difference. It was hard for me to keep my perspective when she began to get a little wild. In truth, I felt helpless, and wondered if her troubles were somehow my fault.

When presented with the opportunity, it didn't take Ron long to come up with a new vision for their relationship. In fact, Ron was able to identify as a chief obstacle to closeness the prior awkwardness he'd experienced just thinking about being Cara's friend again. As he shared with our group:

I just assumed she wouldn't want me in her life. After all, we're different. I'm kind of straight, and Cara's not. She steers clear of any mold or stereotype. Besides, she has her friends and her art. Since our folks divorced, I took over parenting her and have been sort of her guardian and protector. Our older brother Arthur tends his vineyards out in Washington State; we hardly ever hear from him. But now that Cara and I live so close to each other, she's on my mind all the time. I finally got in touch with how much my baby sister means to me, and how simple it would be for me to reach out to her. Making up this vision was the next logical step in the process. . . .

An Approach Centered in Hope and Imagination

As you explore the possibility of creating a new future you'll get a chance to see how things evolve from a picture in your mind all the way to a real-life scenario. At first glance, this may seem far-fetched. Nothing could be further from the truth. Think about it. All great men and women had to envision a world of their choosing, struggle to achieve it, and with luck live to see that world embodied. Jesus did it. Mohammed did it. Even today, Nelson Mandela did it. We tend to focus more on their stories and forget our own. Yet, every time we reach for and achieve a new interpersonal solution to old or unwanted behavior, we contribute to a brand-new world. In fact, all of us are involved in the creation of new worlds as a product of our thinking and imagination. Naturally, this process extends to the kind of relationship you create with your brothers and sisters. We'll let you in on some secrets about how to envision and create the world of your choice, and how to recognize the elements of your vision as they become manifest.

In subsequent chapters we will outline techniques to untangle the threads that bind you to your past in negative or hurtful ways. Our goal is to continue to add freedom and choice to your repertoire of responses available for relating to sisters and brothers. We will show you how to deconstruct some of the barriers inherent in habitual ways of thinking and acting, while you adapt techniques that are more aligned with your adult capacities. Meanwhile, our approach is centered in hope and imagination.

Untangling sibling threads can have unexpected benefits in other areas of your adult life. Research indicates that we tend to replicate sibling relationship patterns in our professional relationships, in our own families of creation, and with our partners. Part of the "magic" in shifting the ineffective patterns established with siblings is the ease with which other difficult relationships improve.

Right now, as you read this book, you are living from some thought, or wish, or desire to reach for something you'd only imagined: creating a new future for you and your siblings. Your thoughts continually move in different directions, and in each moment you have the choice to harness them to what you define as your good. While no one can prevent the inevitable detours or disturbances, the overall direction that we take through our thinking is in our hands. Constantly dwelling on things in the same way and with the same feeling engenders the same future. Imagining and experimenting with different outcomes, especially when we are able to feel their effects, eventually draws us to those outcomes. Albert Einstein wisely remarked that problems could not be solved with the same kind of thinking as that which created them. That's what we're pointing to here.

Keys to Introducing Change

In the beginning, the key to introducing change is to allow yourself to imagine a future that suits you more than the one you have. This often requires a shift in thinking. Most of us are more concerned with observing reality as it is than imagining a new or different outcome. As a result, we lose sight of the powerful connection between our imagining and what comes to us through life experiences. In this chapter we have included samples of sibling relationships in various stages of progress, plus a personal exploration that will help you rewrite the future of your own relationships.

However we view it, we're molding and playing with "reality" as we imagine it differently. Our first attempts at change must come through changing our language. In fact, as Carlos Castañeda said in *The Wheel of Time*, "We talk to ourselves incessantly about our world. In fact we maintain our world with our internal talk. Not only that, but we also choose our paths as we talk to ourselves. Thus we repeat the same choices over and over until the day we die, because we keep repeating the same internal talk."

Psychologists are in agreement with this assertion. Albert Ellis, Aaron Beck, and many others have written exhaustively about the persuasive and potentially toxic nature of internalized dialogue, or "self-talk." Training people to identify, interrupt, challenge, and alter this constant inner conversation has thus become a cornerstone of cognitive and behavioral therapy. We're asking the same of you, knowing it isn't easy. In fact, mastering this process will dramatically change your life.

Behind this innocent set of instructions is a little key to thinking your thoughts instead of having them think you.

Thus, you now have an opportunity to change your language and the way you represent this all-important relationship in your life. The first person who needs to hear about it
differently, however, is you. To speak this relationship differently is equivalent to moving furniture in a room. At first,
shifting the structures may seem to have no point. However,
if you look more closely, you'll see that the act of moving
one piece of furniture shifts the existing relationship with
everything else in the room. Suddenly you've opened up a
space; call it a new vista or perspective in which the parts
can be differently related.

Not all change comes easily, however. Sarah, a successful
clothing designer who is now the owner of her own bou-
tique, shared this:

> Even though I'm 44 and my brother Arnie is 49, I have
> never been able to express my anger to him. My earliest
> memory is of him holding me down when I tried to
> fight him for stealing money from my piggy bank. I
> couldn't have been more than four or five years old, but
> that memory sticks in my mind. From that moment I
> was Arnie's little handmaiden. I guess I learned that I
> was too little to beat him; that he'd get his way no mat-
> ter what. I've continued to do this with him to this day.
> I can be brutal in business, with my own husband and
> children, but not with my brother. To think I can
> change things forty years later is a stretch; on the other
> hand, we've both been through a lot; Arnie lost his wife
> to cancer and his oldest boy has problems with sub-
> stance abuse. I never thought to explore a different
> relationship, but I'm sure we'd both do well with some-
> thing other than our 9-year-old and 4-year-old versions
> of ourselves.

Our Many Versions of Reality

Often sibling relationships don't change because we haven't been able to imagine a future different from our present. Yet, if we were to discuss the future of our sibling relationships with our brothers and sisters, we might be shocked to find that each one has been living from a different past! As we mentioned earlier, none of us can agree what the nature of this relationship is in the first place. That's because, in effect, we all subscribe to different versions of reality. In the instance above, if we were to question Arnie, we would probably find him surprised to discover that his sister's earliest and most prominent memory of him carries such wounding, and from an incident that he considers just a childish prank. But to her it might in fact be a life-altering event. And this is how it goes with people. We perceive things differently, make up what we think is true, and then live as though our perceptions are *the truth*.

Akira Kurosawa's classic film *Rashomon* (1950) illustrates this axiom. A man is murdered. A bandit rapes his wife. Through flashback we discover four different versions of what happened. The result: No reliable history can be assembled from these different versions of reality. What we observe in our own lives is the same: Each of us lives out of the experience of our own interpretations, which are often complex and multifaceted. Although we may compare our different versions (and we often do), we can never hope to emerge with *the one truth* about our relationships. Therefore, when we approach the subject of change, we need to be clear that what we're changing is in fact our version of the relationship, not our brothers' and sisters'.

How Well Can You Envision a Different Future?

In the process of writing this book, one of the unexpected things we had to deal with was the dismantling of aspects of our own relationships to one another. The discomfort of disassembling and rebuilding involves tolerating the uncertainty of a close, intimate, but *different* future with one another. After I know my sister thinks I'm too fat, or she knows I think she's mechanically inept, or my brother knows I know he has trouble meeting the demands of his own wife and children, let alone his sisters—what then?

What comes next depends in large part on your imagination. In fact, one of the keys to improving sibling relationships has to do with how much energy you can invest in thinking differently. To think differently requires faith in a different outcome; you imagine that a new future is possible. It is also true, as Victor Cicirelli's research points out in "Sibling Relationships in Middle and Old Age," that the vast majority of sibling relationships tend to improve naturally as siblings age. Much of this improvement has to do with the overall effects of gaining the perspective of age—learning to accept, forgive, and respect everyone in our lives. In earlier chapters we discussed the power of habits that keep the old sibling relationships in place. On the positive side, we have the habit of loving our siblings. This takes many forms— shared holidays, shared secrets, shared memories, to mention but a few. Doris Lessing wrote, "habit is half of love," and so it is with sisters and brothers. We invite you to consider that the other half of love is consciousness, choice, and a willingness to replace old, immature habits with new, affirming, adult habits.

How Can the Future Be Different from the Past?

Part of the irreplaceable value the sibling relationship has for any individual is that it, alone among relationships, will not change as passage through the life stages occurs. When a parent dies, the role of son or daughter is gone. When marriages end or spouses die, the role of husband/wife is gone. For the most part, however, we take our sibling roles with us all the way through life, since siblings are our longest-lived relationships. In this way, they provide an anchor in a vast sea of relational and role changes.

Mentioned in chapter 2, Adele, a program participant, shares about her sister Joyce, who is two years younger:

> We were raised in a Jewish family. When I was 9 and my sister 7, we were separated from one another. Joyce went to live with an aunt in Washington, D.C.; I stayed in Charleston but was sent to live with my aunt and uncle who are Catholic. I felt responsible for the breakup of my whole family. Not only that, in Catholic school I began to feel like a demon. Here was Jesus on the cross and I was told my people were to blame for his death. Knowing my sister was up north, I felt like a traitor; I must have really been bad to have my father abandon us and to have my sister move so far away.
>
> That early experience placed an indelible mark upon our relationship. I have always felt guilty and apologetic toward Joyce, and she in turn maintains a safe distance from me, as if I really was a demon. It takes all I can muster to begin to work toward a different future.

The dark side of sibling habits includes not only a broad spectrum of repetitive or dysfunctional behaviors but a potentially destructive way of thinking about the future. The habitual way of thinking actually delivers the future as you imagined it. How can you imagine anything else when life with your siblings has *always* been the way it is now? You've failed so many times to express what you want, or to communicate in the way you want, or to have the relationship you want. In fact, you "know" with every fiber of your being how the future will turn out—it will be a reiteration of the past. This type of thinking is invariably a mishmash of attitudes and habits left-over from childhood. It may serve to mask our deeper fear that we don't deserve goodness, as

Adele expressed. At any rate, our desire to venture out and experience more loving relationships is hindered by old patterns of thought.

The Courage to Do Things Differently

To have the courage to do things differently ushers in a new order in the sibling hierarchy. Julia Alvarez captures the flavor of these ambivalent sibling interchanges in *How the Garcia Girls Lost Their Accents*, a novel about the coming of age of four sisters uprooted from their home in the Dominican Republic and relocated to the Bronx. As young adults, the four sisters come together less frequently, and their gatherings are more like lessons in avoiding land mines than sharing tender moments with family:

Yolanda keeps her mouth shut. She is working on a thought about her bossy older sister: Carla has a tendency to lace all her compliments with calls to self-improvement. *Give yourself credit. Believe in yourself. Be good to yourself.* Somehow this makes her praise sound like their mother's old "constructive criticism." Yolanda chooses silence, knowing that her time with her sisters is short, and proceeding with her standard objections to Carla's "little mother" role would disrupt what little harmony the Garcia girls have. Yolanda's new choice is a landmark for her and her sisters. She sidesteps conflict, and—miracle of miracles—her sisters follow suit.

The real world resembles fiction in this matter of shifting old relationship patterns. As Gene Brody points out in "Sibling Relationship Quality: Its Causes and Consequences," every sibling group has a unique, unvoiced balance of power that determines part of the character of the relationship. Jake and his two brothers, whom we mentioned earlier, provide an example of a relationship poised on the edge of growth. According to Jake, he and his brothers have come to a stalemate in their relationship. Although Jake is not optimistic

about their future, he does manage to come up with a vision
that can help move the family in a different direction:

> Right now it's hard to imagine a vision that would
> work for my brothers and me. I really can't imagine us
> coming any closer. It seems like we still have to iron out
> the details of growing up with our particular set of par-
> ents. I would love to feel closer to them both, but I
> don't want to be the only one who thinks that way. So
> I'd have to say that my vision includes all three of us
> coming around to the same way of thinking. All three
> of us wanting to be close at some point in time and
> finding a natural, spontaneous opening for that would
> be the best possible outcome.

What Jake may not realize is that the articulation of his vision is the first step in the process of change.

Francine Klagsbrun, writer, editor, and lecturer, speculates
that we avoid challenging and examining our sibling relationships as adults in part because they have gone unexam-
ined for so long. Unlike parent-child relationships, which
have been subject to exhaustive scrutiny, sibling bonds have
been relatively immune from analysis. In her work *Mixed
Feelings: Love, Hate, Rivalry and Reconciliation Among Brothers
and Sisters,* Klagsbrun writes: "[s]o highly regarded, in fact,
are sibling ties by both individuals and society that since earliest times they have been idealized, turned into a metaphor
for the very best of human relations. We speak of the 'brotherhood of man' as a paradigm of love and loyalty. . . . 'Sisterhood' triggers images of feminist strivings toward a new
understanding by women of each other, a new joining with
one another in friendship and cooperation."

And yet we keep a distance from these idealized versions
of sister- and brotherhood. For whatever reason, we fight
the possibility of change among our siblings, resisting the

inconvenience or suffering we believe may come with it. After all, we are creatures of routine. Change is fine as long as it refers to an upgrade in software or wardrobe—but in a relationship? What we propose, then, is to suspend your cynicism and resignation for a few moments and initiate the following explorations. Then see what happens. We promise that you can always return to your current way of looking at the world and maintain things just as they are. But who knows? Change may happen when you least expect it. After all, the Iron Curtain lifted, the Berlin Wall was dismantled brick by brick, and those whom we thought were our enemies became friends. All things change eventually, including our relationships to our siblings!

Some people are dyed-in-the-wool skeptics and feel that anything that doesn't deal with "reality" as they perceive it is a waste of time. "What good is it to imagine a future I *know* can't happen?" On the other hand, if things are as solid and unyielding as you say, all that might be at risk is greater self-awareness and appreciation of your siblings and yourself as well. Sometimes recognizing the limitations of our siblings and our relationships to them can bring great change and freedom.

A Prisoner of Entitlement

Marjory knows the story of a young woman, Marian, who began working on her troubled and painful relationship with her older sister in a workshop; they continued this work in individual therapy. Elise and Marian are four years apart. Marian describes herself as an invisible child. Elise required enormous amounts of attention and care. She was diagnosed with juvenile diabetes at the age of 9 and did not adjust well to the demands of her illness. Both parents invested a lot of time, energy, and worry into the smallest details of Elise's life. Marian, on the other hand, was healthy and good-natured. As a result, she did not demand much attention from her parents, nor did she receive it. Elise was cruel to Marian and seemed to resent any accomplishment, any small triumph. Marian recounts one of many such incidents from childhood:

> I think I was maybe 9 or 10 years old, so Elise was 13 or 14. She was mean, but I kind of looked at her in awe. She seemed so grown-up to me. Elise told me that I would be getting a terrible disease any day now—just as she had at my age. We shared a room, and she would wake me up and ask me if I felt anything yet. It seems harmless, in retrospect, but at the time, I was so afraid. Elise told me not to tell our parents, that it would break their hearts. I believed her, and waited and waited to fall desperately ill. I was completely terrified.

Marian finally stopped waiting for her terrible illness. More recently, she stopped waiting for her older sister to put her first, to remember her birthday, or to offer any kindness or support. Marian observed: "Elise still operates as though she was entitled to all the attention, all the care, all the concern. I think I'm beginning to understand that she is as much a prisoner of her entitlement as I have been a prisoner of my hunger to have her tell me I'm important to her."

Much of what we know about our siblings is often based on false assumptions or childish interpretations. For example, you perceive that your older sister is bossy and that is all there is to it. Let's agree that anyone observing your sister would conclude that she is bossy. Whenever she acts that way, you react to her shrill voice and superior attitude, annoyed that things never change. The system appears to be static and immutable. She's bossy; you're annoyed—period. Why bother?

But what if her bossiness was based on a single childhood incident in which you fell in a creek and it looked like you almost drowned? (You've probably forgotten the incident, since you were only 2.) Taking this example even further, what if she felt guilty because you fell into the creek? After all, your sister was supposed to "watch" you (even though she was only 5 at the time), and you didn't listen to her. She felt responsible. So, in her mind, in order to protect you, she had to become increasingly bossy and strident for you to listen at all. That strong desire to protect you still shows up as bossiness in the present. And further, if you were honest with yourself, regular talking never got through to you and still doesn't. Another explanation could be that your sister's bossiness is her expression of unconditional love and her desire to protect you. She didn't change at all, but your feelings about her and her bossiness made a giant leap and were transformed.

Something Has to Change

Visiting again with Esther, mentioned in a previous chapter, we observe the fear of relinquishing the past, even if, as in her case, the past conceals a dysfunctional sibling relationship. When she begins to consider a different relationship with her sister Elaine, she panics. Like so many of us, she is used to relating to things as they have been all along, without being able to imagine a new scenario.

Something in this picture has to change. And it's probably me. I get to stay safe and to be myself as long as she's the crazy or controlling one, the one who eats like a pig. I can isolate and refuse to relate because look who I'm trying to relate to. She's out of it. Sometimes Elaine acts more like an animal than a human being. But if I let go of the bleak, uncomfortable picture I have of her, and imagine getting my sister back, if I imagine having someone who cares about me and whom I care about—now that is a vision worth considering. To hold on to it I'd probably have to give up my selfishness, my sense that I know better, my disgust, and my isolation. That's a big one for me. But a lot's at stake.

I need time to think about this, but I'm clear that all the therapy in the world isn't bringing me closer to her. And this is critical to me in my development now. This is the relationship I most need to bring into the present; it lives so much more like a dinosaur or a relic from the past. I'm still circling around it, or around the little girl that I used to be. I need to find ways to make it safe to express who I am and put to good use the tools my adult self has acquired. Come to think of it, I don't like being so inept. I have so much to offer. All my friends see who I am; my partner sees me. Only Elaine has no idea of the person I've become. Everyone receives the benefit from my gifts and talents but her. It's dawning on me what a waste of energy to keep myself so small. Though I've never thought of it this way, I imagine we could both derive a lot more from each other if we were "grown-up" when we were together. Just enjoying each other's company—now there's a vision that I can invest some real energy in.

What we observe with many siblings trying to mend fences is that once we take on the challenge of re-creating this relationship, we discover that we are in fact re-creating ourselves. Stephen Levine echoes this sentiment in his work *Healing into Life and Death*: "The feeling of loss, and being lost, eventually gets our attention and we see that no one can make us happy but us. And we begin to take responsibility. We begin to build the capacity to respond instead of react. And we focus on our resistance and recognize that relationship is work on ourselves."

The Sky's the Limit

With imagination, the sky's the limit; there's no end to what you can dream up. You are not constrained by reality, even if reality includes a sibling who hangs up the phone every time you call. Rather than haunt yourself with versions of the old reality, take this opportunity to radically shift your focus and begin weaving a fantasy version of your sibling future that draws your attention. Imagine what it would be like to one day refer to *that* as reality. Like Esther and Elaine, one sister can change the relationship by herself. We've always assumed that to substantively change a relationship, both siblings would have to participate in some kind of therapy over a period of time. In some cases this is true; in others, a single reinterpretation can shift the whole relationship. Certainly, reinterpretation and revision shift the quality of the relationship for the individual at work, as with Marian and others.

Take the case of James, for example, age 33 and the youngest in a family of six:

> [We were] raised in a Boston Irish-Catholic family; rivalry was part of the setup. With four boys and two girls, we developed a love of physical fights. Dad helped us set up a boxing ring, gave us several sets of gloves, and we learned to box each other. Even the girls were involved. Whoever won escaped washing the dishes or setting the table that night. Although we were taught to appreciate each other's accomplishments, we were fiercely competitive in sports and in school. Maureen's the best diver, John's the best long-distance runner; I play jazz piano, Sean sings well, Kevin's the best boxer, and Marty's a mean cook. Though everyone is good at something, I wish we were all better at listening to each other. Just for once, I wish we'd stop competing for the limelight. But that's a tall order.

James began to picture a different reality with his siblings. Each one continued to exhibit his or her supreme accomplishments, but in his imagination, something new was added into the equation. James imagined a gathering of his sisters and brothers that included space to listen and receive one another just as they were, in a climate of patience and acceptance. After spending time in fantasy, unburdened by his "real" experiences to the contrary, James actually experienced a shift in the family dynamic.

At a family picnic with the whole clan gathered together, James found himself feeling calmer, less driven to "one-up" his siblings. Instead, he offered genuine praise to his oldest brother for an accomplishment at work. His brother literally stopped in his tracks, and James watched as his shoulders dropped and his face softened. To his surprise, his big brother replied: "Hey, thanks, Jimmy! That really means a lot to me." James smiled, put his arm around his brother, and felt warm down to his toes, excited at the huge change that came about because he dared to think and act differently.

We Must Become What We Imagine

Any significant change we make in our lives begins with this process of imagining, or visualizing. It is a cornerstone of cognitive-behavioral therapy and a proven method of reducing unwanted behavior and adding more productive, positive behavior. Top athletes can improve their performance by carefully visualizing themselves in action in their sport. Individuals suffering from crippling social phobias can get up and deliver speeches to five hundred people after careful and thorough visualizing. Naturally, the key to beginning such endeavors is motivation—seeing the need for change, focusing on a different outcome, and adding the critical ingredients of hope and imagination. In fact, we cannot create what we have not first imagined. Although it encompasses thinking and feeling, a further dimension of this process involves embodying the desired future using all of our senses, heart, intellect, and intuition, so that we can draw it into our lives.

More than a mere mental game or calculation, true visioning requires us to go through an internal process of transformation. We must in effect *become* what we desire in our imagination and release the momentum of the past. To draw the new future closer, we need radical desire—the kind of desire that cuts through obstacles and generates energy and momentum enough to step into a new experience. Invariably that comes as a result of transforming old habit patterns. So we come full circle. We must challenge and release old habits while summoning inspiration and vision from a new future.

Setting the Stage

We now ask you to join us in taking advantage of one of the most powerful models of behavior change: envisioning what you want so that you can move toward it. We always recommend beginning a creative exercise such as this one with a time of reflection. As an interesting aside, several participants in our workshops have found that the preparation—that is, the gathering of photographs and other memorabilia—serves as a powerful change agent in their sibling relationships, and even in relationships with parents.

Marjory recalls an experience with a patient, Naomi, who made contact with her parents after several years of estrangement, just to see if she could get some childhood photographs from them. To her surprise, her parents were more than willing to accommodate her; with no questions asked, her mother sent her a package full of old family photos, along with a detailed and tender letter describing all the scenes and situations. Naomi was moved to tears by this package and especially by her mother's correspondence. She sent her parents a letter and a thank-you gift in response, and soon they were back in regular communication on a whole different footing. Naomi was perplexed, too. How had this huge shift in her relationship with her parents occurred without processing all the details of their estrangement? As Naomi pondered and pondered, she also added some of this "magic" into her vision of a future with her siblings.

Exploration 3-1 My Future Sibling Connection
What you will need:

Pictures or reminders of your siblings; 20 minutes

For the second part: construction paper, all kinds of magazines, scissors, glue, crayons, markers, glitter, stickers, etc.
• Choose a time (or create a time) when you will not be disturbed.
• Read through the complete exercise several times and put it away.

Reflection: Sit or lie down in a quiet place. Relax and close your eyes. Allow any thoughts that surface to cross your mind and then leave. When you feel calm and centered, proceed to the next steps.

Allow feelings and sensations to arise and pass on. If recurrent worries surface, open your eyes, make a note in your sibling journal, and return to the exercise. The key here is not to control or hold on to anything, but to let go. Watch thoughts, ideas, or feelings rise to the surface and pass by like a leaf in a stream. You may choose to do some of the breathing exercises mentioned in earlier chapters.

Lights, Camera, Action: Open your eyes and look at the photograph or drawing, and allow yourself to feel whatever feelings emerge as you look into the faces of your siblings. Begin to make quick notes—using words or images—to capture your feelings in the moment.

Do not try to contain or control your feelings at this time. If you are very sad, allow yourself to cry. If you are angry, feel the feeling fully and express the anger in a nondestructive way. When appropriate, allow your feelings to subside.

continued

Look at the photograph again. See if you can summarize your experience in words or images.

You may want to give your family a title that characterizes this moment for you. One of our workshop participants christened her family, "It's a mad, mad, mad, mad world"; later, after working with her vision of a future, she rechristened the family, "Happy Days Are Here Again." See what you discover!

Imaginary lives: Looking at the pictures once again, ask what you would like to have happen. What is the main feeling that you experience thinking about the future of your sibling group?

If strong emotions surface, acknowledge them and allow them to pass. Continue reflecting on the future. You share elements of your life with these people. Your relationship with these people is unique. In truth, no one else has or ever will hold the place that they hold. How would you like to see this relationship unfold in your life?

Intermission

In studying his family portrait, Howard, one of our workshop participants, commented that although he felt very blessed to have good connections with his eight siblings, that there were still some things missing. "I'd like to see more communication from some of the normally silent siblings. I'd like to see encouragement to explore different views when we get polarized around various topics. I'd like there to be enough space for each one of us to express things in a different way or from a different perspective."

Encore

Lights, Camera, Action: Using the techniques of collage (torn or cut images, words, found objects, etc. assembled and glued together either in your journal or on some other surface), begin using words, images, or abstract forms to create a picture of your sibling family as you would like it to be. Let yourself go, be creative, be funny, and imagine a really nurturing, supportive, playful, happy future. Find images that reflect these things. Be sure you and all of your siblings are in the picture. This is not the time to worry about so-called reality. It's playtime!

What Happened

For Howard, creating the collage was an easy task, since he was a graphic artist. He pulled together a stunning pastiche, filled with people talking, elegant symbols, quotations, and telephone wires connecting the siblings together.

Annie, a workshop participant, imagined her large family together on a cruise on a turquoise sea. Her collage was filled with pictures of coral reefs, fish, and happy adults and children frolicking on the beach with the cruise ship in the distance. Having completed her collage, Annie gradually began to relate to her family as her future playmates, almost without realizing it. This subtle shift in her way of relating to her family helped her realize her dream.

Just on a whim, excited by her vision, Annie called her older sister Monica and playfully challenged her to a contest to see who could save the most five-dollar bills toward a family cruise. Monica accepted the challenge immediately, and the game was under way!

Like Annie, you can use these elements to move into a new paradigm, in which the very act of holding a vision elicits feelings of what it's like to live in the future. Once the feelings are in place, your ability to dream, evoke, or call forth elements of a new sibling relationship are easily activated.

We Think We Know Our Siblings

Sharon, an attractive 42-year-old nurse from New Hampshire, speaks up in our workshop about her lucky life. She finally adopted a son (the adoption was very rocky and required her to go overseas and struggle with paperwork and petty officials). Sharon and her husband, Paul, had gone through some hard times and were now pretty happy with the marriage and with each other. As she was thinking about all this, however, Sharon was still nagged by the thought that something was missing. Then, she remembered Elizabeth.

Sharon had seen her older sister Elizabeth only three or four times in the last five years. Each time they had contact it was more painful than the last. The last time was a year ago, after Elizabeth had undergone an operation. Sharon's weak attempt at reconciliation ended only in further disagreement between the sisters about something that had occurred twenty years earlier.

Sharon knew that Elizabeth was extremely unhappy and probably depressed. Over the years she had heard from their parents about Elizabeth's professional and family troubles. She knew from her memories that her sister was remote, aloof, and would never share any details about her myriad problems.

Born only twenty months apart, they were each other's closest companions growing up. When they were children they loved to hike the trails around their New Hampshire home. They were both Girl Scouts and on the ski patrol. They loved outdoor adventures and shared many happy times together.

Sharon remembered when the split happened. Typically, they argued over boys. Sharon was always more outgoing and would pal around with the boys whom Elizabeth (the beautiful one) brought home. Then one day one of the boys Elizabeth had been seeing asked her to go out instead.

Sharon thought it was no big deal. After all, they were just going bowling. But Elizabeth hit the roof; she was certain Sharon had stolen her boyfriend. Not only that, she thought it was some kind of plot that Sharon had been working on. Elizabeth shut down. Sharon was shocked. From that moment on, they acted more like enemies than friends.

From interacting with other siblings in our program and writing a description of her relationship, Sharon realized that although she felt she *knew* her sister, actually she had no idea who Elizabeth was. Moreover, the situation had grown worse because they hadn't spoken for such a long while. In a courageous moment, Sharon accepted the fact that she didn't know her sister and decided to reestablish contact.

Feeling that a call was too risky, Sharon sent her an e-mail introducing the possibility of taking a short trek together. Sharon had already begun planning a trip through Scotland with one of the hiking companies on the Internet. To her surprise, Elizabeth responded the very same day! She was delighted to hear from her younger sister and thought a trek would be great. After studying the Web site, however, Elizabeth got excited about doing a harder and longer outing. Several conversations later, they agreed to go on a three-week hike in Nepal, from Katmandu to the base camp at Mt. Everest.

Unbelievably, the next year she and her sister were going to trek in Nepal. They were going to leave their husbands and kids and go. To top it all off, Sharon choked up with tears when Elizabeth called and informed her that she wanted to cover both deposits for the trip. She suspected that Sharon might need help after having spent so much money on the adoption. Sharon was uncharacteristically speechless when she received the check for the deposit.

Before they had even set out on their journey, Sharon had had many realizations. Most important, she realized that she needed to replace her old images and thoughts about Elizabeth. This was her first chance in many years to really get to know her sister. She was eager to pick up where they had left off.

The Power of Our Thoughts

Our thoughts provide a powerful interaction with life. How we think affects what we observe, which further feeds in to how we think. Our relationships, too, are shaped by our thoughts. Sharon had certain thoughts that led to a certain kind of relationship with her sister. Changing her thinking changed the relationship. When Sharon reported back what had happened, we all wished her a safe and happy trek and wondered if we too should go out on a limb with some of our loved ones.

The mind is an extremely powerful tool. So powerful, in fact, that if you think about lying on a beach under a hot sun, your body may begin to sweat. If you envision a fight or some other stressful situation, you can actually influence your blood pressure. Many are aware of the "white coat syndrome," when your normally stable blood pressure shoots up in the physician's office. These are the principles that shape biofeedback training and other successful methods of self-healing. You are now using this power to change your relationships. As you practice visualizing and imagining new experiences in these relationships, see if you can actually imagine what it would feel like to live in those relationships.

Rebuilding Life Structures

Hank, a retired architect and businessman from Greenwich, Connecticut, described his new project in one of our workshops. At the age of 56 he had retired from a successful architectural firm and embarked on a new career, or, as he called it, a new chapter of his life, which he described as "getting around to rebuilding my own life structures."

The last thirty years I have been hell-bent on establishing a reputable architectural firm, raising two kids, and making a small fortune. The fact that my wife and I split ten years ago and that my daughter never calls have barely made a dent in my consciousness. I was too busy with other things. For so many years I had a good excuse not to talk to my sister Rebecca, who, by the way, dragged me to this sibling workshop. She was too crazy, the kind of person who never had any money and who lived in an ashram. I don't know how it came to me, but I was sitting at my drafting table, glancing through *Architectural Digest*, when I realized that all my money, good reputation, the boat, the house, all the conveniences, what did they matter? If I died in that moment, no one would give a damn. All the people I really loved and whose love I desperately needed were hardly on speaking terms with me. What's so amazing is that that very same night, Rebecca called me.

When we turned to Rebecca, there was a huge smile on her face. A yoga teacher and staff member at a meditation retreat center, Rebecca divulged a secret about her older brother Hank:

I've always been on Hank's case to eat better, to take time out to relax, and to enjoy his life. Usually he would indulge me for the moment and then turn a deaf ear. About a year ago, when my meditation practice deepened, I got the idea to start visualizing Hank healthier and happier. It wasn't hard to do; after all, he is my brother and we do love one another. Then I started working on a vision that would have us be much closer together. It's amazing, though; once I started having that vision, I had to let go of my own feelings of inferiority. I had to let go of the fact that there might be something wrong with me since I never pulled the big paycheck that Hank does, and in fact he's had to come to my rescue so many times financially. So putting forth a vision made me change before it even scratched the surface of our relationship as brother and sister.

We then worked with Hank and Rebecca to determine a vision that would inspire them and which they could each identify as meaningful enough to work together to bring to fruition. They wrote a few paragraphs each, and then Hank condensed his vision into a few words: "My sister is my friend. Who cares how much money she makes? She's as good as gold because she's in my life and I can count on her to be there for me. And best of all, I see that she wants me to be her friend as well. Knowing that is truly worth a fortune."

For the rest of the weekend, Hank and Rebecca's actions embodied the kind of work that brings brothers and sisters together as friends. Watching them laugh and give others advice, we were impressed with how much distance they had covered in such a short time.

As we have described, most important in creating a new vision is the ability to sense the potential inherent in such a change. What would it be like to have your sister as a friend? What if you and your brother learned to communicate? If you can sense the outcome even before you have results, you are on your way to a constructive use of your imaginative powers.

As Esther mulls over the benefits of reworking her relationship with her sister Elaine, she realizes that they are still relating where they left off as teenagers. Neither of them has grown up in the other's eyes, and instead they live within the myth of their teenage differences. When Esther finally experiences the pain of that separation, she also discovers a potential within that very relationship she had written off. Now she is capable of creating a vision. Sometimes that's what it takes—facing our impasse, inactivity, or emotional deadness with our siblings. If, like Esther, we can think out of the box, we may discover a way to be together that includes an adult version of ourselves—and more important, a way that provides enjoyment and a real sense of togetherness.

How to Begin

Begin gradually and slowly. Rather than attempt to transform your entire relationship, begin with a few images of how things might be better. In the same way as when you learn to play the piano you start with scales and "Chopsticks," not Berlioz or Bach, you might want to start with something easy, like imagining one small change in your attitudes and feelings. Then again, if you have a powerful imagination, you may want to start off with an entire symphony. The foolproof thing about working with your imagination is that no one knows if you make a mistake. In fact, it may not even be possible to make a mistake. One cautionary note: Do not be disappointed with the results you get as you begin this practice. Imagine for the sheer pleasure of imagining. Remember that although you may aim for Bach, at first you're more likely to produce "Chopsticks"!

Exploration 3-2 Special Exploration in Consciousness
What you will need:

Yourself and something to remind you to do this exercise; 5 minutes

Stop, Look, and Listen: In the middle of a routine activity such as grocery shopping or taking clothes to the washer, pause, breathe, and take a moment to actually *be* where you are.

Notice the status of your feelings. Are you happy? Sad? Neutral? Imagine yourself one degree happier than you are at this moment. Actually slow yourself down and focus within.

continued

Remember to breathe.
Appreciate whatever's present.
Use the information available
from your five senses: What do
you see, hear, feel, smell, and
taste?

See if you can have a genuine
sense of moving your positive
feelings up one notch. If this is
difficult for you to do using just
sensory information, use your
thinking powers as well.

Focus more on what's in front of
you; see if you can feel what's at
the heart of this experience.
Work to raise your perception of
appreciation, happiness, and
well-being just one notch. You
may also have to work to keep
out negative thoughts or your
list of things to do.

Return to your routine. Has it
shifted in some way?

Observe your laundry, grocery
shopping, or routines from the
new vantage point.

This meditative practice may help free your imagination for the work of creating a powerful new vision for yourself and your family.

Visiting the New Paradigm

Now it's time to return to the vision that began taking shape as you sifted through family images, photographs, and thoughts about your future. In the following exercise, gather all the materials in front of you. Use the centering meditation, if needed, and allow yourself the luxury of entering a new paradigm—a new vision and a new way of relating to your brothers and sisters.

As Alma, a 57-year-old school superintendent, commented in one of our workshops:

I finally realized down deep in my bones that I could start completely over again with my sister. Suddenly, our history became unimportant. The fact that we had all those childhood fights, and that we both grew up feeling unloved, lost ground as the focal point of our reality. All I needed to do was to envision forgiveness and love radiating out to Karen. Then I returned to the vision of how sweet and vulnerable she was as a child, and that brought me back to the essence that I'm striving for, which is to create our relationship over and over again, each day, as brand-new.

Exploration 3-3 The New Paradigm
What you will need:
Sibling journal; 15 minutes

Meditation: Imagine yourself on a new continent, or in a completely new surrounding. All the scenery has shifted.

There is a sense of aliveness and excitement in the air.

Writing and Reflection: Now take a few moments and write from this state of excitement and newness.

What is a new working model for your sibling relationship? What would it look like/feel like to let go of the past? How would you really want it to be, if it could be anything you wanted?

Refine and revise: Review the rough draft of your writing/meditative experience. Create a working vision that reflects the new paradigm between you and your siblings.

Make any additions or changes to your new working model.

Summary
Step 3: Envision a New Future

- Sibling relationships don't change on their own; they change because we've established that we want a different future and we're willing to envision it.

- To set out for change means introducing some discomfort and uncertainty.

- The vast majority of sibling relationships tend to improve as we age.

- If "habit is one-half of love," then the other half is consciousness, choice, and a willingness to replace old, immature habits with new, affirming adult habits.

- Thinking about the future in a habitually dark, negative way actually delivers the future as we have imagined or expected it. Therefore, we become jaded or cynical about the possibility of introducing real change into our relationships.

- Any significant change must begin with our thinking and imaginative powers; this is the cornerstone of cognitive-behavioral therapy.

- We begin envisioning small changes and work our way up; little by little we can see how far-reaching the effects of imagination are. Through practice at the level of imagination, it becomes much easier to deliver change in the realm of action.

Seeds of Change

- ❏ I am beginning to take note and to examine outmoded ways in which I "predict" or negatively imagine the outcome of my sibling relationships.

❏ I am willing to suspend my disbelief about how relationships change and apply new thoughts and visualizations to the sibling experience.

❏ This commitment to a new vision for relationship must be reinforced repeatedly. It is a conscious decision I take on because I am excited about the prospect of transforming my relationship to my sisters and brothers.

Grains of Hope, Pearls of Wisdom

✓ Even though things may not have changed as yet, I am willing to be patient and continue to imagine a different form of sibling relationship through the power of my thoughts.

✓ I am exploring the use of my imagination to envision new outcomes and relationships with my friends and associates as well.

✓ Opening a vision of a new future gives me new energy and incentive. I am grateful to acknowledge that change is possible in this area of my life (and, by extension, in all other areas).

CHAPTER 4

Explore New Modes
of Contact

We hardly ever realize that we can cut anything out of
our lives, anytime, in the blink of an eye.
Carlos Castañeda,
The Wheel of Time

By looking at the quality of our contact and the way we interact as siblings, we have a starting point from which to explore the overall nature of our relationships and determine
what may be missing. This chapter approaches several important subthemes, including how we approach or distance
ourselves, the current state of our communications, and
what you might call the topography, or overall condition, of
our relationships. Other themes include the ongoing impact
of birth order and further exploration of the dynamics of de-
identification.

Is It Worth It to Rock the Boat?

When he considers the possibility of relating differently to
his brothers, the initial steps become obvious for Jake, middle brother of three, whom we mentioned earlier. As he
pointed out:

Simply being more available for one another just as brothers would go a long way in my book. We're pretty much there on demand when our parents need us, but we don't arrange things or try to get together just by ourselves. Somehow, in our family, we never developed an autonomous relationship with each other—a relationship that exists outside of our relating through our parents.

There are a lot of things we need to heal, a lot of injuries that have never been acknowledged. We need to go back and talk with Edward because he feels so much separation at coming out and declaring himself gay and not feeling us supporting him. We need to take more time with Christopher because he feels we don't take much interest in his children or his wife. Now I realize that we all need to heal the separation that's crept in between us. We need to do the repair work by being more connected and more interested in each other right now.

In some cases the path to a transformed relationship is as easy to chart as Jake's. His vision is clear. He knows what he wants and can see a path toward it. Jake could begin with small, even humble gestures to bring the brothers together on their own. He could start to speak of the fun times first and work his way to the injuries, slights, and omissions that have accumulated among them. This is not to say that any of these steps would be easy. Jake and his brothers have to answer the important question: Is it worth it to me to rock the boat? All of us, in fact, will have to answer that fundamental question. What do we gain by upsetting the status quo? On the other hand, what do we lose by continuing the old relationship-defeating patterns? What do we lose by not being known, as adults, by our sisters and brothers?

It is often said that before you set out to change the world, you should clean your own house. Our position, supported by research, anecdote, myth, and legend, is that the path to a fulfilled, meaningful, happy life begins within the family of origin, with our first companions, our siblings, and then reaches out to the rest of our adult community.

Identify Built-in Structures of Relating

An important early task in moving toward our imagined sibling relationship is to clearly identify structures that hold the relationship in place. By structures we refer to the actual behaviors, including modes of contact, and specific activities that you take part in with your siblings and through which you are related. We also refer to something subtler, which is the emotional climate that surrounds your sibling contact. Do you approach a meeting with a sister or brother with a feeling of dread? Joy? Anxiety? Do you start out hopeful and wind up disappointed?

Participants in our workshops often voice the fears and uncertainties that accompany attempts to change the set patterns and habits of relating to one another (or of not relating). One of the first things we have to do as a group is clear out these stored-up fears of ridicule, rejection, discomfort, or disapproval. Harry, a participant in our first workshop and a 35-year-old public relations executive from New York City, exemplified this with his preprogram calls to us. He first inquired: "How much time will I have to spend with my sister? Will I be able to get away from her if I need to?" As we talked, he disclosed that he had not spent more than two consecutive hours in his sister's company since they were in high school. He was petrified—afraid she'd blame or punish him for inviting her; afraid she wouldn't enjoy herself; afraid she couldn't stand the thought of spending uninterrupted time with him. It is natural to have some fear or uncertainty in undertaking the transformation of a key life relationship. In this case, our nervous brother needn't have worried. His sister was perfectly happy to spend two days with him. In fact, for many years she'd been longing for nothing more and was afraid to approach him.

In several instances, we've worked with people whose anxiety is so great that they cannot sleep or eat for days before a planned meeting with siblings. A dramatic case in point occurred with one of Marjory's patients, who responded to making rare contact with her brother and three sisters with full-blown psychotic symptoms, thus requiring hospitalization. Most of us fall somewhere in the middle of this spectrum between bliss and psychosis when we plan or participate in activities with our siblings.

Ultimately, we want our relationships with our sisters and brothers to be smooth enough to guarantee that we will not become psychotic after spending Thanksgiving with them! For some of us, however, that will require dismantling of the old habits, practices, structures, and, most important, the emotional significance of events that transpired between us. The fifty-thousand-dollar question is: How?

In other instances, the feeling of distance or discord may be so familiar that it is hard to imagine a different outcome. It may seem that there is no place to begin, no possible foothold that will support the initiation of a different kind of relationship. This impasse is well illustrated through the example of Therese, a 43-year-old schoolteacher from Connecticut, married with four children. A workshop participant, she described her relationship with her only sister, Emma, three years older, as abusive and injurious. Emma, age 46, never married and has devoted her life to founding and directing a nonprofit organization in their hometown of Boonton, New Jersey. According to Therese, Emma has been nasty for as long as memory. They rarely have contact. Therese avoids family situations that include Emma and thus has stopped celebrating Christmas, Thanksgiving, and other major holidays with her family of origin. This pains her elderly parents and leaves Therese lonely and depressed, "celebrating" her separation and distance from her family in defiant isolation. This also deprives Therese's children of the opportunity to be connected to their aunt, grandmother, grandfather, and other maternal relatives. However, Therese has begun the journey of change. She attended our sibling workshop. Participating in all the activities, Therese altered some of them to suit her stubborn insistence that Emma, alone among siblings on earth, was really too horrible to approach directly.

Degrees of Separation

There are many degrees of impasse in sibling relationships. When Jo Ann speaks of her friend David, she's disappointed that he sees his brother Carl only during Christmas and other family events. Carl rarely calls or visits. What's more saddening to Jo Ann is that Dave doesn't consider that out of the ordinary.

"Oh, that's just the way it is," Dave told Jo one day while they hiked the countryside. "Course, we used to be closer when we were young," Dave continued, "then Carl got married and moved upstate. His wife didn't care for me, and the truth is, we no longer had much in common."

"But this is your one and only brother," Jo Ann exclaimed. "If you had the chance, wouldn't you be closer?"

Dave shrugged. "Hadn't really thought about it. Not every relationship is meant to be close."

Of course, he's absolutely right. At the same time, knowing their history provides some insight into their connection. Dave and Carl were fierce competitors for their parents' affection. While the parents were undoubtedly loving, supportive, and conscientious, they didn't show much emotion. The playing field was thus cool, constrained, and nondemonstrative. Thinking their parents didn't care, the brothers competed harder for what was available. In the name of this competition Dave did mean and cruel things to his younger brother and still feels guilty about it. Insofar as it is not discussed, he can avoid his guilt by avoiding closeness with his brother. Of course, Carl looked up to Dave but lost most of their battles. Carl avoids feeling helpless and unsafe by not contacting David. They've both arranged their lives as though they were only children. Jo Ann observes that the sad part for her, as a friend, is to see how Dave now keeps himself distant from most people, especially men. Sad, too, is the missed opportunity to "grow up" the childhood conflict between these two grown men.

Evidence in the research literature lends support to part of Dave and Carl's distance and separation. According to Victor Cicirelli in "Sibling Relationships in Middle and Old Age," the natural pattern of the sibling relationship throughout the lifespan begins with proximity, intimacy, and conflict during early childhood; moves toward distance as the siblings mature; and may be at its most distant during early adulthood. According to Erik Erikson in *Identity, Youth, and Crisis*, the developmental task of the early adult years is to establish autonomy through career and family of creation. At this time, family of origin necessarily takes second place. More recent research carried out by Agnes Riedmann and Lynn White in "Adult Sibling Relationships: Racial and Ethnic Comparisons" (in Gene Brody's *Sibling Relationships: Their Causes and Consequences)* indicates that as individuals age, especially in the United States and other highly industrialized Western countries, there is a pattern of return to closeness among siblings. In our highly mobile society, where divorces, remarriages, and nontraditional living arrangements are common, adults in middle age and older are relying more and more on their sibling connections. Certainly for the baby-boom generation, this trend is in full swing, regardless of race, class, ethnicity, and location.

There is ample evidence to support some difference based

on the gender mix of the sibling group. Sibling pairs and groups of brothers are more likely to be distant and even estranged than pairs and groups that have at least one sister. In research carried out by Victor Cicirelli and by Agnes Riedmann and Lynn White, sister pairs and groups are least likely to report distance and estrangement. For immigrant populations in the United States, lifetime ties to siblings decrease with the length of time here. Thus, new immigrants tend to rely very heavily and in some cases almost exclusively on the sibling network. They also tend to have larger sibling groups. As time passes, however, and the newcomers begin to acculturate, patterns of sibling connection more closely resemble the national norms.

By Default, Not by Design

Although we may choose not to be close to family members, often it's by default and not by conscious design. With our siblings, the degree of closeness can be as random as how we wound up in the birth order. For most of us, however, our relationship to brothers and sisters evolved unconsciously within the parental matrix. This matrix provided certain rules, a context, and ways of interacting that we blindly accepted. Participation was largely by tacit agreement and by condition of being born into the family. Early on, we were unaware that the family matrix also existed within a larger social and cultural matrix. None of us was fully formed or fully aware of our impact on one another. And so our sibling connections developed from those beginnings, with rules from our parents, and for the most part a life of their own, independent of our conscious thinking or deliberate plan.

Acting Consistently with Our Birth Order

Jake relates from his family life with brothers Edward and Christopher:

The issue that escalated our whole family into action centered on our parents' fiftieth wedding anniversary. One year ago when we gathered for Thanksgiving, I broached the subject and my mom got really upset. She didn't feel there was anything for her and Dad to celebrate, even though they had been together forty-nine years. My brothers and I tried to talk them into it, but things only got worse. Edward declared he didn't want to visit again and went off sulking. Christopher tried to placate everyone, without really listening, and I got so angry I could have punched him out. Later I shared with him that I couldn't hold back my feelings, and we sat down for a long talk. Some hard truths got told back and forth. But even now we keep a respectful distance from one another. And I do feel closer to him, in a funny way. Christopher's always the oldest, and was always trying to smooth things over. Edward, my baby brother, is like a lost soul; he vacates as soon as there's any sign of conflict. And as for me, consistent with my birth order, I always seem to be in the middle, trying to fight with or sort out everyone's madness.

Much research and speculation surround the effect of birth order in the development of siblings. Alfred Adler, an early disciple and later outcast of Freud, postulated that sibling birth order determined the course of an individual's life. He was not the first. In the 1870s a "science" of birth order emerged, stating that firstborn children had clear and permanent advantage over their younger brothers. In the 1870s, sisters didn't count in the equation of power and success in the world. At that time, of course, primogeniture ruled, so that the firstborn male had the obvious advantage of inheriting the family land and wealth. Later researchers pointed out that the author of these early studies was himself a firstborn, as was Freud. As the youngest son in a large family, Adler naturally had different ideas about the implications of birth order.

Esther, the baby in the family, comments on the power struggle between her and her older sister:

> Our patterns of interaction are predictable: Elaine will call in a state of panic and do everything in her power to recruit me. Dad has diabetes and Mom has a heart condition, so we're constantly fussing over them. When I tried to convince our folks to adopt a healthier lifestyle, Elaine hit the roof. She didn't want to upset them. I went along with her opinion just as I always have. I'm afraid to say no. As the baby I feel more comfortable letting her decide things; that way I don't have to have an opinion. Of course I still fight and resist her every step of the way.

Francine Klagsbrun, writer and lecturer, observes in her book *Mixed Feelings*: "The techniques the youngers use in their struggles differ from those of their more powerful older siblings. The youngers may be overtly competitive, showing their feelings by yelling, fighting, or sulking, as opposed to the more restrained and subtle skills of the olders." Taking a closer look at your relationship may yield some interesting awareness, hopefully freeing some of the energy bound up in maintaining rules and regulations of birth order long after the need for them has passed.

Despite extensive research into the long-term effects of birth order on success, achievement, economic status, education, and other variables, there is no consistent finding that firstborn children experience significant advantage when measured over the lifespan. Nor is there support for the theory, long held by many middle children, that no one cares about them. This finding surprises many middle children, who have made a career out of the certainty that things just aren't fair.

In our discussions and experience in writing this book, Joel and Marjory began to see more clearly how much Jo Ann carried as the oldest. She felt responsible for the positive outcome of every meeting. If we didn't accomplish all that we said we wanted to, she became snippy and dictatorial, as you might expect from a person in charge. At first we went along with this structure. It certainly seemed familiar. But after a time, the wear and tear of carrying this whole project, at least psychologically, began to cause pain for Jo Ann, and discomfort for Marjory and Joel, who in turn began to rebel in fairly characteristic ways. We had to stop the action, talk about the underlying dynamic, and then, as adults, reassign roles and responsibilities more in keeping with a project among equals.

It took both Joel and Marjory by surprise that Jo Ann seriously considered the success of our undertaking to be primarily her responsibility. It surprised Jo Ann that her younger siblings didn't realize this, and more, that we didn't blame her for the failure to meet every timeline and goal. All three of us were surprised by these invisible rules that had eluded our conscious efforts to bring equity into our relations. Exploring the issue in depth, each of us felt responsible for the project in his or her own characteristic way. When we fell behind schedule each of us tended to blame ourselves.

Even when we're trying to be conscious, we lapse into unconscious patterns. That's part of the game. However, as adults we can learn to choose how we relate to our siblings. Through books, movies, and other media we receive multiple messages about relationships; we observe friendships, other siblings, other families, and contrast relationships that work with those that don't. At any given moment, then, we have the option to develop a new and different connection. Or do we? Perhaps that's the crux. We shrug our shoulders like Dave, Jo Ann's friend, and consider the way our life's relationships have turned out to be a done deal. In fact, we could be dreaming, imagining, and investing ourselves in a totally different future. The key lies in our desire. And our desire for something different can only be born out of a sense that in fact it does exist. It is possible for us to have entirely different, more viable, and even satisfying relationships with our sisters and brothers.

Toward a New Future

Designing and implementing a new relationship entails a different structure for contact and the way in which we relate. It is usually more powerful to begin this process in thought than in deed. Think and imagine before you suggest or attempt new behavior. In this way, you can begin to shift the subtle, emotional climate within you so that you can approach the relationship with greater ease, enthusiasm, and freedom.

For example, if Dave had the desire, he could begin to think about his little brother Carl in new and unusual ways. How nice it would be to go horseback riding with him again after all these years. What if Dave invited Carl and the kids to stop at his house instead of going directly to the grandparents'? Then he could enjoy his nephews and his brother. Dave is a good cook. He could invite the whole family to come for a cookout and they could see his new place. These are not thoughts that Dave usually entertains about his brother, sister-in-law, and nephews.

We arrive at a new perspective usually by observing what doesn't work, what doesn't fulfill us, and then by imagining examples of what does work. Dave and Carl have innumerable possibilities. But maybe a couple of more visits a year and one or two horseback-riding ventures would be all they needed to kindle a renewed sense of closeness. Within the comfort and pleasure of these simple gestures of closeness, more substantive psychological change is then possible. It might be that a new era of closeness is ushered in for Dave and Carl with the addition of *one* additional telephone call, or *one* unexpected invitation.

Research actually bears this out. In Agnes Riedmann and Lynn White's large study of African-American sibling relationships, summarized in their work "Adult Sibling Relationships: Racial and Ethnic Comparisons," participants rated their reliance on siblings at the top of the scale whether or not they had close contact. The perception was that in critical situations, sisters and brothers are 100 percent reliable and number 1 on the list. Surprisingly, this held true for sibling groups in close contact and those in very minimal contact. Further, those who felt they could rely on their sisters and brothers, no matter what, reported a greater sense of well-being and comfort, a greater readiness to meet life's challenges, than those who could not.

Where to Start?

Esther, mentioned earlier, describes an experience of one phone call that made a difference in her relationship:

We seem to have this one mode of interacting, which is to argue and make a big drama out of everything. However, one phone conversation stands out as different from the rest. One morning I got a call from Elaine, and I was shocked to hear from her. She usually calls me after ten P.M. even though I've told her I go to bed early and can't talk late. But this one Saturday she called, and we had a really nice conversation. She told me about her girls, she talked a little bit about Tony, her husband, and then how worried she is about Mom and Dad. Because I was wide awake, I was able to reflect back to her what I was hearing. I wasn't pulled off center by her drama; in fact I felt grounded and clear. The upshot was that she really opened up to me in that conversation and I did, too. At the end she told me, "You've really been a great help," almost as if she were shocked that something like that could happen.

And I think that's part of the problem. We have been so locked into big sister, little sister that we have never had a chance to try on different roles these last forty years. Once I wanted to go to New York to see the play *42nd Street*, and I called her daughter Dana, asking her to go. Dana said to me, "I can't, but why don't you ask Mom? I bet she'd love a Broadway musical." It shocked me at first, but then I got used to the idea. I liked it. So I called Elaine and offered her the invitation. Immediately she started moaning and groaning about how much work she had to do and how the house needed painting. So we ditched the idea. However, it did raise some questions for me. How come we never go on outings? How come we only talk on the phone? Then I thought to myself, What am I talking about? I can't even be in the same room with her for more than ten minutes. Suddenly that seemed wrong. It seemed like the only sister I have on earth should want to spend time with me and I with her. Although it means trying on a different set of behaviors and expectations, to tell you the truth I wouldn't know where to start.

Perception Rules

We are modest beings. The feeling of being close to your brother and his family may be achievable by two extra visits a year, gifts for his kids, or a few e-mailed notes. One barrier to closeness is the effort we imagine would be necessary to achieve that closeness. We imagine that closeness entails tons of work and daily contact. However, it is possible that closeness is a matter of your attitude coupled with a few changes of your habits. An interesting result of some adult-sibling research indicates that perceived closeness among siblings is not related to proximity or interaction. Additional data from the study mentioned above underscored that among Asian-American families and Latino families in particular, which tend to be the least proximal among sibling groups and the most likely to be closer to family immigration, perception rules. All middle to late adult sibling groups reported perceived closeness and reliance on siblings in an emergency whether they actually had contact or not, and whether their siblings actually gave instrumental or material support during times of crisis.

All relationships are held firmly in place over long periods of time by certain patterns and practices. We call them structures because they acquire mass and substance through years of repetition. They may actually *feel* solid to you and to your siblings. These patterns are difficult to see because they have surrounded the relationship for decades, back to childhood. They appear to be the way the world is, rather than a structure that was actually set in place as we were growing up. In many cases, we weren't the authors of the early sibling structures. They may have come to us from generations back or have been an innovation of a parent. Then, our individual temperaments and interactions added weight and mass to these early structures.

Joel reports on an incident with a colleague during an all-important briefing for a major contract. They'd flown to Denver the night before, rehearsed their presentation, and went into the meeting early the next morning. His colleague, Bernard, got an urgent call in midconference and without a second thought, excused himself. His oldest brother had been rushed to the hospital with liver failure. Bernard went right back to the airport, took the first plane home, and met his other siblings at the hospital. His brother didn't survive, but Bernard had the opportunity to be with him and tell him all that was in his heart before his brother died. They ended up getting the contract anyway, though they had to return to

Denver to do so. Joel reports that he wasn't the least bit upset or angry with Bernard. He would have done the same thing.

Setting the Stage

At this moment pause to reflect on the network of interactions and contact you have with your siblings. We'll be asking you to take an inventory, so prepare yourself, as if you were going to count every item in a warehouse. An inventory is a process of taking account, through actual observation, of everything that exists in a particular place at a particular time. This doesn't mean you count *only* the nasty things or, conversely, the nice things. You'll be counting *everything*. So relax, take a breath, center yourself using our centering exercise in chapter 1 (or one from appendix A), or a relaxation technique of your own, and take out your sibling journal. Identify the present modes of contact you have with your brothers and sisters. Remember to include everything.

Exploration 4-1 Structural Inventory: Our Modes of Contact

What you will need:

Sibling journal; 20 minutes

Lists and landmarks: On a sheet of paper or in your journal, describe the following:
The What: What are our preferred modes of contact (i.e., phone, e-mail, family visit, etc.)?

Who seems to prefer what? (For example, do you like to e-mail, and she calls you back? Do you hate electronic communication and prefer Sunday dinners? Etc.)

How we make contact:

- Talk on the telephone
- E-mail each other
- Fax each other
- Write
- Visit
- Do fun things

How often we make contact:	• Is our timing predictable or unpredictable? What tends to alter or affect it? • Are there hidden assumptions about how much or how often we can be in contact? • Is there a sense of duty to our contact?
Where do we meet?	• Are there places you avoid? Places where you always meet? • Who chooses where you meet (including cyberspace)?
Who arranges this? Do you take turns?	Is there a sibling who serves as social secretary or who tends to initiate and facilitate your gatherings?
Reflections: Evaluate the quality of these contacts.	Look at each incident and decide whether it is enjoyable or excruciating, whether it supports your vision for the relationship or is destructive. How will you look back on it ten or twenty years from now?

Intermission

In the first part of this exploration we completed an inventory of contact habits. These habits are not good or bad. For example, a habit of going out for a drink might be a "bad" habit if the family has a history of alcohol abuse. In another family, two brothers going to a bar might be seen as a positive breakthrough in their relationship. So the habit itself is not good or bad. The context makes it so.

Exploration 4-2 Reactions to Structural Inventory:
Our Modes of Contact

What you will need:

Sibling journal; 10 minutes

Lists and landmarks: Now list all of the habitual thought processes that accompany the who/ what/ where/ how/ when of your typical interactions, as they now exist.

Remember, this is an inventory, not a judgment or evaluation, of the state of your relationship!

Some possible habitual reactions and thoughts might include:

- Recitation of complaint (He never . . . They always . . . etc.)
- Oh, goody-goody! I can't wait!
- Forgetfulness
- Resentment and/or impatience
- Martyrdom
- Anxiety, fear, expectations of being judged

Witness: Note any thoughts, feelings, or sensations that arise as you complete your inventory.

Write these down if you feel they'll be of value to you.

Reflections: Review your inventory and add anything you may have forgotten, or that comes to your mind as a result of this process. Whatever you are thinking and feeling is fine. Allow it to be.

If you'd like to make note of any of this, do so now, while the memory is fresh.

If you need to express some emotion, of course do that at any time.

What Happened

Just as in industry, or in twelve-step programs for that matter, the purpose of an inventory is to see exactly what's there, and what isn't. When you take an inventory, there is no judgment. Factory owners don't say, "Oh no, we have 8,014 widgets! I can't accept that! In fact, I won't even count them."

Although you're looking at behaviors and contact rather than widgets, the methodology remains the same. Later, when you have seen what is present, you can make decisions about what to value, what to keep, and what to discard.

Setting the Stage

For now, you need more objective information. In addition to the particulars of the who/what/how/when/where of your contact with your siblings, it's helpful to inventory the content and quality. Since this is a subjective inventory, it may be more difficult to assess. For example, you may have had a blast at that bar mitzvah, while your brother was in agony. You may have been moved to tears at your nephew's first communion, while your sibling was furious. However, remember that this is your evaluation. Try not to be swayed by the experiences and judgments of others.

Exploration 4-3 The Content

What you will need:

Sibling journal; 10 minutes

Lists and landmarks: Consider topics discussed and topics that are not discussed when you're together.

In your discussions how often do you bring up the following:
- Death or care of your parent(s) as they age
- Problems and pride about your kids or theirs
- Health issues
- Details of partnerships/marriages
- Your/their money situation
- Anything painful and/or incomplete from the past
- Any topic of known or suspected controversy
- Real issues of deep concern to you

continued

Would you share intimate information with your sibling(s)?	• Is there some variation— that is, would you tell one sibling and never breathe a word to another? • Do you rely on an "intra-family communication network" to transmit awkward or important information?
How would you characterize the content of your relations and communications?	• I can be *totally* real, myself • *Sometimes* real • I'd sooner walk the plank or chew metal than truly be myself with my siblings
Reflection: Is there anything else you'd like to add that would further clarify the content and quality of your contact and communications?	Any thoughts, feelings, additions, or amendments come to mind? Notice how you feel, and make note of anything that comes to mind that you may want to pursue.

What Happened

As you review and evaluate the previous two explorations, we encourage you to look at some of your communication patterns and practices with your siblings. As food for thought, consider the following questions: What topics are taboo? At what point does communication come to a halt between you? Are there thoughts/events that *must* be shared, and from your point of view, what constitutes family gossip?

As is true in other areas, old communication patterns are often invisible. Two sisters, Mollie and Angela, volunteered to be interviewed for this project. Angela is a highly skilled health-care professional and Mollie is a housewife with 14-year-old twin daughters. She's just returned to her local community college to start work on an undergraduate degree. As it turned out, they demonstrated their invisible patterns perfectly in this interview. Angela, the older sister, who admitted she'd spent her childhood pushing her little sister around, actually *never* let Mollie answer a question without interruption or contradiction. In fact, Angela answered every single question first, even those questions prefaced by her little sister's name! When this was pointed out to Angela, with Mollie present, both of them were shocked and denied that it was so.

When they listened to the tape, they were flabbergasted. Our interview quickly took an unexpected turn. For a moment, the sisters just looked at each other in silence. Having directly perceived their patterns, with evidence in the form of an audiotape and a neutral witness, they experienced a shift in consciousness. At this critical juncture, they were free to experience the reality of their interaction and begin to imagine a different style of communication. Mollie admitted that she always felt inadequate and inferior to Angela because she'd never gone on to college. Now that she was realizing this dream of hers, she had a little more courage to meet her big sister head-on, approaching equality. Angela had suspected this. She, in turn, felt like a failure because she'd never had children. Their father had made it clear that the purpose and value of women, including his daughters, was to produce and raise healthy offspring. Mollie was shocked to hear that Angela felt inadequate. She noted that Angela had rebelled against everything their father had said was "proper conduct" for a young lady. Angela saw the truth in this and had a glimpse into something deeper about herself—she was a rebel, and she was willing to sacrifice for what she considered to be right for her.

Setting the Stage

In the following exercise, we'll ask you to use the data you collected so far to produce a moment of clear insight for yourself. If you have the inclination and the luxury of time, look back at all you have written, drawn, imagined, and noted thus far.

Exploration 4-4 Back into Contact
What you will need:

Sibling journal with list from last exercise; 20 minutes

Reflections: Returning to your list, review the nature of your contacts and communication patterns, expanding your list.

Fill in more of the story or rationale that keeps you from being in contact, or being constrained by the contact you do have.

Take time to challenge some of the underlying assumptions whenever they become visible to you.

If you have restraining forces that keep you from relating (and you're the one who's the most optimistic), then imagine what restraining forces must be acting upon your siblings.

Imaginary lives: Now consider: What would light you up in terms of interaction? What kind of experiences would help you draw closer? Jot some notes on these now.

Most important, drawing on the future that you identified in the previous chapter, what types of contact coincide with and in fact amplify the kind of sibling relationship you've decided to have?

Encore

What you will need:

Sibling journal; 15 minutes

Change characters: As a final touch to this exploration, fill out another list from your sibling's point of view. Imagine what thoughts he or she holds about being in contact with you.

If appropriate, speak to your sibling and explore these assumptions together. See if you can agree on a type of structure or contact that may provide more relatedness between you.

What Happened

You may not believe in it right now. You may not feel you deserve or can actually have it. Or you may feel that you're the only one who wants it and you know you'll have no support from your siblings. Never mind. Return to your cherished, heartfelt desire. If you could have the best sibling relationship imaginable, what would it look like?

The three of us made up this exercise and tried it out on ourselves first, to see how it worked (we did this with all the exercises in this book before we included them). The results we obtained surprised us, gave us food for thought, and provided a road map for changing our relationships. We discovered that we operate out of an assumption that we're very close, that our relationship has freedom, balance, love, and all manner of good things in it. However, what we actually saw was that there were elements of denial and even of fantasy in which we lived—especially between Jo Ann and Marjory. We saw areas of constraint that had been invisible for a long time, since adolescence, when we'd discovered a way to shift our constant fighting to a more harmonious way of relating. What emerged was conflict!

We saw clearly that we lived in a conspiracy of harmony, and that under the surface we were unwilling, even frightened, to share negative feelings with one another. Vivid pictures of long-suppressed howling fights between us surfaced. There was a time when we lived in a fragile truce that could be shattered at any moment. Joel crept around us and mostly avoided taking sides as we battled like titans for power and control. We've had to gingerly reopen the possibility of disagreement without devastation in our meetings and conversations. This seemed very threatening at first, but as we practiced, and gained adult experience in negotiating differences, our relationships became more genuine, more comfortable, and more resilient.

Observing De-identification

As we begin to dismantle structures of contact and con-nection that haven't worked for us, we are automatically led to the unmasking of different areas where we've been on au-tomatic, or functioned more from a role than from who we really are. As a natural part of the jockeying for position that takes place in a family, each child carves out an exclusive ter-ritory. In their work *The Sibling Bond*, Stephen Bank and Michael Kahn call this process "de-identification." If a sister is good at writing, her brother will probably excel in math. If he's subdued, she may turn out to be the loudmouth.

In *Sibling Rivalry*, the movie mentioned in chapter 2, Janine goes out of her way to be happy (i.e., different), and Marjorie, her sister, goes out of her way to disapprove (while hungering for her own freedom of expression). While they may not seek the same lifestyle, they desperately want each other's love and acceptance. But while making space for each other's eccentricities, they unwittingly wind up sup-pressing their strong, inner urgings and sense of freedom.

In our family, Jo Ann, the oldest, was the "perfect" child. She excelled in school, rarely got into trouble, and was an all-around impossible act to follow. So Marjory, through de-identification, became the "wild one." Always in trouble, creative, volatile, she kept far away from her big sister's world of perfection. When Joel, the youngest, went to school, teachers and administrators looked at him with great apprehension. Would he be another hellion, or would he be the editor of the school yearbook? Joel decided to choose the middle ground, acting worse than Marjory some years and as good as Jo Ann in others, which further confused every-one and gave him a sense of his distinct identity and value.

De-identification is thus an important way we identify who we are in the context of family life. If an older brother is a hard act to follow, then it behooves the next sibling to create a to-tally different act. However, at some point, we must discover that it was only an act; that in fact we are much more than this narrow set of characteristics we claimed for ourselves. A natural part of our growth process, then, will be to "re-identify" or reintegrate the parts we discarded because in our minds they were so heavily connected with our brother or sister's "turf."

Setting the Stage

In this exploration we attempt to free up some of the energy we use to maintain our stereotypes. This will give each of us more latitude to experiment in relation to our siblings, to express ourselves more fully, and, we hope, to relate to others with the same freedom.

Exploration 4-5 Take Back Your De-Identifications!
What you will need:

Sibling journal; 15 minutes

Consider what roles each of you has played in the family.

You may wish to check back with earlier explorations, particularly those in chapter 1.

Lists and landmarks: List each of your siblings and your own name. Next to each name, write the predominant characteristics and the predominant role that sibling has carried within the family.

For example, the eldest child is often the caregiver for the group or, under adverse conditions, the self-appointed "sergeant-at-arms." The middle child is often the rebellious one, the scapegoat, or the creative nonconformist. And often the youngest is the spoiled brat, or in some circumstances the "lost soul" or one who can get away with murder.

Pow-wow: After you have deliberated on the roles for each of your siblings, you may wish to confer with them and see how they personally represent themselves.

Write several roles next to each brother or sister's name.

continued

Change characters: Now exchange these roles. Try on one that doesn't suit you. For example, imagine being in charge if you're the youngest or being the rebel if you're the oldest. Write a few sentences to describe what it would be like to think and act "out of the box."

Or consider times in your life when you actually learned or replicated qualities that were once solely identified as another sibling's stock-in-trade. What was it like?

Reflections: Finally, sit back and relax. Imagine having open communication with your siblings. Imagine the feeling of accepting the roles you've each adapted, while at the same time leaving room for each of you to express yourself more completely.

What would it be like? What kind of communication would occur between siblings truly de-identified with their original roles?

What Happened

Each of us plays a character in the play of our lives. Our sisters and brothers play complementary roles. The goal of this exploration is to identify which roles we are playing and to determine if they are the most likely to give us satisfaction.

Softening Our Automatic Responses

Finding new methods of communication boils down to discovering the areas in which we've been relating on "automatic." Invariably these include some of the patterns of de-identification, as we described above. Dismantling dysfunctional patterns of communication thus means acknowledging knee-jerk reactions and finding ways to sidestep these automatic patterns, understanding that they no longer serve us. As is true in other areas, these old patterns are often invisible.

One of the things we observed in many sibling groups is that the communication styles from childhood are out of place and no longer appropriate to the adult siblings. Sibling rivalry, childish criticism, complaining and whining about one another, and jockeying for position are behaviors expected among children. In adults this behavior is anachronistic. It is almost like looking through a periscope to the past. You can see the templates—the old styles of sibling interaction at work.

To make it more humorous (or tragic, depending on the point of view) adults will swear they don't like the behavior and don't want it to recur. Or they will deny that their interaction replicates the domineering older sister/passive little sister routine, as Angela and Mollie did. Yet this old, automatic behavior does recur. Unproductive modes of relating recur without your say-so, without your permission, and often (some would say usually) without your conscious awareness.

Thus, moving from a dysfunctional to a more positive sibling relationship may begin with first being able to see through the automatic relationship-defeating patterns. Remember the Garcia girls in Julia Alvarez's novel *How the Garcia Girls Lost Their Accents*. No matter what Carla (the "bossy older sister") says, Yolanda hears an echo of their mother's critical and censuring voice. It is not the behavior *per se* that creates the experience, negative or positive, but the perception of that behavior.

Sometimes we inadvertently resort to automatic behaviors when we feel uneasy or out of sorts. This happened while the authors worked together designing workshops. Jo Ann and Joel had begun discussion before Marjory had entered the room, and her knee-jerk reaction was to feel not included. Though she couched her sniping in humorous teasing, nevertheless she aimed a few shots at her sister. Jo Ann got defensive. Although momentarily enjoying it, later on Marjory sensed that she may have hurt Jo Ann: "Not a pretty sight! Squashing my beloved older sister is *not* in service to our vision of our sibling relationship! Coincidentally, it isn't in my personal vision of who and what I want to be as a human being. Now what? It's easy enough to apologize. But to be really effective (and redemptive) we need a new behavior, a new automatic ritual, if you will."

A Ritual of Unkindness

Marie and Marla, sisters who came for a few therapy sessions with Marjory as part of Marie's ongoing individual treatment, were almost at the end of their rope with each other. Marie was privately considering whether she should simply cut off contact with her troubled and troublesome older sister, and had arranged these sessions when her sister came on a rare visit, passing through on her way to her home in the Midwest. These women had somehow reversed the stereotypical older sister/younger sister roles. Marie fussed and mothered Marla, and Marla, helpless and depressed, lashed out with impotent, childish rage. Marie was the logical, practical, successful sister. Marla was just a mess. Nothing in her life pleased her and she was openly jealous of Marie. From her point of view, Marie had always gotten everything she ever wanted, and she, Marla, had been deprived.

Not much in the way of jealousy and resentment was hidden between these sisters. This was even a matter of pride for them. There was no vile, nasty thought that they would not share with each other. Marla admitted that she often fantasized about her sister's death. Marie did the same. She told Marla that her life would be much more peaceful and serene without her older sister's drama and depression. Once, when the sisters had not spoken to each other in several months, Marla left a message on Marie's answering machine describing in detail a violent dream she had had where Marie had been crushed by a train. Marie found this to be completely devastating, though she was by no means innocent of these kinds of cryptic and toxic communications. Perhaps the strangest part of this relationship was that the sisters continued to cling to each other and struggle to work on their relationship.

The first ground rule we established was that both of them had to monitor their conversations and stop sharing every single nasty, violent, creepy thought they had about each other. They drafted a list of forbidden subjects, including a twenty-year-old disagreement about who was responsible for ruining their mother's cashmere sweater! In the short time we had to work with the sisters, we focused on dismantling some of their hurtful and damaging habits before we began the task of building better ways of relating. The wounding and rewounding had to stop. Marie did not sever ties with Marla. She worked within as well, replacing her automatic negative thoughts and associations regarding Marla with neutral or positive thoughts. Marie would actually look at a sunset she loved, or a beautiful city nightscape, and get herself all riled up imagining how Marla would put her down for loving these scenes! In this way, Marie ruined many private experiences with her almost compulsive comparisons and imaginings about her sister. Marie discovered that it was difficult for her even to imagine Marla doing well, being happy, and having fun. She didn't recognize herself if she wasn't the one on top.

The first step for Marla and Marie was to witness their self-defeating behavior patterns. This aspect of witnessing is critical. Without creating space for differences, we remain trapped in our past expectations and negative predictions. Our focus in this chapter has been on re-creating your vision, while practicing awareness and choice in the face of automatic and unwanted behaviors. Once you know what you want to create, you can then explore what gets in the way of fulfilling that vision.

Putting the "Fun" Back into Dysfunctional

It is possible that the difference between a functional sibling relationship and a dysfunctional one is a series of relationship-defeating patterns that have never been defined, questioned, and verified. For example, the very same practices may exist in a functional relationship—such as talking on the phone monthly, or having a picnic yearly—as in a dysfunctional relationship. (We're back to *Rashomon*.) If you haven't examined your practices or opened them up for inspection, you may continue replicating what hasn't worked. For example, what is delightful for you may be disgusting for your sibling, and both of you may continue to be completely unaware of this. Many practices that sisters and brothers share come from prior generations. There are virtues in having a look. You may discover a destructive pattern that belongs to a great-grandparent. Or you may discover a pattern your parents set in place that nourishes your whole family experience. That is the case with Jacqueline, below.

A Ritual of Kindness

When Jacqueline discovered that she had free long-distance service on Sundays, she decided to initiate a family call to see how her siblings were. Now, this is no ordinary call. Jacqueline lives in California and is the older sister of Delores and Nicole, whom we introduced in an earlier chapter. Today there are thirteen siblings in all, and ten of them have three-way calling. Thus, Jacqueline initiates the call at 8 A.M. Pacific time. She reaches Roberta in Chicago and Andrew in St. Louis, who in turn connect with Evan in Dallas, who tracks Nicole and Delores in Atlanta, who contact everyone else. Sometimes the call takes two hours, but the ritual remains the same. Everyone checks in and gives an update on his or her life. New babies, old flames, new jobs, old fights, new illnesses—every family event is reported and everyone is given the appropriate condolences, congratulations, or kick in the butt, as Jacqueline puts it. Delores feels that this ritual of kindness was not really Jackie's invention but a hand-me-down from their mom, who taught everyone to look out for the next child down the line. To this day they maintain that tradition, and their vision for the future is to spread the contact and caring through the generations, and, they hope, beyond their family of origin.

It All Begins with Vision

Whatever the outcome of your observations and insights, whatever you come to as a worthy structure for interacting with your siblings, it all begins with vision. It begins with seeing something that may not have been there to begin with (in the case of a difficult sibling relationship), or was there early on and got lost as you grew up. And it may not necessarily need a complete overhauling of the relationship. Perhaps a few strategic phone calls or lending a hand when a sibling moves from the suburbs to the country is all that's needed. Keep your inventories handy and think up creative ways to enhance contact. Meanwhile, now that you've formulated a vision and found ways to strengthen it through new structures and practices, it's time to move deeper with your sibling relationship. In chapter 5 we clear the path for healing and integration.

Summary
Step 4: Explore New Modes of Contact

- According to Erik Erikson, the developmental task of the early adult years is to establish autonomy through career and family of creation. Thus, we turn our attention away from our siblings; however, as we age, we tend to reestablish that earlier bond of closeness.

- The impact of birth order greatly affects sibling development and in particular the perceived differences among siblings according to where they fit in the family structure.

- All relationships are held in place over long periods of time by certain patterns and practices, which we refer to as "structures." Designing and implementing a new relationship entails creating a new structure for contact and relatedness with our siblings.

- To begin, we can take an inventory of these structures and determine the true nature of our interactions, in terms of both quantity and quality.

- Although we might imagine closeness to require great effort and an extraordinary amount of contact, we are modest and adaptable beings. In reality we may discover that a change in our personal attitude coupled with a few behavioral changes may be all we need to feel "closer."

- Communication is another aspect of the structure that holds our relationships in place. The way we represent the sibling relationship in language is an important clue to how we feel about it and experience it. We must be the first to describe it differently if we are to witness the changes we desire.

- De-identification is an important way we identify who we are in the context of family life. We take on different roles or areas of expertise to avoid our siblings' "turf."

- At some point, with de-identification, we must discover it was only an act; that in fact we are much more than this narrow set of characteristics we claimed for ourselves. A natural part of our growth process, then, will be to "re-identify" or reintegrate the parts we discarded.

- It is possible that the difference between a functional sibling relationship and a dysfunctional one is a series of relationship-defeating patterns that have never been defined or questioned.

- Creating a vision and reinforcing it through the invention of new structures and patterns of interaction are the first important steps we must take in configuring the sibling relationship of the future.

Seeds of Change

❑ I am noticing interesting characteristics about how I relate to my siblings (and how they relate to me) based on our particular birth order.

❑ Having taken an inventory of our modes of contact, I am beginning to see disparities/similarities between the way I define who we are and how much we're in contact.

❑ It is helpful for me to take a closer look at the content as well as the nature/type/frequency of our interactions.

❑ I have been able to distinguish relationship-defeating patterns from those that help our relationship(s) to thrive.

❑ I look forward to more quality contact and am willing to initiate this.

❑ I am venturing into new territory, exploring and taking on qualities and characteristics I used to associate with my brother/sister's "turf."

❑ My communications are shifting; I am much more conscious about the ways that I represent my sibling connection to others.

Grains of Hope, Pearls of Wisdom

✓ What gives me hope is realizing that making change is not a huge, earthshaking matter. I can send one or two more e-mails a month or call my brother more often and it makes a big difference.

✓ As I study these sibling connections, I am relieved to understand that I am not to blame for their unconscious origins, especially as related to our birth order and family constellation.

✓ I am willing to create a more deliberate impact now—through how I envision, communicate, and establish actual contact with my siblings.

CHAPTER 5

Heal Past Wounds and Misunderstandings

At times it was hard to tell if we were pilgrims on the path or clowns in the circus, but the next step was always the same: to let go into love, to deepen mercy and awareness, to put down the load as we were able. A moment at a time. Lightening the burden. Healing.

> Stephen and Ondrea
> Levine, *Embracing the*
> *Beloved: Relationship As a*
> *Path of Awakening*

The fifth step involves healing past wounds and misunderstandings. Often events that occurred in the past have left their imprint on us, making it difficult to approach or trust our siblings. Those wounds take time and conscious effort to transform. In some cases, recent wounds also take their toll and call on all our resources for healing. That was the case with the Grant sisters. "We've come here to heal the loss of our brother," Sheila, 32, explained. She was the youngest of three sisters who had traveled from Syracuse, New York. Vicky was 35 and Lucinda 38. Their brother Stuart had been killed in a car accident eight months before the workshop. He was the baby of the family.

"I have no idea how we can ever heal this wound," Lucinda, the eldest, shared with everyone. Vicky nodded her head in assent and added, "Without Stu I just don't feel whole inside; there's an ache in my heart every time I try to do anything. It's so unfair that he was snatched away like that."

The next step in our process is to release the hold that the past has on our present life. In this chapter with courage and grace we revisit hurts of the past, not as an invitation for re-wounding, but with an eye toward lessening their impact on our lives today. The major work has to do with making these wounds conscious and using that consciousness, through a series of structured explorations, to step out of our old ways of perceiving and experiencing our sibling relationships. The fifth step is thus an invitation to heal past wounds, no matter when they manifested or in what way they caused a rift in our family connection.

Once Vicky, Lucinda, and Sheila had shared their initial story, the whole group exhaled simultaneously. This would be no easy thing to heal. Although most people come to our workshops to heal the loss of relatedness or contact with a sibling, here was a reminder to us of the ultimate loss. We commissioned the three sisters to make lots of room for their grieving process and asked the group to support them, acknowledging that there are no fixed guidelines or protocols with something as complex as losing a loved one. In the course of the weekend, the three sisters shared memories of Stuart, wrote individual good-bye letters to him, meditated, prayed, and finally brought his photo into the center of the room for a farewell ceremony.

Out of this experience everyone gained insight into the value of focused intention; there was certainly no guesswork or misconstruing the three sisters' wish to heal and be free. From that the group began to understand the miraculous and completely unpredictable way in which the healing process unfolds, once we've staked ourselves to its purpose.

Hard to Dismiss the Past

Other members of the group began to focus with greater intention on issues with living siblings. Adele, 55, one of our workshop participants mentioned earlier, relates a memory of her younger sister Joyce:

> To this day I cannot forget how my sister Joyce treated me when I was down and out. Joyce was always more successful than I was. She was interested in business; I loved the art world. I made paintings; Joyce made money. Some twenty years back I had so little money that when I called her, I had to reverse the charges. She got on the phone, found out it was me, and refused the phone call. I was so humiliated. But she may have never forgiven me for making her walk home barefoot when I discovered her out with her friends wearing my brand-new shoes, fifteen years earlier. I guess we both liked to get even. And with all these old tapes we have going on in our heads about each other, I doubt either of us has the slightest inkling of who the other one is.

We can dwell as much as we want on the desired future, and it is important to do this and strengthen our envisioning muscles. At the same time, chief among our stumbling blocks are the powerful and tenacious wounds and conflicts that plague us from the past. Memories of these wounds can be reactivated at a moment's notice. Even years later, when that sibling teases us, or seems threatening, the memory of the hurts, wounds, and conflicts floods back into awareness.

You know the feeling. Your rational mind tells you that the hurts were in the past, that they're long gone. Yet the memory of the broken doll still comes to mind and at the slightest provocation you feel enraged. It's not the broken doll that's the problem. It's the old feeling of powerlessness and injustice that is so hard to overcome. Based in fear, guilt, or resentment, these kinds of childhood wounds keep us stuck.

When we take a closer look, we see that the feeling of being stuck or resistant is an unconscious manifestation of the past hurt or wound. The incident itself may have been forgotten. However, the process gets stuck because the feelings fueling it have not been acknowledged, accepted, and laid to rest. Any attempt to visualize a happy or more fulfilling outcome invariably becomes mired in cynicism and resignation. Although we give lip service to an ideal of closeness, deep inside we believe that things will never change.

Tired of Being Alienated

Natalie, a workshop participant in her late forties and co-owner of a home-furnishings business in Detroit, shakes her head in disbelief when presented with the possibility of healing an old wound with her brother Maxwell, 42:

> There's no way things will ever be different between the two of us. After all, Max and I haven't spoken for thirteen years. Ever since we caught him dipping into the "till" in our family business, I can't imagine trusting him with anything.

Although she felt that her family was in breakdown around this issue and immobilized, Natalie came to realize that there were no accidents and that she had chosen to attend the workshop because she was tired of being alienated from her brother.

> The truth is, I don't really care that he took that money from us so long ago. What kills me is that he didn't trust me enough to ask in the first place. I would have gladly given him whatever he wanted; after all, he is my brother.

But we never had a chance to talk because Max vacated the scene. Whenever there was a problem, we'd ask, "Where's Max?" And he'd be gone. Now that he's drinking so heavily, I can't even imagine how to start again.

Part of Natalie's work involved healing her own wounds and lack of trust. This centered on forgiveness for Max's actions and then, stepping deeper into the process, on gaining a sense of understanding and compassion for her brother's motivations and his own sense of inadequacy and mistrust. But first Natalie had to allow her cynicism and disappointment to take center stage.

Setting the Stage

Among the many reactions to the possibility of healing past wounds, we've witnessed anxiety, disbelief, cynicism, and denial. Before we embark further on this journey, take a moment to see what kinds of thoughts surface about your situation.

Exploration 5-1   Quick Check

What you will need:

Just yourself; 3 minutes

Reflections: After reading the past few paragraphs, check in with yourself. Can you listen in on your thoughts? Right now are you open-minded and eager to hear the rest of the discussion? Do you hear yourself saying "yes but" or "my (hurt, wound, abuse) is different"? Is there any feeling of resignation in saying, "My situation will never change"? Whatever you are saying to yourself is fine. The important issues are first to continue even if you are cynical, and second to accept your current state and don't try to change it.

When we began to offer our Sibling Revelry Workshops, we often heard, "But you don't know *my* sister [or brother]. He [or she] is *hopeless*." In a few cases this may be true. Research carried out in Gene Brody's *Sibling Relationships: Their Causes and Consequences,* indicates that a mere 7 percent of full sibling sets in the sample population report estrangement, and those estranged are most likely brothers. The presence of a sister in the sibling group seems to ensure against total estrangement.

These hurts form dialogues within the mind (conversations between the operating mind [ego] and the supervisory mind [superego]). The dialogue is usually designed to protect you (don't show him your feelings or he'll make fun) or boost you up (she's a fat slob). These conversations are the conscious traces of the old childhood wounds. The problem with all this is that in the end, the original (unhappy) conversation always seems to win over the newly designed and superimposed conversation.

In fact, most of us suffer to some extent from what might be called the "looped tape syndrome"—the tendency to play and replay tapes of the past and act as though these old conversations still exist. This universal syndrome actually keeps past injuries alive in the present. The slightest provocation, such as a missed birthday call from your brother or a comment from your sister at dinner, will trigger your tape to replay its endless version of how much your brother hates you or your sister thinks you're awful.

Andrea, a dear friend and colleague, illustrates this point. She is still insisting that her older sister Renee apologize for being unavailable for her twenty-six years ago during a personal crisis! Andrea has minimal contact with this sister—her only surviving relative—because she feels that Renee did not meet her emotional needs then and is insufficiently remorseful now.

Although at first she may not be open to it, Andrea needs

to see how much she's feeding into the problem. After all, the underlying event happened twenty-six years ago, and no matter how Renee might be feeling, Andrea still bears the brunt of the anger. As a social worker, she readily understands how she continues to rewound herself by shutting her sister out and not attending to the sources of her own anger and hurt. What is lacking, though, is an intention to heal. No matter what experiences we go through vis-à-vis our brothers and sisters, sooner or later, in order to set the healing process in motion, we have to be willing to take responsibility for the problem. That means looking beyond blame, guilt, or the feeling of powerlessness that we have associated with the past. Otherwise we continue to view the past and our role in changing the future as beyond our control.

The Overwhelming Sense of Powerlessness

In the 1998 movie *Hilary and Jackie*, we observe Jacqueline du Pré, world-renowned cellist, competing with her older sister Hilary, originally the star musician of the family. We can see the wounds develop between these sisters as they try to make good in the world and still hold on to each other. Observing their dilemma, Hilary might think: "I adore my sister Jackie. I will do anything to make her happy, even if it makes me miserable." And from Jackie's point of view: "I never wanted anything to come between Hilary and me. But in the final analysis it was my fierce ambition that separated us. No matter how hard I try, I cannot succeed in bringing love to my life the way she has."

What started out as love and closeness turned into competition and misunderstanding. An ingredient essential to Hilary and Jackie's dilemma and common to most wounds from the past is a sense of *powerlessness*—i.e., life happened and there was nothing we could do to change or prevent it. Stories then live on in our minds telescoped into injustices, hurts, or complaints we suffered (or imagined that we suffered) as we were growing up.

Old ideas about the world and our place in it die hard. Unless they are brought into the light and examined, our childhood memories and opinions pretty much govern our present-day point of view. Take the example of Joel's friend Jay, who raised a Doberman pinscher, Zack, from a puppy. Jay played with his dog every day, flipping him over, having Zack bite a sock and pull him around the room. Jay disciplined him with a newspaper, if warranted. Zack clearly learned that Jay was bigger and stronger. Zack grew into a large, menacing-looking dog, although still a teddy bear underneath. One day Jay told Joel, "It's clear that Zack still thinks I'm stronger. I hope he never figures out that I'm not!" Growing up, we're all like Zack. We think our older brother is still bigger and stronger, our sister smarter, and that we're small and weak.

And we suffer as a result. When we were small, our powerlessness was real. The problem is that our feeling of inadequacy does not change as we grow up. The feeling gets filtered, twisted, and rearranged for our adult purposes. However, the victim-perpetrator plot remains intact. Our purpose in this chapter is to examine this "plot" and the various complaints, concerns, and incompletions that may accompany it, getting them out of your mind and onto paper. You might ask: Why put them on paper? Won't this process open old wounds and stir up trouble?

Writing down the feelings and impressions evoked by these exercises helps organize the amorphous swirl of complaints, concerns, and incompletions into concise statements, which can be viewed more objectively by the grown-up mind. This creates emotional distance that allows for review and reappraisal. Then we have a choice as to starting the real work of healing.

Our goal is to allow our stories to be heard and received by the grown-up mind. From that vantage point we can see the limitations of the victim-perpetrator perspective. The victim was a child and so was the perpetrator. When you raise children you realize that occasionally they really do want to kill, maim, or humiliate you or their siblings. That is the normal working of a child's mind. When we realize that the evil older sister or the pesky younger brother was just acting out his or her part in a larger drama, the wound seems less intentional and even less hurtful. And we come to understand that the victim and the perpetrator both suffer and are wounded in these childhood wars.

The Importance of Your Intention

Most humanistic psychologies hold that the conscious intention to change is the actual leverage point for change. We hope that the storytelling, exercises, and journal writing we present in this book reinforce your healing intentions by creating a point to focus upon. Then your intention operates almost with a life of its own. It may draw certain data and information your way or provide a forum in which you can work on different issues. Your intention to improve your relationships with your siblings may not only have urged you to purchase this book; it may have been the force behind completing a certain exercise or initiating a healing conversation. This process works in mysterious ways.

As we mentioned earlier, the simple act of observing changes the chemistry of your relationships. You enter into the observation and inadvertently become a catalyst for change. Mounting evidence suggests that the very intention to heal attracts healing energy. Whereas normal thinking may be compared to diffused light, intentionality has been compared to a laser beam. It can focus and concentrate energy so that deep healing takes place.

Sometimes it is difficult for us to consolidate our real intentions in regard to healing. We have so much of an overlay from difficult past experiences holding us back. This is the case with Shelley, 39, one of our workshop participants. Far from Tennessee, her home state, Shelley reminisces about her older brother William, 41, from whom she is estranged.

> I don't really know how to let go of the hurt and rage I feel toward William. In high school he went out with my best friend Abby and they became very close. They were even planning to get married. For some reason, though, William insisted on putting me down in Abby's presence, and she finally got angry with both of us. First, she drifted away from our friendship and later she left Will for some other guy. To this day William believes I plotted to turn Abby against him. He's never forgiven me, and I've never forgiven him for cutting me off from my best friend. That was years ago. Although we're long overdue to make amends, I don't know the best way to do it. Mom says William feels as badly as I do, but I'm afraid to take the next step.

Wounds and hurts can be witnessed and understood within the larger context in which they took place. This larger context is the family, with its economic issues, marital discord, or other problems and secrets. To gain even greater distance and compassion, we must see the family in the even larger context of race, class, culture, and era. When viewed this way, observing the key players acting in a manner appropriate to their age and circumstance, wounds often heal or lessen in impact. That, in turn, helps us peel off the label and identification we have given to these injuries as "personal."

How We Heal

A big debate centers on how we actually heal the hurts and pains of the past. Is healing equivalent to letting go? If so, the act of letting go resembles a "we lose/they win" proposition. If I give up my anger and resentment, will this person walk all over me? I don't want to be hurt again. Viewed from that perspective, it's clear why we sometimes hug our tapes and interpretations more closely than our siblings! Then how can we point to certain emotional wounds and say with conviction that they're healed? In some cases, healing may seem too much like mandatory forgiveness, and having to forgive too much like condoning unacceptable behavior. Letting go does not mean capitulation to the whim of anyone—sister or brother included. As in the Sufi proverb: "Trust in God, *and* tie your camel." That is, let go, as an act of radical inner liberation, and remain grounded in reality.

Many thinkers have turned their attention to the difficulty of genuine healing of emotional wounds. In *The Creation of Health*, Norm Shealy and Carolyn Myss summarize their views both on healing and on having your say:

> The experience of shedding troubled emotions and completing long-awaited conversations with family and friends brings to an appropriate conclusion all of the energies a person has set in motion during the course of a lifetime. This is a deeply healing process that allows the necessary moment of letting go to occur without residual guilt or angry emotions being retained by family members or friends. Though grief is present, it is not grief mixed with the crippling feelings that come from not having the final opportunity to say what is in your heart.

In fact, letting go serves as a philosophical underpinning to much of the humanistic therapeutic model. Some say we can tell we've truly released a hurt or wound when our thoughts no longer return to dwell on it; or when our thoughts do return to the incident but there is no longer a great deal of emotional energy attached to it. Others say we just learn to adapt more capably and efficiently but that the initial wound remains forever part of our psyche. We urge you to find a workable sense of the *feeling* of letting go, and not to be afraid to fake it until you make it. Use the strength and energy of your capable, adult self, and if you must invent letting go, do so! What's critical, however, is to remember your underlying intention.

We hold to a rudimentary idea of healing. On a physical level we know that wounds heal; we can see the process in action. On an emotional level, we assume that wounds heal, but we may not be privy to the mechanism. We do have clues, however. Emotional wounds heal with time and experience, often indicated by a release or change in feeling.

Acknowledging the Gap

At some point we come to a gap between the external recognition of our wounding process and our internal response. This gap is not fully explained by modern psychology. Essentially it's a mystery. The gap occurs after the work of recall—after writing or telling the story in which the healing of the hurt takes place. Some people refer to it as an insight or "aha" experience; others call the gap transformation; still others call it grace. Whatever you want to call what Mariah Gladis refers to as that "moment of healing," in her unpublished manuscript, "Exact Moments of Healing," usually you must put some effort into it before it unfolds. The end result is catharsis and healing.

In order to approach the gap, we must enter a state of being unlike our ordinary waking consciousness. In his book *Too Much Is Not Enough*, Orson Bean captured this state perfectly when he described his biology teacher's experiment:

Mr. Bartlett finds a cocoon in the woods and brings it to the classroom. We crowd around as he takes a razor blade and neatly slices it in two. The cocoon looks empty. "There's nothing in there," says one of the kids. "Oh, it's in there," says Mr. Bartlett. "It just doesn't have a shape right now. The living, organic material is spun right into the cocoon. Caterpillar is gone; butterfly is yet to come." We stare in wonder.

"Real transformation," says Mr. Bartlett, "means giving up one form before you have another. It requires the willingness to be *nothing* for a while."

In our approach, we do not separate healing from transformation. In fact, for us, they are one. True healing takes into account the inner life we live day to day, which is a composite of the workings of body, mind, and spirit. To let go is holistic in nature, because it takes into account all the related parts of us. And letting go fundamentally occurs as an energetic event. We release any charge we may have held around an issue by letting it rise to our awareness, by feeling its effects in our bodies, and by releasing the habitual thought pattern that embedded it in our consciousness in the first place. Healing is both a process and a practice. If you find that you automatically drift back to habitual, painful patterns of thought, consciously remind yourself that your goal and intention is to soothe and heal.

While swimming laps one summer day, Marjory observed a sibling interaction at the shallow end of the pool. Jason and his little sister Katie were swimming around. Jason kept posing challenges to Katie: "Swim backwards!" Katie would give it a good try, and invariably, Jason would respond: "Katie, you did that wrong. Now watch me!" Jason must have come up with ten different tricky water maneuvers for his sister to try (and fail).

Some time later, Katie was sitting off by herself, looking a little despondent. She told Marjory she just wasn't a very good swimmer and couldn't do anything right. Despite attempts to reason with her, Katie knew the truth: According to her brother, there was something wrong with her. It's easy to imagine Katie carrying this conviction with her into her later life—easy to imagine the resentment and pain, the barriers she will feel unable to overcome. Should Katie internalize her brother's impatience and conviction of her imperfection, we would design for her a process of uncovering and awareness, gently challenging the "truth" of a young boy's efforts to master the world through his compliant little sister.

Through this process of storytelling, healing, and letting go, we hope to create a context for something wholesome and entirely new to emerge in your sibling experience. We want to give the adult Katies and Jasons an alternative to these "frozen misunderstandings," as Stephen Bank and Michael Kahn call them in their book *The Sibling Bond*, and the years of suffering they might experience.

How to Let Go

As we have seen, letting go is no easy task. Many of the wounds that we inflicted or received as young siblings were intense or unrelenting. In the *Washington Times*, Wade F. Horn, Ph.D., Director of the National Fatherhood Initiative and former United States Commissioner for Children, Youth and Families, describes the unsettling nature of sibling rivalry:

"Unfortunately, sibling relationships are among the most competitive we will ever experience. Ever since Cain and Abel, siblings have been competing with each other for status, power, and affection. And like Cain and Abel, sibling rivalry can turn violent. According to research reported at a recent meeting of the American Psychological Association, 65 percent of a sample of 202 college students said they had experienced some sibling physical abuse, resulting in injuries to 17 percent of that group, with 4 percent requiring a visit to a physician."

Often we have difficult, convoluted experiences that have not been fully healed or laid to rest. However, with rare exceptions, these wounds and hurts are past, not present. Yet, we live as if the past could reappear at any time. The fact that your brother beat you up thirty-five years ago is probably not good evidence that he'll do it again now. But deep inside we live in fear that the wounding or unkindness will be repeated, and instantly we react as the same helpless being we once were. In order to deal with that essentially outdated emotional baggage, we need to get it out on the table.

The process brings to mind these famous words from His Holiness, the Dalai Lama: "Changes in attitude never come easily. The development of love and compassion is a wide, round curve that can be negotiated only slowly, not a sharp corner that can be turned all at once." (As quoted by Bo Lozoff in *Deep and Simple: A Spiritual Path for Modern Times*.)

Naming the Wounds of the Past

The following exercise involves making lists of the hurts and complaints you can remember from your childhood. Initially, bringing the memories of these painful episodes into consciousness might activate some of the old emotions. The focus in these exercises is not to fan the flame or build a new list of resentments, but rather to expose these thoughts and feelings to the light of day. We keep things unconscious or hidden by not naming them. We then can convince ourselves that the experience (and its pain) is unreal. As we discussed a few pages back, we want to allow these memories to rise into consciousness so that we can acknowledge them as real. This act of naming immediately begins to dispel their influence. We can breathe, relax, and admit, "Yes, this painful event happened. I lived through it. I can now feel and release the feelings associated with it."

Setting the Stage

In the exercise that follows, fill in the blanks at the end of each sentence. If possible, allow the child version of yourself to express itself along with the adult version. As you air sibling issues, you may find yourself unearthing feelings that were unanticipated, unexpected, or of deeper emotional content than you imagined. If so, you've tapped in to a potential gold mine.

It is helpful to remember that you have not entered into these exercises to settle old scores. Stay focused on your intentions and goals in the present. Although it may be awkward or difficult to acknowledge the woundings, allow the feelings that rise to be expressed without censoring or changing them. No one needs to see or have access to this material if it feels inappropriate to you. During the process of writing this book, we had to grapple with the power of some of our own long-sublimated conflicts.

In addition, if you feel overwhelmed by the intensity of your recollections, slow down. Sometimes one or more sessions with a mental-health professional can help you to clear your mind and control your feelings of being overwhelmed. In particular, in families with a history of violence, the uncovering of these memories can be quite painful. Use your networks of support and give yourself permission to go only as far and as deep as best serves you.

The following sentences are jumping-off points. Use them as a guide. If one doesn't apply to you, move on to the next one. If a question of this type enters your mind, please add it and answer it in your sibling journal.

Some of the exercises in this book are designed to be shared, and others are designed to be kept private (and shared only if your sibling is directly involved in this process). These exercises are designed to be kept private. The words and ideas that you write might be unnecessarily hurtful to siblings to whom you are not very close.

You should do these exercises on separate sheets of paper outside your sibling notebook. We have a powerful ritual at the end of this section that can be followed to help end your suffering over these issues.

Exploration 5-2 Healing Wounds from the Past: Sentence Completion
What you will need:

A few sheets of paper; about 40 minutes for all sections
We *do not* recommend that you use your sibling journal

Lists and landmarks: Complete the following sentences for each of your siblings.

I strongly disagree with my brother/sister in relation to _____
I wish my brother/sister would/would not _____
I feel wronged by my brother/sister in relation to_____
The hardest thing for me to do in relation to my brother/sister is _____
I'm afraid of my brother/sister when _____
I feel guilty about my brother/sister when _____
I feel sad about my brother/sister when _____
I feel misunderstood by my brother/sister in relation to _____
I wish I could communicate to my brother or sister when _____

continued

> I'm angry at my brother/sister
> about _____
> I will never forgive my
> brother/sister for _____
> I'm afraid I will never be forgiven
> by my brother/sister for _____

What Happened

This exercise is designed to make the unconscious conscious, and to make the unspoken spoken. There is great power in this simple exercise.

Exploration 5-3 Healing Wounds from the Past:
Fear, Anger, Guilt, Hurt

What you will need:

A few sheets of paper; 15 minutes this section
We *do not* recommend that you use your sibling journal

Mapping the territory: Take another sheet of paper and create four columns (see illustration on page 167), under the headings of Fear, Anger, Guilt, Hurt.

In each column write your key starting sentence: What I'm afraid of; What I'm angry/resentful about; etc.

Fear: What I'm afraid of
Anger: What I'm angry/resentful about
Guilt: What I feel guilty about
Hurt: What I'm hurt about

Having reread this sentence-completion exercise, summarize the essential items that you fear, resent, or feel hurt/guilt about in the columns provided.

Examples of table for Exploration 5-3 Healing Wounds from the Past: Fear, Anger, Guilt, Hurt

	Fear	Anger	Guilt	Hurt
Tom	My brother John will give up on me	Always having to be subservient or he'd beat me up	Not paying back the money I borrowed	Knowing he doesn't really respect me
Sally	My older sister will leave me behind	Always having to be nice and polite	Putting Magic Marker on her favorite dress or throwing it away	She doesn't really care about me (she told me this over and over)

What Happened

This continues the work of the preceding exercise. With prompting you will associate with the four words and remember new and different things. Remember, this is an exercise in remembering injuries not to get even but to heal them.

Take Courage: You're on Your Way to Healing and Integration

One of the central themes of our book is that both courage and generosity are necessary aspects of letting go of the past. Holding on to a clear vision of the future is also helpful. Remember that you are on your way somewhere. If you have the choice to drop some baggage, it may make your journey easier.

So we are asking you to summon courage and generosity now as allies to assist you in this process. As we move forward, there is much we will recommend to accomplish this important objective of letting go. Remember that letting go is a process that occurs in time. Do not expect instant release from childhood hurts (although you may be lucky and experience just such a catharsis). Be gentle with yourself and your siblings.

What Needs Healing?

Consider an intention that may prompt you toward healing something in relation to your brothers and sisters. You've had a chance to unearth the aches and pains, acquainting yourself with the troublesome conversations that have held the sibling dynamic in place.

Now we pose the question: What needs healing? What needs to be released? What do you need to let go of? What no longer serves your highest good or that of your siblings?

Reviewing the columns you wrote about fear, anger, guilt, and hurt, ask yourself which of these have outlived their usefulness or which of these you are willing to give up. Are you willing to let go of your fear, anger, guilt, or hurt for a more fulfilling relationship with your sibling? Which of these seems to hold you back from a more fulfilling relationship?

Setting the Stage

There are powerful forces afoot. In this exploration you will have the conversation of a lifetime. You will say it all. Too bad you will be the only one to hear it. Leave yourself enough time and reasonable assurance of being left alone for this exploration. This exploration is especially recommended for those siblings with whom you have some unresolved conflict or difficulty, including estranged or deceased sisters and brothers.

Exploration 5-4 Allow Healing to Happen
What you will need:

Separate sheets of paper; 20 minutes plus
We *do not* recommend that you use your sibling journal

Reflections: Find a photograph or other representation (baseball glove, Barbie Doll, etc.) of your sibling. Take some time to reflect on the picture or item.

Allowing yourself to settle into a meditative and reflective state, begin to bring the image of your brother or sister more deeply into your mind.

Memory Lane: Call to mind your brother or sister; see if you can experience their presence with you. As you study the image, consider who or what needs forgiving.

Allow forgiveness to enter the picture. It may be clear who needs to be forgiven in the situation; it may not.

Lights, Camera, Action: Now, take a breath and begin to write a letter to your sibling.

This letter is for your eyes only. Write whatever comes to mind, and especially those things you would like to have said but withheld. Let it all out. Tell him what still hurts or what you resent about him. Tell her what you're afraid to express and why.

Witness: Once you've completed your letter, sit in silence. Allow any feelings that have come up to be present.

Sit and breathe and allow yourself to feel whatever you feel. You may want to add a postscript to your letter.

Reflections: Focus again on the picture or representation of your sibling. When you feel connected, read your letter aloud as though he or she were in the room with you and as committed to healing and letting go of this injury as you are.

See your sibling sitting there in front of you. See if you can actually feel his or her presence with you. Use a photograph, if that helps you.

Intermission

This can be intense work. You are making contact with old material and with the hurt child inside you. As an aside, this may be a perfect time for milk and cookies. Like any great play, your life has conflict, triumphs, and failures. With you as the central actor, you need to be able to flow smoothly between action and reflection, victim and perpetrator, and between the play and the audience. Now for act 2.

Exploration 5-5 Allow Healing to Happen: Put Yourself in Your Sibling's Shoes

What you will need:

A few sheets of paper; about 15 minutes

Change characters: This is the tricky part. Shift to your sibling's thoughts, and sense and feel what lies undisclosed. Have the thoughts that he or she would have. Imagine that your sibling is taking in this new information you have provided them.

Some people actually switch and sit opposite where they were. Like a great actor, become your sibling.

Once you feel focused in your sister/brother's world, take up your pen and a new sheet of paper. As your sibling, compose a letter to yourself about the things you heard in the last letter.

Remember, be a great actor and hold your sibling inside as you write. Imagine how he or she would respond. Feel free to make it up. You may be surprised that you have more insight into your sibling's perspective than you imagined.

Reflections: When you have completed your sibling's letter to you, again come into stillness and silence. Feel whatever there is to feel.

Remember to keep breathing.

Lights, Camera, Action: Read this letter to yourself out loud, as though you were that sibling.	For this part you may want to look at yourself in a mirror, or have a photograph of yourself nearby.
Witness: Again, allow some time for feeling, reflection, and silence.	For many people this can be intense. Even if you initially feel no reaction, you have heard what you needed to hear and the work inside you has begun.
Reread both your letters and notice what has shifted in relation to the conflict. What remains the same?	Keep noticing your feelings; remember to breathe.
If there is anything you would like to write down to complete this exchange, do that now.	Make sure you have included all of your hurts and resentments about this issue.

What Happened

When all the hurts and resentments have found their way to your paper, create a conscious turning point. Decide in favor of healing; let your original intention take over, writing whatever comes into your heart. That may include asking or seeking forgiveness; it may not. You may want to ask yourself what you need to give up in order for healing to happen. If feelings arise, welcome them. Sense how your intention has paved the way for this shift in energy. Then sit back and enjoy the sensations, both happy and sad. Acknowledge your part in letting go. Invoke prayer, if that feels right. Ask for a change, and likely it will come. For this is the part where grace has a role to play, and it's important for us to get out of the way once we have done our work. Then we can let the unseen complete what we have initiated.

Example of a Variation

Therese, one of our workshop participants, addressed her letter to God. She was estranged from her only sister and was too angry and hurt to address her directly. She has generously given us permission to reproduce part of her letter here.

Dear God:

In my next life I would like to have a sister, a real sister, someone who loves *and* likes me. I have always wanted a sibling who would be a pal, someone to call on the phone and talk about work, husbands, and our parents. How I have longed for someone who would let *me* talk, who would be a good listener.

I wish I had a sister who wasn't always so ready to argue, to snipe, to ridicule and put me down, and to boast about herself and dominate. Instead, she would be kind, sympathetic, intuitive, sensitive, and cheerful. I've always wished for someone with whom conversation could flow naturally, in a balanced way. I've always wished I'd had a relationship that was based on equality and respect, instead of mistrust, jealousy, and competition.

God, you got real mixed up when you sent me this sister—I think she's more of a *brother* than a sister. She has grabbed onto the masculine traits assigned to her by our parents and won't let go. She delights in emphasizing that she's "one of the guys"—especially when it comes to competitiveness. She delights in pushing me around physically and mentally.

I'm *not* one of the guys, and I'd like to feel that that was O.K. I wish I had a sister who didn't make me feel like I was a lesser person because I am not like her. I wish I had a sister who could keep her hands and her sharp remarks to herself.

It's hard for me to imagine this because I've never had it, but an ideal sister would be someone I could meet for coffee to talk about everything and nothing, to people watch, to be enclosed in our own special world. An ideal sister would call me up in the middle of the week and invite me to do something fun for the weekend, like go shopping or ride bikes or go to a museum, or just drive around and do errands together. I'd look forward to spending our time together. It would be relaxing and fun, not some kind of traumatic, competitive, life or death event.

In my old age, I'd have a sister who would be my connection to the past, and to the outside world. If I got sick, she'd be there as an advocate for me. I'd be her advocate, too. We'd look back at our lifelong tie and laugh at all of our silly disagreements. We'd hold hands and help each other up stairs. I could talk about my unconventional ideas without fear of ridicule and mockery. We could love each other, just like sisters should.

Therese

Moving Toward Completion

Taking a close look at the roles we play in our relationships is one of the most important parts of letting go of past hurts. This means having the courage to look at the source of pain or perceived unkindness. It means being willing to be honest with ourselves first, and then with our siblings. Letting go, however, involves more than studying our interactions. There is a point where it's important to share our experiences and perspective. Sharing delivers us to the point of real letting go because it helps bring about completion and validation.

Setting the Stage

Human beings use rituals to mark life passages. Societies have parties and rituals around birth, coming of age, marriage, and death. One of the things that we would like to add to our modern society are rituals that signify turning points in people's growth and maturation. This is one such ritual. Please take this as a bare outline and use it to help create your own perfect scenario.

Exploration 5-6 Completion Ritual
What you will need:

The sheets you have written in the last few explorations; barbecue pit, fireplace, outdoor grill; 25 minutes

Gather the papers you have written in the last few explorations into a pile. Assemble a small "funeral pyre" and place your writings on top. Clear other flammables away. Be sure you are in a safe area for this activity.

If you do this outside, be sure the area is safe for a small fire. Use a barbecue pit, metal trash can, or Hibachi. Indoors you can use a fireplace. You might want to invite some friends and your spouse. (Siblings can be invited and they can also do the exercises. Do not read each other's papers.)

Reflections: Say a few words or read from a favorite poem or the scriptures. A section that moves you dealing with death might be appropriate.

A part of you is dead and you are about to burn it and spread the ashes.

Lights, Camera, Action: As you read the section, light the fire. Watch the flames and feel the complaints and hurts die away.

Say good-bye to this part of yourself in a solemn and respectful way. Spread the ashes where they will do some good, such as in a garden or at the base of a tree. Afterward have a nice wake.

What Happened

As Norm Shealy and Carolyn Myss explain in their book, *The Creation of Health:*

> Completion is the opportunity to bring to a close—literally and figuratively—the open wounds of your life. Completion is the counterpart to creation. We want to see the energy we set in motion in our lives come full circle. We want to see our children grow up; we want to learn why some of our relationships failed; we want to see our businesses flourish. Wherever there is incompletion in our lives, there are strings attached, though these attachments may be unconscious. We remain tied through the invisible strings of our creative energy to all that we have set in motion. That is perhaps the dynamic that is responsible for causing us to re-create certain situations in our lives until we learn the lessons and can finally break the pattern by applying conscious choice.

And Finally . . . Validation

The final element in the process of letting go is to be validated for who we are and what we have experienced or suffered in relation to one another. Validation is not to be confused with condoning or judging one's actions. It does not provide proof that anyone is right or wrong; it simply allows us to transmit the heart of our experience and be received by one another, to be seen, heard, and felt for who we are. Then we no longer feel alone in our struggles.

At this point, if it's appropriate, take the opportunity to share with your brother or sister the pain or hurts you are releasing from the past. If needed, use a friend for support. You may also choose to enlist the help of a therapist if your issues are deep-seated. Keep a record of these experiences in your journal. Now that you've completed this work, sit back and relax. Realize in this moment that your relationship has undergone tremendous change. By unearthing these conversations from the past and being willing to face them, you have altered the chemistry of your interactions forever.

Prayers

"May all beings be free of suffering. May all beings be at peace. May all beings meet their pain with mercy and loving-kindness. May all beings make room in their heart for their pain and the pain of all sentient beings, who, too, want only to be free." (Buddhist prayer adapted by Stephen Levine.)

Prayers are our connection to the unseen. They comfort us and help us release resistance. And the rest of what they do is part of the mystery. The following prayer is dedicated to Patti LaBelle and the inspiration she provides, not only through her magnificent singing but through her recollections of her sisters, three of whom she lost to cancer. During one of her televised concerts Patti spoke about the importance of cultivating gratitude, urging us to pay attention to these wonderful beings who are our brothers and sisters, for we don't know how long we'll be graced by their presence.

A Prayer for My Sister/Brother

Jo Ann wrote this prayer. Feel free to write your own or use this one.

As I sit here bringing your image to mind, I can feel your presence near me and can almost hear the sound of your voice. Becoming very still, I breathe slow, measured breaths. It seems as if I can see your smile. In these precious moments I feel you close to me.

The basis for our connection is and always has been a mystery. I don't know why or how we came together and developed the relationship that we did, and I realize it's not important to know. What is important is that I stay tuned to how precious you are in my life. You are a continuous shining presence. May my love for you become even more pronounced and more deeply felt.

Despite all that we have been through, we are still here for each other. There is something that makes us more than friends, on the one hand, and more than relations on the other. We know each other way beneath our skins in the place called soul. And we're together. Whatever time we have is precious, and beyond that I recognize that our ties are eternal. Whether near or far, you remain forever in my thoughts and in my heart.

I sincerely pray you have the best of everything—the best of health, the best of prosperity, the best of love, creativity, and friendship—and an ongoing sense of how much you're loved. May you always live with adventure, joy, and growth as your companions and the feeling of contentment in the way your life is unfolding.

Remember that you can lean on me anytime and draw strength from our connection. If anything remains incomplete or unfinished, I pray that time will help us heal and come to a place of gratitude, centeredness, and peace. May you know love in its deepest realms; may you experience profound joy and freedom in your life. And above all, may our connection as brother/sister grow to be a source of endless love, support, and inspiration for one another.

Summary
Step 5: Heal Past Wounds and Misunderstandings

- Chief among the stumbling blocks to creating a new sibling relationship is the power and tenacity of

wounds from the past. We cannot move forward with
our healing if our inner resistance from these injuries is
too great.

- These hurts form inner dialogues, or conversations, between the operating mind (ego) and the supervisory
  mind (superego), which are designed to boost or protect our self-image.

- As in the looped-tape syndrome, these conversations
  tend to repeat themselves as the predominant argu-
  ments in our minds, and we tend to act as if they are so
  and as if we are locked into the victim/perpetrator consciousness.

- Common to most early wounds is a sense of powerlessness; i.e., life happened and there was nothing we
  could do to change things.

- When we were small, our powerlessness was real; the
  problem is that our feeling of inadequacy doesn't
  change as we grow up.

- Reviewing and writing down hurts from the past helps
  create emotional distance that allows for review and
  reappraisal. Wounds can then be witnessed and understood within the larger context in which they took
  place. That in turn helps us peel off the label we have
  given to these injuries as "personal."

- To heal or let go means to release any charge we may
  have held around an issue by letting it rise into our
  awareness, feel its effects in our bodies, and release the
  habitual thought patterns that embedded it in our consciousness in the first place.

- Letting go is not an easy task. We often live as if the
  past could reappear at any time. It takes a conscious

commitment to begin to heal these wounds and courage and generosity to stay with the process.

- Completion is the counterpart to creation. Wherever we have the opportunity to move toward completion in our lives, we free up considerable energy that was held captive in wounds and self-defeating patterns.

- The final element in letting go is to be validated for who we are and what we have experienced or suffered in relation to one another.

Seeds of Change

❑ I am willing to dive more deeply into childhood wounds and take on the work of inner healing.

❑ In this process I discover conversations that tend to repeat themselves in my mind and ones I have subscribed to as victim/perpetrator.

❑ I am releasing the sense of powerlessness held over from my childhood as I get to the heart of this wounding.

❑ Writing and reviewing has helped me establish emotional distance. I am seeing the larger picture; in fact, I am grasping how all my family members suffered some type of wounding, not only myself. I am willing and ready to let go.

Grains of Hope, Pearls of Wisdom

✓ This process is helping me move toward profound freedom and acceptance of my past.

✓ I no longer have a need to hold my siblings (or myself) accountable for the wounds of the past.

✓ I experience the courage and generosity it takes to heal.

✓ From His Holiness the Dalai Lama: "Changes in attitude never come easily. The development of love and compassion is a wide, round curve that can be negotiated only slowly, not a sharp corner that can be turned all at once." (In Bo Lozoff, *Deep and Simple: A Spiritual Path for Modern Times*.)

CHAPTER 6

Invent New Family Legends

Human beings are perceivers, but the world that they
perceive is an illusion: an illusion created by the description that was told to them from the moment they
were born. So in essence, the world that their reason
wants to sustain is the world created by a description
and its dogmatic and inviolable rules, which their reason learns to accept and defend.

Carlos Castañeda,
The Wheel of Time

The sixth step involves creating new family legends. But first
we must study our families and learn what legends are
already in place. For two of our workshop participants,
Martin, age 39, a corporate lawyer, and his sister Ellie, 35, a
computer troubleshooter, there was a clear legend that developed as they were growing up. Martin was aware of being recruited at age 7 when his mother began suffering
severe bouts of anxiety and depression and his father's work
took him on the road several months a year. The message to
Martin was: "Take care of your mother; she needs all the
help she can get. Take care of your little sister and make sure
you both behave!" Martin became the little caregiver, husband to Mom and father to Ellie. As a grown-up, Martin has
an ex-wife who is in and out of institutions. His two kids
also seem unable to care for themselves. However, his sister
Ellie has started to turn her life around and defy the family
legend. This has helped Martin see his own entrapment.

In this chapter we address the invisible world of legends. A legend is a story handed down through generations and popularly believed to have a historical basis. We all have legends we've grown up with; perhaps the story has created an imprint on our consciousness such that we no longer need even to tell it out loud. Nevertheless, legends shape how we view our world. Although you can't see or touch them, these stories are woven through your life and impact how you act, how you choose your friends, and how you treat your brothers and sisters.

The main purpose of a legend is to provide safety, predictability, and a shared identity through which we relate. The common stories that define all families often concern money, being taken advantage of, safety in the world, health, autonomy, opportunity, being responsible, the kind of work you do, how you relate to others, and the importance of extended family, loyalty, and love. These legends can form invisible ties that bind you to a glorious or horrendous past. From the readings and explorations in this chapter you will begin to unearth and shed light upon the stories that shaped your personal development; you will also understand how people are conditioned by the particular legends that they grew up with.

You Write Your Own Ticket

Corey, a dark-haired 41-year-old from Dallas, seemed older than her sister, as we greeted the two women entering our workshop. However, we were surprised to learn that Caitlin, blond and petite, was not her younger sister but her twin.

Well, she's a few minutes younger than me, but we're fraternal twins, born on Christmas Eve. I look like Dad; she's the spittin' image of Mom. Mom called us Christmas angels, and Dad said we could have whatever we wanted. That's where our family legend began.

Caitlin, a little less sure of herself, chimed in:

The family legend that was handed down to us was basically "you write the ticket." Dad's father made money in oil; Dad has a cattle ranch, and we both feel like the world's our playground.

As we shared stories from our family experiences, some of the workshop participants playfully asked if they could trade their family legends with Corey and Caitlin's. If only it were that simple.

Guidelines on How to Live Life

Every family has legends. These family legends are stories—whether apocryphal or true—that have some kind of moral or guidance that directs the family, describing how to live life, what one can expect from the world, and what's possible. They arise out of the zeitgeist, or the time, place, and particular circumstances that together shape the destiny of a given family or group of families. These legends can stretch back for generations. They may arise out of the race, culture, or ethnic group with which the family identifies. They may be variations of some larger legend, such as the legend of unlimited individual opportunity that characterized the United States for so long. Family legends do not have to be consciously passed along; in fact, they are often unspoken, yet powerful and directive nonetheless.

Coming to Terms with Your Family Legends

In her book *Like Water for Chocolate*, Laura Esquivel weaves into her fanciful narrative the legend most deeply affecting the family experience, created by Mama Elena, who insists that her youngest daughter, Tita, must stay on as her guardian in old age and never marry. But Tita and Pedro are in love and wish to marry. When at last Tita takes matters into her own hands and opposes the family legend, she must go to war with her mother's ghost in order to become free.

Most of us don't have supernatural foes preventing us from living our lives in freedom; however, all of us must come to terms with our own family legends and family ghosts. Our ghosts are likely to be invisible and just as powerful as Tita's. As in Martin's case, although he is beginning to see the pattern, he still feels victim to the family dynamic set in place earlier. Martin laments the fact that he seems to attract helpless women who need to be taken care of, and can't seem to teach his children appropriate autonomy. Underneath the surface he still feels as if his job is to care for the mothers and little sisters of the world. To break through the legend Martin, like Tita, must go to war with the ghosts of his mother and father.

Our purpose in this chapter is to examine the legends that we have in place with an eye to teasing them out of the fabric of our lives, and evaluating their usefulness to us in the present. If necessary, we will also take some steps toward transforming their substance and giving them happier endings, and us more freedom and possibility.

How Legends Get Started

First we observe how the legend evolves from the story. Through a series of repetitive experiences we begin to formulate conclusions. Like the proverbial blind men touching the elephant, we are convinced that life is hard, thick, thin, resilient, or trunklike, depending on which part of the animal we are touching. And from there the story accumulates until "history repeats itself": the so-called legend is born. Even stories that never actually happened can exert influence on the present. The family makes them true (whether in fact they are is not as critical as the impact they have on the family dynamic). In many cases the tendrils of those stories start generations in the past and extend to and entwine future generations.

Once we identify the legends that hold us captive, we can choose to create a different future. Taking this radical a step means we are willing to acknowledge that what we held as our common history may in fact be neither true nor largely relevant; it also means stepping out of the so-called trance that, in effect, held it, and us, in place. We began the process of letting go on a personal level in the preceding chapter. Our task in this chapter is to let go on an impersonal level. That is, to let go in terms of the family identity and dynamic, and perhaps beyond that, to let go of elements of our sociocultural history that no longer serve our unique, individual purposes. The first part of our task in this chapter is investigative and evaluative, the second inventive or imaginative. We want to acknowledge the legends we carry with us, keep what serves us, and then re-create them in such a way that our future sibling relationships are happy ones.

We Stick Together

Erica, age 27, and her sister Eliza, 25, were perhaps the youngest members of a particular sibling workshop we ran. Although silent for much of the workshop, Erica was definitely not emotionally "quiet." Thus, we were happy when she at last shared with the group.

> I'm the oldest of three children and our names all start with E, something my parents thought was precious but we kids hated. Eliza's 25 and Ethan's 23, and he's definitely the baby. We grew up in Avalon, New Jersey, but we live in Moorestown. I'm a fitness instructor. My sister and I are close but the real problem is Ethan, our

baby brother. He's a wreck. I don't know what happened to him, but ever since he turned 21, he started using drugs, showing up late for work, and just hanging around smoking and drinking with friends.

Eliza, heartened by her sister's confession, also decided to break the ice:

We just don't know what to do with him. He talks about making films but never does anything about it. And he has so much talent. You should see the video he put together for our parents' twenty-fifth wedding anniversary. But now he's like a foreigner; he's virtually dropped out of our family altogether.

For Erica and her sister Eliza, this was an especially difficult problem because Ethan's behavior threatened the fabric of the family's relationship and built-in pattern of closeness. "We stick together through anything" was evidently the family legend. It was certainly true that they all pitched in when their father's business went bankrupt. That's when Eliza dropped out of school to work as a waitress and Erica got a second job. And when their mother developed uterine cancer, the whole family rallied. But now that Ethan was unreachable, the family was in chaos. Ethan laughed at his sisters' attempts to draw him out and felt they were useless. Of course, he wouldn't have been caught dead in a workshop of this nature.

For the remainder of our workshop the two sisters focused on prayer and meditation as well as talking through their resistances. They decided to stop calling Ethan "the baby." And they realized they could refrain from being part of the problem by making room for their brother's quirkiness while also holding the expectation that he be an adult. Finally, they agreed that their family legend was worth holding on to.

As Eliza shared:

> We stick together as a family, and I'm not letting go of that. What this workshop has helped me to see is that you continue to go to bat for your family members even if they're unresponsive. Ethan doesn't have to conform to my expectations in order for me to love him. I still love and care for him even if I have to adjust to the form in which it comes through. But he can never complain that my love wasn't there for him.

Erica agreed with her younger sister. They made plans to continue meditating together after the weekend workshop. At the same time, they relaxed their expectations and demands of Ethan. Not surprisingly, four months later we received an e-mail telling us that Ethan had shared at length with his sisters and had agreed to go into family therapy with them.

Starting New Legends

In a leadership program in an inner-city high school that Marjory led some years ago, she met a charismatic young man named Andre. He came from a large family that was very poor. In his entire family and extended family, no one had ever finished high school, let alone gone to college. At the time, he was in the eleventh grade and was experiencing some pressure from his cousins and siblings to quit school. Andre loved school. He was smart, eager, and very well liked by his teachers. He confided in Marjory one afternoon that he was the only 16-year-old male in the family who had not yet been to jail. Andre was certain that he'd rather go to college than to jail, and on his own, he began to shape a variation of his family legend. Ultimately, he did make it to college. It remains to be seen whether the legend in his family will change with him or if he will be an oddity—the exception that proves the rule. One of his sisters graduated from high school last year, the first female in the family to do so. A new legend may just be starting in this family.

It takes courage to start new legends. First we become aware of the stories circulating around us that have influenced our behavior, then we choose a new direction. At the heart of this process, as with everything else we've suggested, is the willingness to make conscious what has unconsciously driven us. That means being willing to observe ourselves much more closely and determine the underlying patterns that drive our behavior.

In the Levitt family we have come to observe a set of conflicting legends that were handed down to us from our mother's and father's sides of the family. From our maternal grandmother, Betty, we learned to appreciate culture, beauty, and music. She was the epitome of stylish living. Legend has it that she went on wild shopping sprees, occasionally spending the rent money. Her extravagant tastes and habits lent credence to the legend that she must have been a wealthy Russian Jewish princess; we had always sensed something aristocratic about her. Needless to say, her legend filtered down to us. Jo Ann and Joel in particular seem to have inherited a love of spending without necessarily being able to make ends meet. This exotic legend lived on in our family, in direct contrast to the legends of our father and his family.

Tales from our father's side were more humble, had more to do with thriftiness, loyalty to the family, and the kind of personal grit and determination that created two teachers and an engineer out of a poor urban family. There is a famous story about Nellie, our paternal grandmother, who helped run the family grocery store. Someone came in and wanted an eighth of a pound of butter and she replied, "Why don't you just bring in your bread and I'll butter it."

Every family has stories that are so pervasive and powerful that, in a sense, the family organizes around them without being conscious of the source of influence. For us, legends of suffering and penury on the one hand and luxury and generosity on the other seeped into family life and influenced us. We learned many lessons and derived different habits and behaviors from the collision of these legends brought to us by our mother and father.

Legends As Training Ground

Some legends are developed in a more conscious framework as a way to train family members and to create a modus operandi for the family to get along. Such is the case with the previously mentioned Adams sisters, Delores and Nicole. Nicole shares one of her family legends:

I could hardly wait until I was nine years old. I knew that Mom was having another baby and this one was going to be mine. Now, I don't mean literally mine. But the way Mom and Dad raised us, each child would care for a younger one down the line. Remember, we were fifteen altogether, fourteen after Jimmy died. In a sense you became the caretaker for that new baby, feeding and diapering and doing everything to look out for the child's welfare. At three o'clock in the morning, if the baby was crying, sure enough I'd hear Mom say, "Nicole, get up and see what the baby wants." I used to think Mom never did anything except give orders. But now I realize her genius. She had us all caring for one another. And to this day, I feel like Andrew, who was my official baby, is still my offspring. That way of taking responsibility has affected all of us very strongly; not only do we look out for each other, but also a good proportion of the fourteen of us are managers in our everyday jobs. Mom taught us well!

The importance of these legends seems to be wired into the human psyche. Legends are used to motivate members and indoctrinate new members in all organizations. Think of the legends of the long hours, hard work, and creativity that were the hallmark of the early days of Microsoft, or stories of valor of the Marine Corps. Young recruits in any organization are steeped in legends and traditions that mold them into a marine or a software engineer. The emphasis on safety of the chemical company Du Pont or the exemplary commitment to quality at the automotive division Saturn keep employees of these companies behaving in ways that are consistent with the organization's vision of their own volition (even when no one is looking). The same pattern can be seen in families. The purpose of the legend is to provide assurance that the family members will abide by the rules—even when no one is looking, even when the rule makers are long gone.

Yet, the indoctrination of a marine is nothing compared to the indoctrination of a child into a family. While the legends of business, the military, and education are powerful and important, the family is the prototype for all of these systems. Starting with your first breath, family stories permeate the air you breathe. Everything around you supports the stories. If the moral of the story is that you are frugal and thrifty, then the furniture, car, house, and even the dinner-table conversation (or lack of it) will support that story.

Gene, a 32-year-old workshop participant, reminisces about his family life; he was raised in Manhattan but lives in Vermont, where he works as a ski instructor.

My parents' motto was similar to Joseph Campbell's: "Follow your bliss." My mom is an opera singer; my dad teaches comparative literature on the graduate level. We were brought up with excellent education and opportunities; in fact, dinnertime provided a constant exchange of information and ideas—history, music, literature, politics, you name it. My sister Leslie edits at Doubleday, so you know she's good. This motto goes back generations; everyone must do what they love and excel in; Grandfather was a justice of the peace; we have corporate lawyers, landscape architects, and artists in the family. I even have a cousin who studied to be a shaman. Now the only problem is that my family's mad at me for moving so far away. So I guess you could amend my family legend to read, "Follow your bliss but stay in Manhattan."

The Moral of the Story

Family legends often contain a built-in moral. The moral might be that we are smart, or that we might not be rich but we're "good" people, unlike most of those rich people. The legend or the actual story that family members tell will show the moral as the only logical conclusion to the story. These legends are internalized and help us know who we are in the world. When we act contrary to the legends, we feel like we are betraying the family (even if they are all a thousand miles away, or long dead and buried).

In our extended Jewish family, there was a larger, cultural and religious legend, based on grim reality that we had to stick together. You could trust other Jews, but never, ever trust a Gentile. World War II and the Holocaust were close enough to be an object lesson that allowed for little contradiction. Our maternal line, except for our grandmother and a few of her husband's kin, were killed in concentration camps. For the generations that preceded ours, hostility toward Jews was not merely a legend but a cruel fact of life.

The same kinds of bitter legends have shaped the lives of African-American, Latino, and Asian-American families. Yet, our generation has not lived in fear as our parents did. Gradually, we've rewritten that part of the legend, and our lives have expanded accordingly.

Setting the Stage

In the following exercise, you will have an opportunity to explore the legends and stories that influenced and helped to create your family experience. While you are looking at the legends of your family it is interesting to think about legends in other families, particularly ones you know well. Sometimes it is easier to see legends everywhere but in your own corner. From there you can decide if the same legends are relevant to your life.

For some this is a tough exercise. It may seem that your family has no legends. If possible, introduce these concepts to your siblings, parents, or other relatives and see if anyone can see the stories that made your family what it is. Legends are most powerful when they are invisible. Use whatever medium or method most appeals to you. Some useful methods include collages, sketches or diagrams of your own invention, lists, or genograms. (A genogram is a representation of the family that looks like a family tree. Squares represent males; circles represent females. Straight, unbroken lines indicate direct bloodlines from one generation to the next.) You may already have a sense of these guiding stories and the ways in which they shaped your family's history. If not, the following exercises will assist you in unearthing the key features of your "story." Begin by mapping the legends of your family.

Exploration 6-1 Legends of Your Family
What you will need:

Sibling journal; 15 to 20 minutes

Lists and landmarks: Write a few statements to summarize your family history.

Recalling stories that are told and retold about your family's beginnings, summarize the ones that most likely contributed to your family's sense of itself and its mission and role in the world.

Mapping the territory: Now write some brief statements that summarize the way your family treats any of these areas: health, work, money, communication, relationships, religion, sex, education, individuation, family cohesion (i.e., all for one, one for all), and family secrets.

Choose the areas that strike you as relevant to your family. Note if there are different versions that come from your father's side as opposed to your mother's side of the family.

In your journal create two separate columns.

On the left side, write at the top, "It's okay," and on the right side, "It's not okay."

Sometimes it is tough to see the legends. If the legends are still not apparent, try a different approach. Look to the result of the legend.

On each side of the column, fill in (particularly as you recall what it was like growing up), the things it was okay and not okay to do in your family.

For example, it's okay to work hard in exchange for getting a bigger allowance, but it's not okay to ask for money. It's okay to talk about how babies are made, but it's not okay to talk about sex.

Reflections: Write three or four core statements from these patterns that summarize your family legends.

Review both sets of statements, and see if there are any significant patterns or ideas in common.

Intermission

This might be an interesting conversation with your parents, aunts and uncles, and even grandparents (if they are alive). Try starting with a question such as, "What are the important principles of our family and where did they come from?" Or, "What do we stand for?" Another way to approach this is to question what kinds of struggles the family went through in the early days and how those struggles are perceived today. Your brothers and sisters may also have ideas to contribute to this discussion.

Setting the Stage

Ask your siblings to explore family legends with you. If possible, you may want to broaden your search by including your parents in the conversation. Gather information from members of your extended family as well, if appropriate. Even old friends of the family can be a good source of information about your family legends.

Exploration 6-2 Legends of Your Family

What you will need:

Sibling journal; pictures, album, tape, glue, scissors, possibly magazines (to cut up); 20 minutes this section

Mapping the territory: Create a family album of legends that coincides or moves chronologically like a photograph album (you may even want to insert portions of this album side by side with your actual photo album).

Legends do not have to be elaborate, or noble. Often, core legends are quite simple: "Work hard and be honest," for example. Don't overlook the obvious!

In studying family stories, be sure to distinguish the positive legends that keep the esprit de corps of your family intact.

If some are difficult to digest, try defusing the more intense legends by making them into movie titles, soap opera titles, or jingles for commercials. Have fun and lighten up in the process.

Memory Lane: Now that you have a sense of the legends that shaped you and your siblings, see if you can trace them not only through your life but through the lives of your siblings as well.

How have these legends influenced the way you learned to relate to your sister or your brother? What are the freedoms and constraints of your family legend?

What Happened

These are powerful stories that mold people's lives. Some people rebel against these legends and some swallow them hook, line, and sinker. As in many of the explorations in this book, we suggest that you focus on bringing what's unconscious into conscious awareness. Once the legends are out in the open, you can decide which to embrace and which to discard.

Illustrating the power of a legend at work is Stan, a 52-year-old very successful businessman who came to our workshop feeling depressed, dissatisfied, and empty. He seemed to have everything that anyone could want—a devoted and intelligent wife, healthy children, a beautiful home, every material object under the sun, and so on. One thing was missing for him, though: a sense of passion and meaning. We discerned a powerful family legend at work in Stan's life. He was raised with the family legend that the oldest son followed the father into business, worked unbelievably hard, made lots of money, never complained, and served as financial adviser and support for all of his siblings. His father had done this. His grandfather had done this. And now it was his turn. Stan occupied a role in his extended family that had been waiting for him since birth. His two sisters and his brother, though adults with families of their own, still looked to him to oversee their financial well-being, and he did so without complaint, but at great cost to himself.

Stan viewed himself as a stranger to his family; in the words of Thomas Wolfe in *Look Homeward Angel:* "Which of us has known his brother? Which of us is not forever a stranger and alone?" No one knew of Stan's feelings of anger, resentment, and bitterness. No one knew that he had wanted to be, of all things, a teacher. He wheeled and dealed and took care of his sisters and brother, his own family, and even his parents as they aged. What was his problem? His father had done this and his grandfather, too. Stan felt completely stuck inside this legend. His siblings were deeply caught as well. They had no idea how to take care of themselves and had, in some ways, never fully matured. They looked up to him as an "almost father." His brother in particular had spent his life in rebellion and had never really supported himself.

In order for Stan to revise the family legend, he would first need to take a long, hard look at his life and what the effects of being everyone's caretaker actually cost him in terms of stress, dissatisfaction, and alienation. Then he would need to make some important decisions.

Although many of us have come to the point where we recognize that we're caught in these negative cycles, it often takes a family crisis, such as a death or a major illness, or financial breakdown, for us to gather the strength to move on. After all, the legend provided a modus operandi and a means of managing life's uncertainties and changes.

Rewriting the Family Legends

Once we have explored our family legends and grasped how they influence our lives, it's time to begin reworking the script. That was the case with the twins mentioned earlier, Corey and Caitlin. While sharing with them in our group circle, we wondered what had brought them to the sibling workshop if, as they had shared, their lives were based on the ability to write their own ticket. Corey responded:

> Well, life isn't all peaches and cream. Caitlin says I need to slow down; I'm stressed out working as a CEO for a big conglomerate in Dallas. I've got hypertension and stomach problems. And whatever I do, I always seem to be dominating poor Caitlin.

To which her sister nodded her head and added, "We're probably different from anybody else in your workshops because we're twins and we're close. Our problem is learning to let go of one another and make decisions on our own, not getting closer together."

When we asked Caitlin what work she did, she responded, "Oh, I work for my sister. I'm her writer and chief PR person."

We then encouraged the twins to use their family legend to good advantage. After all, we reasoned, if they could write their own ticket, then they could do that in any realm that mattered to them, to which Corey responded, "I never really thought much about molding our relationship. As long as I've known Caitlin we've been joined at the hip."

It was Caitlin who finally came up with a vision that would adapt the elements of their family legend into a more balanced future for both of them:

> We have written our own ticket all through our lives. Now we write in the freedom for each of us to speak for ourselves, allowing more space between us for individuation and self-expression, along with the continuing solidarity and twin-soul connection we already share.

Corey agreed that that was a perfect revision of their family legend, and then she playfully cautioned Caitlin that they should each write her own separate version, in case they needed to individuate a little more.

The Strongly Knitted Family

A central myth in the Levitt family is the sacredness of independence within the context of a strong extended family. We each have a lot of latitude in "doing our own thing" and being on our own; however, it's the strongly knitted family that provides the background for such freedom. It's all for one and one for all, as long as we're talking about the family unit, but if we step out of that boundary then it's us against the world.

Ours is not the only family with the legend of sibling and extended-family support. Research indicates that siblings of nearly every racial group in the United States consider their brothers and sisters to be a source of instrumental and psychological support. Asian-American families lead statistically, with the greatest perceived sibling support, though the actual delivery of resources and support may never materialize. The same is true for African-American sibling groups, though the net of family obligation extends beyond the boundary of full-blood siblings to include half, step, and others considered to be siblings. This fact is pointed out in Agnes Riedmann and Lynn White's "Adult Sibling Relationships: Racial and Ethnic Comparisons."

As is true for our family, many of the myths and legends of American families stem from the immigrant experience. The most potent legends have to do with triumph over unimaginable odds and eventual prosperity and success. It does take an extended family network to accomplish this. For Betty, our maternal grandmother who came to this country without her siblings, her deceased husband's family and a few cousins provided material and psychological support. In a larger sense, this accords with the underlying American myth that we live in "the land of milk and honey." Of course, this myth is not relevant to Native Americans and African-Americans, who experience a radically different past. Yet, present generations still participate or are influenced by the legend of rugged individualism set loose in the land of opportunity.

Updating the Legends

In the process of rewriting the Levitt family legend, we agreed that the sacredness of independence was important to our strength as a family unit. However, we didn't want it to stand out like a sore thumb. We wanted to strengthen the myth of our power to be there for one another and to remain interconnected. The new Levitt family legend sparkles with elements of the old and the new and sounds something like this:

> We are a strong, cohesive family. We are not afraid to stand alone; we know we can each succeed in our individual endeavors; and yet we come together to create works that are greater than the sum of us individually. We love our spirit of play and adventure. We each have wonderful contributions to make to our family, and we are truly reliable and present for one another as we go through life's experiences.

Exploration 6-3 Inventing Your New Family Legends
What you will need:
Sibling journal; 15 minutes

Review the myths and legends you defined in the explorations above.

Select one or two key statements about your family you wish to retain. Write these down on a new sheet of paper.

continued

Reflections: Now go back and reread your future statements from chapter 3. What is the future relationship you want to create with your siblings?

Examine the key elements that will bring you fulfillment and add these into this equation.

Rescripting the play: Now rewrite your whole family legend, including the past qualities you wish to preserve and the future elements that will bring joy and love into your lives.

It may sound strange but many legends are actually designed and never really happened.

Pow-wow: Check with your brothers and sisters and refine this statement, based on their hopes and wishes for the family's future.

If your siblings are not participating in these exercises with you, try to include your sense of their values in your design.

Change characters: What would you want, by way of freedom and permission, if you were your sibling?

If there is a toxic legacy or legend that has wounded you and your siblings, be sure to include healing as a part of your new legend.

What Happened

Jake, who has three brothers, mentioned that this exercise was illuminating for him.

This gave me a chance to think about my family in a different way. Everyone in my family is hardworking and has a good livelihood. The legend is that you work hard to care for the children and to uphold appearances that all is well, but as far as intimacy is concerned, we don't score very well. I'd like to amend the family legend to include working hard at relationships as well as working hard at our careers. It would mean a lot to have that to look forward to as well as a respected name in our fields because of our different achievements. Now I feel inspired to approach my family. Although things haven't changed between us, at least I have a sense of a direction that can transform our interactions.

Vivian, a 52-year-old workshop participant from Delaware and a marriage and family therapist, commented on the process of rewriting legends:

I can hardly believe what a Pandora's box this process opened for me, despite my years of "therapizing." What I've come to realize is that my family legend has to do with keeping secrets. So it's no wonder it took me so long to unravel it. We have many stories that are hush-hush. Starting with my great-grandmother—she made off with a man half her age, then my uncle fell in love with his wife's sister and left his wife. Then my parents divorced, and no one ever talked about it, and finally my brother dropped out of our family with no explanation—it's amazing how dedicated my whole family's been to keeping secrets. No wonder I always encourage my clients to sort out the truth. Now I have work to do, and it feels like I've awakened from a dream. I have this overwhelming need to know the truth, and it's burning like a *fire* in me. I can see that I need to tone things down a bit, while I sort out fact from fiction. In fact, I nearly scared my dad half to death when I asked him to tell me the real facts about his divorce. So I'm proceeding with a little more caution. The next step is searching for the right time and place to talk with Danny, my lapsed brother. I guess my new legend will be "The truth, the whole truth, and nothing but the truth, so help us God."

In his recent work *Love and Survival*, Dean Ornish, M.D., comments on some of his family legends, chief of which has to do with identity and enmeshment:

> Growing up in my family . . . the unspoken message from my parents was this: "You don't exist as a separate person; you are an extension of us. Therefore, you have a great capacity to cause us joy or pain. If you act right, we will be so proud of you. If you don't, we will suffer. If you really mess up, we will *really* suffer—and if we suffer enough, we will die and leave you all alone. Since you don't exist separate from us, then if we die, you'll die, too. And it will be your fault." In short, as they once wrote me, "Dean as healer Dean as slayer." When the stakes are this high, the stresses can get very intense.

Many of us can relate to growing up with that kind of family legend. In fact, it sounds like the emblem for a generation of codependents. At any rate, through this focus, and undoubtedly by bringing heart and consciousness to the family, transformation can occur from the inside out. As we mentioned in the beginning, the mere act of noticing something that drives your experience is enough to turn the tide. In fact, there really is no legend that cannot be transformed through consciousness. It may take patience and effort. It may take a gutting or reworking of the old scripts. Although we don't guarantee a painless path or sudden glory, we highly recommend a view toward the past and the future that lets in more light.

Summary
Step 6: Invent New Family Legends

- Every family has myths or legends that have some kind of moral or guidance directing the family in how to live.

- These myths can stretch back for generations, and though often unarticulated, they nevertheless serve as powerful directives to family interaction. In a sense the family organizes around them without being conscious of the source of influence.

- Through a series of repetitive experiences we begin to formulate conclusions about life, which are then woven into a story, and from there "history repeats itself." These legends are swallowed and internalized, helping us know who we are in the world and what is expected of us.

- The ultimate purpose of these legends is to provide safety, predictability, and protection from chaos.

- Once we identify the legends that hold us captive, we can choose to create a different future and a different story line to support that future.

- The legend of siblings providing valuable support to one another extends to nearly every major racial group in the United States.

- Many of the myths and legends of American families stem from the immigrant experience and have to do with triumph over difficult odds.

- Through tracking and developing conscious awareness, we can transform these legends in our lives so that they become more relevant. We can selectively sift, retaining positive elements and refining or adding in others, which support the kind of sibling and family experience we desire.

Seeds of Change

❑ In reviewing my family experience, I am coming to see the particular myths or stories that held our family together and gave meaning and order to our lives.

❑ I am becoming aware of how these family legends affected my sibling relationships in particular.

Grains of Hope, Pearls of Wisdom

✓ Gradually I am learning to penetrate the details of our "story" to uncover the unconscious mechanisms at work and gain a deeper appreciation of our shared history.

✓ From this work I've gained inspiration about ways we siblings can now be in relationship to one another.

✓ I am excited about the prospect of rewriting my family legends so that they reflect the growth and maturity of our new connection.

Chapter 7

Make Room for Differences

love is a place
& through this place of
love move
(with brightness of peace)
all places

yes is a world
& in this world of
yes live
(skilfully curled)
all worlds

e.e. cummings,
The Complete Poems

I am learning that the key to survival is love. When we love someone and feel loved by them, somehow along the way our suffering subsides, our deepest wounds begin healing, our hearts start to feel safe enough to be vulnerable and to open a little wider.

Dean Ornish, M.D.,
Love and Survival

You and your siblings are different. You have different strengths and weaknesses, likes and dislikes, even though you come from the same family. The seventh step provides the opportunity to sort out some of these differences so you can accept your sisters and brothers exactly as they are.

Joel often shares his feeling of being totally different from us, his sisters. It is curious how we are different from him and from each other. He's a husband and father; we're both single and live alone. Our talents, our interests, even our forms of expression are different. And yet, there is some intersection of our personalities that defines us as siblings. What is that? And the next question: How is it we're so different and yet still experience such closeness?

In this chapter we shine a light on our differences, the little quirks and idiosyncrasies that once upon a time kept us apart. This is all part of the process of allowing family members (and ourselves) to grow up, not in biological terms but as a means of coming to know and experience who we truly are, as distinct from our childhood perceptions.

Making room for differences is an important step. All the work you've done up until now has helped clarify not only the kind of relationship but also the kind of life you want with your siblings. At some point in this process some of you begin to see that your old way of relating isn't working; at the same time, a possibility for a new way to relate presents itself. You may have the vision but not know specifically how to achieve it. This chapter outlines some tools toward that end. In some cases it may be as simple as focusing on things your sibling accomplishes or attributes that are different from yours. In other cases, you may want to practice giving up resistance to the ways that you're different from each other. That will lay the groundwork for coming to accept these differences as gifts that enrich your family life.

Although you're not complete in this process, you've made great progress in exercising consciousness. (And who *is* complete?) To become conscious means to become aware, noticing what lies beneath the surface, much as when we turn on the light in a room, we readily see the room's contents. When we turn on the light of our inner knowing, what gets illuminated are the dark areas, cumulatively referred to as the "shadow." In these exercises we stress developing the ability to bring into conscious awareness those dynamics and attributes that were formerly relegated to the shadow. In equal proportions as we come to know and embrace the shadow, we are brought in touch with the light.

What is left now is to reinforce and strengthen all that you have set in motion. This involves a continuous process of witnessing the strengths and achievements in your siblings as well as opening space for differences to show up. For the most compassionate stance we can take is based in consciousness: the willingness to be present for all that shows up, without falling into the habit of dismissing, denying, or discrediting what we see. After all, that is what we seek in life—the experience of loving and being loved unconditionally. In the words of Thich Nhat Hanh: "Seeing and loving always go together . . . Great understanding goes with great compassion."

Working with the eight steps will help us move in the direction of appreciation and acknowledgment by peeling off the layers of judgment and dissonance and seeing the true nature of our siblings as multifaceted beings who, like ourselves, are worthy of being loved. Take away the conditions we hold or the complications and conflicts, and the core experience of love becomes available.

Crises Bring Us Closer

Brought up on a dairy farm in southern Wisconsin, Emily, 47, shared that she couldn't have wound up with three more-different siblings in her family than if she had hand-picked them herself:

> First of all, no one ever guesses my real origins as a farm girl. Right now I do fund-raising for a large firm in Madison. My brother Ernie, 44, true to form, still works the family farm. He's so set in his ways we invariably go head to head. It's not like there are sparks; it's more like a continual cold war. Then there's Roxanne, who's 39 and a reporter in Chicago. She's outgoing, vivacious,

and lives a life of danger. She'd be the first in the family to volunteer for bungee jumping off Mt. Everest, if it came to that. She and Merle used to be my dolls; at least that's what I called them growing up. As the oldest, I got to dress them and curl their hair. Ernie thought it was a waste of time; he only wanted to know who'd gather the eggs or milk the cows. Merle's out in San Francisco now, working for a museum curator.

When questioned about what she wanted from our sibling workshop, Emily shared that the family was facing a crisis and she needed to learn some new coping skills:

Ernie's just been diagnosed with prostate cancer and his family's up in arms. My sister Merle's depressed and Roxanne lost her job to a younger reporter. I'm not as worried about her; I know she'll spring back, but all of a sudden our whole family is out of kilter. I just came from a visit with Ernie, and I'm sick. I've never seen him like this. Something needs to happen, but I don't know what. After all, I'm the oldest and in some ways still setting the tone for the younger three.

When we explored these issues further, Emily came to understand how much the family had played up their differences as a modus operandi, using their different skill sets, temperaments, and locations as an excuse for pulling apart and staying apart. Now, with Ernie's diagnosis, there was an opportunity to come together. Emily admitted that that scared her.

Emily then focused most of her attention on her relationship with Ernie, letting go of her resistance to his tight-clad way of being. As she dialogued and experimented with letter writing, she felt some physical resistance of her own disappear, as if holding him at arm's length was no longer a pre-caution she needed to take.

> This is the first time I've ever had a chance to welcome our differences. Even the notion that you can acknowl-edge or validate someone for the fact that they're differ-ent is strange to me. I mean we were brought up to think alike, to be solid citizens, and to go back to the earth. That didn't get us very far, except for Ernie, of course. But I am coming to see the strength in our dif-ferences. It takes getting used to. But it's broadening my perspective.

And indeed it will. Allowing for differences opens up new possibilities for expression and interaction within Emily's family. There's less need to defend or keep up appearances. A subtle relaxation and enjoyment can then be present. In fact, it gives everyone room to breathe.

As Emily worked on a new vision and a reworking of some of the family legends that had kept her brother and sis-ters separate, she felt a softening in her heart and a renewal of her love for her brother in particular. Afraid that she was taking too much of the group's time, she was reassured by other members that there was plenty of time for her process and plenty of room for her tears (which were copious).

The Seventh Step As Continual Practice

Of all the steps, the seventh is in some ways the most dif-ficult. It requires the willingness to consciously commit to the strength and longevity of our relationships by letting love be the dominant influence. This is not a one-time event. This is a decision you make and reinforce over and over by breathing new life into the relationship, by being willing to laugh, or forgive one another, or keep your perspective when discrepancies or evidence of old habits pop up. That is exactly the time to consciously honor and reinforce the vision for your siblings that started you out on this journey in the first place.

The seventh step is a practice that you must engage in continually—much like piano lessons or meditation. The more you practice, the better you'll get, the easier it will become, and the more muscle you'll develop.

Two very important tools assist you in your practice. The first is to actively take note of and allow for differences that show up among your siblings. The second is to forgive or accept differences or discrepancies of your own, which in the past you may have used as a foil for separation. By doing so you create a climate of acceptance and appreciation, giving everyone the message that there's plenty of room to show up as they are.

Honoring differences is a practice that for many of us is new. We're used to judging or disallowing those qualities that are different from our own and attempting to homogenize our family experience.

Honoring differences is twofold: First, it requires us to acknowledge ourselves as we are; second, we must acknowledge our siblings as they are, or, as in the instance above, allow both sisters to be who they are without stamping "wrong, misguided, or mistaken" on any of their behaviors.

Honoring differences requires courage. When our idiosyncrasies pop up, we can then say to ourselves, "Thank God, I'm human." And then let go. Not dwelling on or deriding these problematic behaviors gradually allows them to lose their significance or cease to cause such a stir. Finally what we are left with is spaciousness—room to be ourselves and compassion for one another's foibles. This is a powerful and practical stance that we can take out into the world with us.

In therapy, particularly group therapy, we learn to resolve sibling rivalries by working through our projections with other group members. We then take this new strength back into those problematic original relationships with sisters and brothers. We're reversing the therapeutic order here, learning to resolve and accept inside the original peer relationships. You may notice spaciousness in all of your peer relationships as you clear up and clear out some of this "sibling clutter."

Setting the Stage

The following exercise provides the beginning steps to help you make this practice more conscious. By taking a look at your differences and your similarities, you begin to chip away at the barriers to closeness and acceptance. And you derive a more complete knowing of each of your siblings.

Exploration 7-1 How We're the Same— How We're Different

What you will need:

Sibling journal; 15 minutes

Lists and landmarks: In your journal, write the name of one of your siblings. Then make a list of traits.

On the next page, include another sibling and repeat the process.

Change characters: On another page, complete this exercise as if you were each sibling.

Sibling #1 (then repeat for each)

How we're different.   How we're the same.

Write the traits you hold in common and those you consider to be differences.

Imagine what each sibling's list would look like.

Encore

Exploration 7-2 How We're the Same— How We're Different

What you will need:

Paper for everyone, or just have a conversation with your sisters or brothers; 15–30 minutes

Lists and landmarks: If the relationship is such that you could ask each of your siblings to complete lists of their own, by all means ask them.

For those of you who are not comfortable in working directly with your siblings, this material can be brought up as an informal conversation rather than an "exercise."

All of you switch and compare lists.

See how each views the others. This can be great fun as long as you each take it lightly.

What Happened

We are not the same as our brothers and sisters. To move on in our development we need to accept them as they are and feel that they accept us as we are. Because we are in the same family, we thoughtlessly assume that we should somehow be the same or at least similar. We do this even when we know from years of experience with this person that this is not so.

Having completed the explorations in our sibling group process, Stephanie, a 57-year-old physician from Virginia, remarks on the differences between herself and her younger sister Bonnie:

I always held my sister at arm's length while we were growing up. Maybe it's because she was so good, so angelic, it made me feel like a rat. She was easy to take advantage of. When I was 14 and she was 12, my mom wanted her to move into my room, because she was getting too old to share a room with our brother Phil. Though no one consulted me, I finally let her move in, provided she follow the rules. I drew an imaginary line across the center of the room. On her side was the bed and the window; on my side the closet, my bed, and the door. For two years Bonnie had to knock and ask permission from me before she could enter her own room. Poor kid, she hardly ever complained.

Although it was pretty unconscious, I think I made it up that she deserved this meanness because she was so nice and everyone loved her more. In fact, I'm certain that part of my motivation to become a physician was to gain my family's love and approval. Bonnie never had to strive so hard; it seems she had it easy in life. She became a legal secretary, married, and had five kids. To this day she's still as kind and considerate as she can be. And you know what? I don't fight it anymore. I don't resist her kindness because I know it's really genuine. And I don't resist my own differences. Even if I am crabby and a little self-absorbed, I'm a damn good physician and I have other strengths to call upon.

As with Stephanie, you may discover that these lists of similarities and differences are a Rorschach for yourself in relationship. Often they tell us more about ourselves than do our siblings. The most important aspect is not that there be agreement about your lists of similarities and differences, but that you see clearly, acknowledge, and appreciate that the fundamental characteristic of relationship is that we see things differently. Even the similarities we choose to focus on are different for each of us.

Now, the differences between us add spice to life. Once, Marjory said to Jo Ann, "I totally understand Joel's love. It took me a while to realize that he doesn't demonstrate it the way you and I do. It's there, like an underground spring."

Jo Ann didn't understand what she meant. Reflecting further, however, she began to see the point.

Some love must be grasped without frills or cards on your birthday. Looking for similarities or predictable behaviors in those we love can blind us to the love that's actually present. Joel's style is different; where we might hope for him to be more solicitous and outgoing, calling once a week to chat, for example, it's very clear that whether he calls or not has nothing to do with the depth and quality of his love. Some of us require a dog-and-pony show in order to know we're loved. Some of us can see through the externals and grasp what has been present all along.

Stop Resisting the Way They Are

With Esther and Elaine, two sisters we met in earlier chapters, the differences expand not only to the sibling in question but to the family as a whole:

Both my parents have serious health problems that aren't improving as they age. But the key thing that arises for me now is that out of the four of us, I'm the best equipped to make decisions in our family. Elaine has a husband and four kids and a very severe eating disorder. I've tried to get her into therapy, but the one time she went to a session, she said, "The guy told me I had a lot on my plate. Do you think I want to pay someone to tell me that?" She has never been interested in therapy or twelve-step programs like I have, and it's hard to see her caught up in her own abuse. I often find myself judging her, especially when it comes to her un-willingness to do her inner work.

So I look at her, I look at my folks, and I realize there's very little consciousness about how to really nurture or take care of ourselves. That makes me very sad. Though I work hard on my own issues in therapy, it's hard to keep banging up against these differences when we're together in the real world. I'm learning to pray for all three of them and allow space for them to be different. Not that I want to let go of trying to change things, just that I want to stop resisting the way they are.

The key here has to do with giving up the fight. If Esther can observe the way her family members are without pushing against them or resisting, she can free up a lot of energy to direct any way she sees fit. Then she will have stepped out of an old behavior pattern that keeps many of us prisoner—that of fighting or struggling against things that have wounded us but which we're powerless to change. Dropping resistance, she can take a deep breath and experience newfound freedom.

When we can accept the contrasts we see in one another without using them as a basis for conflict, we have taken big steps toward allowing diversity to enrich us. This does not mean forsaking conflict or escaping real problems. It means generating relationships that are spacious and accommodating of our differences.

Setting the Stage

Breathe and relax. Center yourself and review your lists of similarities and differences. If you have a copy of your siblings' lists, review them, too. Spend a few moments just sitting with your expanding awareness of yourself in relationship to them.

Exploration 7-3 Accepting Differences

What you will need:

Sibling journal; 15 minutes

Now take a moment to review the ways you and your siblings are different.

Lists and landmarks: Make a list of any traits you find troubling in your siblings.

Next to each trait, answer some or all of the following questions: "What would happen if I allowed my sibling to be who he/she is without trying to change him/her?" "What would happen if I stopped having any objections to this behavior or trait?" "How much do I share in this trait or behavior; or resist displaying this trait or behavior?" "Does anyone else in my family have this same trait/behavior?"

Settle back, breathe, and relax fully into this exploration. You may want to make up liberating or meaningful questions of your own as you consider a radical alteration of how you've behaved with your siblings.

Reflections: Now take a step further and consider ways in which differences among you actually serve to enrich or broaden your perspective.

Write any feelings or impressions that arise as you complete this process.

What Happened

Continuing our venture into the world of contrast among siblings, this exploration has an added twist. In addition to looking for differences and similarities, we are asking you now to study your reaction to those traits. Consider the possibility that the differences are not really that important. Your negative reaction was programmed a long time ago. As a matter of fact, instead of being a problem, the negative trait could be helpful to you and your family. See if you can re-frame it. And finally, take time to reflect further on ways to drop your resistance and release the hold of these differ-ences. You may find yourself far more relaxed when you are again in the presence of your siblings' differences.

Welcoming Differences As Gifts

Daniel, a massage therapist from Rye, New York, reflects on his relationship with his brother Arthur:

We grew up in San Diego. Arthur's 46 and I'm 49, but we don't have the personalities of siblings in typical birth order; in fact, we're reversed. Arthur's a bank president; I'm a massage therapist. He has a wife and three kids, two dogs, an SUV. I'm a loner. To draw the comparison further: his life resembles a Norman Rock-well painting, and mine a Salvador Dali.

I think he pulled away from me when we were teens and I started experimenting (you know, with sex, drugs, and rock and roll) and he only wanted to run the Junior Business League of America and participate in the Na-tional Honor Society. Art was threatened by my free-dom. Eventually we went our separate ways; I came to the East Coast; he stayed in San Diego. But time has a way of wiping out differences, and recently Art's been helping me sort out some financial problems. And in the middle of his midlife crisis, he's gotten "experimen-tal"—I don't mean crazy or acting out, but picking up on his old hobbies, snorkeling, backpacking with his kids. For the first time we're in a position to see and welcome each other's differences.

For Daniel, the notion of "being different" doesn't have a negative ring anymore. He no longer has a need or compulsion for his brother to emulate him, be like him, or cater to the same principles and way of life. Needless to say, this has been tremendously freeing.

It's taken me a long time and some years of therapy to finally admit Arthur into my life as he is. I think I stopped trying so hard. Always comparing and competing, I finally let go of wanting my brother to be a carbon copy of me. When I finally did that, I got a sense of who he really is. And who he is is someone special, considerate, hardworking (though a little compulsive), devoted to his family and to me, his only brother. In the final analysis, those differences turned out to be a gift in our relationship.

More Like Lamb Curry

Anjani and Anil jokingly refer to themselves as the Bobbsey Twins from New Delhi, even though they've both lived in New Brunswick, New Jersey, for years and they're not twins. Their family emigrated to the United States after their father opened a dental practice in Queens. Anil studied and then taught physics at Rutgers. Anjani finally caught up with her older brother by teaching comparative literature at the college level. She was the first to speak:

We jokingly use the term Bobbsey Twins because Anil and I basically straddle two worlds. We grew up Indian, but we're American. I'd just as soon eat macaroni and cheese as lentils and dahl. Anil wouldn't be caught dead in a kurta or a Nehru jacket. Yet we still have the Old World values, deep respect for our elders, willingness to sacrifice for the family, et cetera.

"Except that Anjani doesn't believe women should serve men. I believe in that fervently," Anil added, tongue-in-cheek.

We wondered if in fact there were some differences between them that were harder to accept, despite their good-natured joking around. This time Anil spoke in earnest:

"The truth is I don't feel as successful as my sister. Even though we both teach at the college level, she's much more outgoing. She has published more than I have. And she really does feel American, like macaroni and cheese. Inside, I'm more like lamb curry."

When we dialogued with Anjani and Anil, both came to see that it was Anil's reluctance to accept his own differences that had placed some distance between them. He was always trying to catch up with his sister, despite the fact that she was the younger of the two.

"If you're a little lamb curry, I like that about you," Anjani confessed. "Besides, I often feel like any minute somebody's going to blow my American cover. Let's face it: I'm not blond and blue-eyed. I'm Indian."

For Anil, it was a revelation to discover how much Anjani judged her appearance and on that basis considered herself unacceptable. He began telling her what a beautiful sister she was and that her olive skin and dark hair were her assets, not her drawbacks. Together they began a practice of appreciating each other's good qualities, as opposed to resisting what they had presumed to be their differences.

Although it poses a challenge to distinguish our differences, it's a very important part of growing up within our sibling relationships (and indeed within all relationships). Again, this is a conscious, deliberate process we've embarked upon. We're actively individuating from our siblings; that is, we're sorting out who we are and making room for each of us to show up with our distinct personalities. This may mean taking on roles or behaviors that you gave up years ago to avoid the anxiety of direct competition with a sibling. In some cases this requires courage because the individual siblings and the sibling group, as our earliest peer connections, tend to reinforce sameness and homogeneity just as our adolescent peer groups did. Consistency of role and behavior is also an earmark of relationships that endure through time. In short, there are many forces that conspire to keep us all acting exactly as we've always acted, and it may take effort to shift these patterns. The result, however, is an undeniable freeing up of energy within our sibling relationships. Instead of subduing or suppressing our personalities, we come as we are. Instead of looking for idealized companions, we allow siblings to show up as they are, which frees us to interact spontaneously and move our relationships to the next level.

Seventh-Inning Stretch

If you've come this far, you are to be congratulated. Undoubtedly you've woven skillfulness and new vision into your sibling relationship, and it will take its place in the world as a more deliberate creation.

In baseball we have a seventh-inning stretch. We would like you to take a break now and read through your sibling journal. If you've done the explorations over a period of days or weeks, you will notice some changes. (If you did them in one sitting, take a break!) These explorations have set in motion some fundamental shifts in how you view your sibling relationships. Each of the first six chapters had explorations in different areas. We designed them in order to help you strengthen your ability to witness and accept what was present and to clear out any lingering pain, remorse, or anger in order to make space for something new. Taking on the seventh step will add to your resourcefulness and skill, gradually conferring feelings of openness and compassion in relation to your sibling family.

Summary
Step 7: Make Room for Differences

- The most compassionate stance we can take is based in consciousness, the willingness to be present for all that shows up without trying to dismiss, deny, or discredit what we see.

- Working the eight steps will help us move in the direction of appreciation and acknowledgment by peeling off the layers of judgment and dissonance, and seeing the true nature of siblings as multifaceted beings who, like ourselves, are worthy of being loved.

- The seventh step, allowing for differences, is in some ways the most difficult. It requires the willingness to consciously commit to the longevity of our relationships by letting love become the dominant force.

- By that means we honor and reinforce the vision that started us on this journey in the first place.

- Two tools that help reinforce our commitment are: (1) taking note and allowing for differences among siblings, and (2) observing, acknowledging, and making space for our own differences to show up.

- In observing our similarities and differences, we are learning that we do not need to be in agreement or homogenized; in fact, we are observing that one of the fundamental characteristics of relationship is to see things differently!

- When we can accept the contrasts we see in one another without using them as a basis for conflict, we have taken big steps toward allowing diversity to enrich us.

Seeds of Change

❑ As I allow space for differences to show up, there seems to be more latitude both for my siblings and for myself to show up as we truly are.

❑ This ability to allow for differences is now spreading to other significant relationships in my life.

Grains of Hope, Pearls of Wisdom

✓ I take courage from this growing ability to see my siblings as they are and to have them see me as I am. Greater freedom and compassion have naturally entered our experience as a result. Best of all, we're having more fun!

✓ "Seeing and loving always go together . . . Great understanding goes with great compassion." (Thich Nhat Hanh, *The Sun My Heart*)

CHAPTER 8

Honor Your Strengths

The true nature of healing is undefended love.
> Joan Borysenko, Ph.D., as
> quoted in *Love and Survival*
> by Dean Ornish

The eighth and final step involves honoring your strengths and those of your siblings. There are many creative ways to accomplish this task. Nicole Adams, whom we interviewed in an earlier chapter, describes a project that she set in motion for her family's annual reunion. She is one of fifteen siblings in an African-American family from Chicago:

> I decided it would be such a great surprise for us to sit together and hear what we each have to say about one another. So I sneaked around with my little tape recorder, and every time I had a chance I would record a few short words. If you were one of my siblings, I would ask you what you learned from the next oldest sister or brother. Then I asked the same thing about Mom and Dad. Delores told me that she learned not to be afraid to die from her next oldest brother Sammy, who died about two years ago. She was with him till

the end. I learned never to waver in choosing my life's
direction from my next oldest sister Roberta, who became a minister, just like Dad. And all of us agreed on
Mom and Dad's contributions: my father taught us we
could do anything. Mom gave us the wings to fly.

Though Nicole's large family is now spread all over the
country, and two of the original fifteen have died, her ongoing project keeps the family in touch and keeps alive the
memory of those who have passed on. What's important is
how she has managed to make conscious the network of relationships crisscrossing her large family, reminding everyone to notice the gifts they receive from one another. In this
chapter as well, our intent is to bring sibling relationships
even more into focus, taking stock of the good things we receive and the strengths each sibling brings to the relationship.

Acknowledgment and Appreciation

Appreciation of one another's good points and the ability
to recognize how your siblings have enriched your life
strengthens everyone's participation in that relationship. The
chief tool here is acknowledgment: the ability to distinguish
strength and to share it. This can have considerable impact.
For example, Jo Ann reflects on a time when Marjory spontaneously expressed her appreciation, and this so deeply affected her that she shifted her feeling about herself from
despair to acceptance. Similarly, both sisters acknowledge
that the way Joel brings up his boys gives them a feeling of
completion in terms of the family dynamic, particularly to
witness such demonstrative affection from father to sons.
Few barriers can remain in the face of genuine acceptance
and appreciation. If there is no danger, there is no need to defend.

A Family Venture Grows Out of Appreciation

Les and his sister Maxine were thrilled to attend our workshop in the Berkshires because they called it "B&B heaven." Les, 51, an exercise physiologist and former college professor, and his sister Maxine, 49, run their own B&B in southern Vermont. "We never dreamed of doing a family venture until Maxine quit her job managing a hotel in Bennington. With both our kids grown, we were casting about for the next thing—you know, a modified midlife crisis. Then Max had a brainstorm."

To which Maxine responded: "It was so obvious I couldn't believe it. With Les being a fitness nut and me an ace manager, running a health-oriented B&B in the Green Mountains was a natural for us."

We wondered if they had always been able to work together like this.

Les responded quickly: "Not at all. I always thought Max was too uptight and too obsessive-compulsive. For years we didn't get along."

> And for my part, I thought Les would never amount to anything with his laissez-faire attitude. He's a free spirit, but so disorganized you wouldn't believe it. It wasn't until I gained a lot of weight that I really needed to call upon my brother. I knew he would give me the lowdown on working out, strength training, the whole package. When I finally saw him in action, I got real inspired. He's so good at what he does. And he's my brother!

Les, for his part, started drawing on his sister's expertise to get his business organized. And just for fun he began e-mailing her silly stories and occasional words of praise. Then finally they came together, drawing on the best of their talents to run a very successful B&B.

Acknowledgment Grows Through Repetition

Our sibling connection grows from our conscious attempts to put it to good use, to hear each other's foibles and follies, and sometimes, just to e-mail each other silly jokes. In some instances, appreciation bubbles up spontaneously. Seeing your brother do something you wouldn't dare to attempt yourself brings up feelings of pride and satisfaction. At other times it's important to make deliberate gestures, reaching out to each other. Like any other practice, acknowledgment grows through repetition. And sometimes it can bring home to us a deeper sense of our impact on each other.

Somewhere in the shadowy strands of the past, we find little jewels buried. Along with the first hard lessons about power, competition, and other aspects of rivalry, we may also have learned more gentle lessons. Our siblings are our teachers and sources of compassion, generosity, comfort, and acceptance. Often, these aspects of the relationship are overlooked. Uncovering them is part of the work toward greater harmony in the present.

As a matter of fact, if Joel considered his sisters stupid for not knowing how to surf the Net, or figure out what was wrong with the water heater, he never said anything about it. In fact, one cold February day he waited hours when Jo Ann accidentally locked her keys in the car.

"He didn't even think twice about waiting with me until the AAA man came to help me unlock my car. That afternoon and his quiet, steady devotion still bring tears to my eyes. There's something so unwaveringly calm and present about Joel. With him as with my sister, I know I have two lifelong friends."

Setting the Stage

Now consider your connection to your brothers and sisters. Take a moment to explore the ways your sibling relationships have grown or changed. In order to reinforce what you love and what works in those relationships, it's important to voice your positive feelings and acknowledge one another. The more you acknowledge what is working, the more those aspects are amplified.

Exploration 8-1 Gifts We Receive

What you will need:

Sibling journal; 10 minutes

Lists and landmarks: Fill in these sentences:

The gifts I receive from my brother/sister are _____

Gifts I feel I've provided for him/her are _____

What I love about him/her _____

What I want to acknowledge to him/her _____

What I want him/her to acknowledge about me _____

What I now see that he/she has provided for me _____

What I'm now ready and willing to provide _____

Setting the Stage

If you can create the setting in your family to voice these acknowledgments, so much the better. Gather together with your siblings and go around the circle. Don't forget to take turns! This is probably the group where you first learned about turn taking, waiting, and sharing. Bask in the love that is present, or help it make a stronger appearance if it's been hiding. If you are completing these exercises on your own, you can create a circle of siblings in your imagination. Use a family photograph, if you have one. Extend the results of this exercise into the real world by communicating something you appreciate about each of your siblings directly to them. Send a card, a fax, or an e-mail. Or make a phone call. If you have lost track of a sibling, or if he or she is no longer alive, you can still send thanks and acknowledgment in a quiet moment of meditative thought.

Exploration 8-2 Acknowledging Each Other

What you will need:

Just your siblings; just 5 minutes
(it works great with spouses and kids, too)

Lights, Camera, Action: In a quiet moment when you are together with your siblings, ask one another, "What would you like to be acknowledged for?"

For example, a sibling might want acknowledgment for dealing with the nursing home for your mother.

Then other siblings affirm that, or add separate acknowledgments for gifts/strengths that have made a difference to them.

In this example the acknowledgment might be worded: "Janice, I would like to acknowledge you for taking care of the communications with the nursing home and for being willing to take time to visit Mom every week. It means a lot to me."

Each person takes a turn.

Simple acknowledgment is a powerful way to reconnect people to the love they have for one another.

Share any feelings or responses that have come up as a result of having been acknowledged by one another.

What Happened

Acknowledgment is a powerful way to thank people for what they've done or who they've been for you. If you must do these exercises without a sibling present, return to the processes described in earlier exercises. Use a photograph or some object that represents that sibling. Speak to the photo, or take turns writing acknowledgments as though you and your sibling were in dialogue.

For some families, recollecting goodness may automatically bring up recollections of conflict. If this is true for you in your family, try to soften the painful feelings that arise. You may need to return to earlier chapters and express more of your hurt, disappointment, and anger. It takes courage to change the patterns of a lifetime. Give yourself plenty of time, encouragement, and uncritical acceptance. Consider this—if you have spent forever hating a sibling, being able to come up with even one good recollection is an awesome achievement.

Drawing More Deeply from Our Strengths

In chapter 7 we practiced the art of allowing differences to be present among our siblings. In this chapter we expand that process by going a layer deeper. What we want is to continue to unearth strengths and observe differences but this time with an eye to understanding how they contribute to who we are as a family. Can we learn to distinguish and draw more from these strengths and differences as we recognize their role in contributing to our core identity and sense of connection?

Stephen Bank and Michael Kahn, in their groundbreaking work *The Sibling Bond*, identify optimal relating among brothers and sisters to include what they call a "constructive dialectic." That is: "We're alike, but different." This is challenging and creates opportunities for us to grow. Relationships of this sort are characterized by vitality and strength

focused in a positive direction. In this kind of sibling relationship, the growth of one member is offered to the others
in a way that makes joining and benefiting natural and safe.
However, a "constructive dialectic" does not emerge out of
nowhere. Often, it takes conscious individual work and ongoing positive choices to make the most of our differences.

Robert, 39, identifies the nature of the "constructive dialectic" in relationship to his older brother, Gerald, 42. From
Lexington, Kentucky, the two boys grew up more or less as
equals, with the usual sibling fights and frolics:

> When we got into our teens, however, it seemed as if
> we were going separate ways. Gerry went out for foot-
> ball and did all the "guy things." I stayed home and
> wrote poetry. Now that we're grown, Gerry plays golf,
> goes hunting, watches football games, and manages a
> very successful business. I didn't want any part of that.
> I got teased mercilessly through the years, not only by
> Gerry but also by Mom and Dad. After all, a true South-
> ern gentleman doesn't dabble in the "feminine" arts. But
> what I can see now is that Gerry was claiming the mas-
> culine side of life and I was developing my feminine
> side. Not that I'm gay. I'm just more interested in spiri-
> tual things.

In our workshop, we asked Robert how the "constructive
dialectic" was finally reconciled.

> After a long separation and a lot of bitterness, slowly
> things changed. I had moved north to get away from
> my family. When I entered the ministry, my parents be-
> came more accepting. However, Gerry was still angry
> with me; he wanted me to help him run the family
> business. I have no head for business whatsoever. So I

wrote him letters, went to visit, and finally relegated the whole thing to prayer. It seemed like God would have to intervene. And sometimes, when you least expect it, that does happen. Four years ago Gerry made the first tentative contact. He was going through a painful divorce and needed to talk about it. So we talked. I wouldn't say I counseled him, but he seemed to feel better afterward. So I began corresponding. And we'd see each other on holidays. The crowning touch came last year, however, when Gerry asked me to preside over his wedding. I helped him and his wife-to-be to create a beautiful ceremony, and I married them on the first of June. The whole family came together, and in its own way it was a special healing time. Ever since then, it seems there's room for us to be different.

The Next Family Experiment

James, age 33, mentioned in an earlier chapter, used the Sibling Revelry Workshop material to introduce a constructive dialectic with his five sisters and brothers from Boston. Having returned for a second workshop, he shared his insights from the first workshop experience:

My family is fiercely competitive. It goes back to the early days when Dad put boxing gloves on all of us and taught us how to fight. The subtle message that came through was, "It's okay to be strong and demonstrate your strength to others." However, the not-so-subtle message that came right along with it was, "Don't advertise if you're a weakling." For some reason, I took it on to challenge that in my family. After all, I am the youngest, so you can imagine how many fights I won. But I'm winning in a different way. Now I go out singing with Sean, a professional singer and songwriter, and he's amazed because I don't have much of a voice. Give me a couple of drinks, though, and that doesn't matter. I run along the Charles River with John, and he slows down so I can keep up with him. I invite my sister Marty to dinner, and watch her laugh as I roll out the meatloaf. Needless to say, she's a chef in the best restaurant in Boston. But she wolfs it down good-naturedly. I think my whole family caught on that I was going to be weird. Not just a jazz pianist and a peroxide blond, but someone to challenge our strengths and make us stretch a little bit to let in the differences. And the thing that makes me the happiest is that they let me get away with this. I think they see me as the one who initiates the next family experiment, and like anything else we've taken on, they don't want this one to fail!

Families have different ways of coming together and different methods for solving problems in common. A friend from the pool in Marjory's neighborhood told her that what works for her three sisters and brother is to gather together around a card table and play Rook. She said that within five minutes they're laughing like crazy, teasing their brother and accusing him of cheating (she insists that he really does cheat), and immersed in the sweet familiarity of being a family. Once they've played cards, they can settle any problems or issues they have to face without rancor or conflict. This may sound odd, but not until they'd finished their game of Rook did the five of them decide what to do about their frail elderly mother after the death of their father.

Oddly enough, in some families being close comes about as a result of keeping rivalries alive and active. This is the case with Sam, Louie, and Ethel, all in their eighties. Jo Ann learned about these siblings through Sandy, a co-worker; Sandy is Sam's daughter.

At Each Other's Throats

It seems that Sam, Louie, and Ethel have lived on the same block in a town north of Albany since childhood. Ethel moved into Louie's house fifteen years ago, after his wife died. Since his arthritis was nearly crippling, it was helpful to have Ethel's support with meals and housecleaning. And Ethel, who had never married, was happy to have company. Although visiting their house, you'd never know it. On his frequent visits to fix a toilet or replace some cove molding, Sam would hear Ethel and Louie swearing at each other downstairs: "You son of a bitch." "Why, you little asshole." Coming downstairs, Sam would say, "You two are like an old married couple, always at each other's throats," to which Ethel would reply, "Up yours."

Once a week Ethel cooks an extravagant meal for her two brothers—a tender roast, a plump chicken; or every so often, sirloin steak and potatoes. If Sam tries to compliment her for the food, she invariably chides him, saying, "Up yours." If he picks up a dish to take it to the kitchen, she says, "Put the goddamn dish down."

All three siblings have a tacit acceptance of this feisty manner, even though it is sometimes startling to Sam, who doesn't live with it every day. However, he's catching on. For her eighty-sixth birthday, Ethel served an elegant dinner to her two brothers. Louie carved the roast, and Sam settled in place with his secret gift in the freezer. When it was time for dessert, he took the Carvel ice-cream cake out of the box and placed it on the table in front of Ethel. All three of them had a laugh when they saw the cake's inscription: "Up Yours."

Distance Sometimes Improves the Connection

Unfortunately, there is no fail-safe recipe for bringing sisters and brothers closer together. Sometimes, paradoxically, it is creating distance that does the job. Marjory worked with Warren, age 29, who was in the habit of leaping into action whenever his sisters or brother called him. The baby of the family, his life was filled with family-this and family-that. He reported his many obligations: a niece's First Communion on Sunday, driving Mom to her doctor's appointment on Monday, attending his oldest nephew's soccer game on Wednesday, and so on. He never, ever said no, and, not surprisingly, he had very little life of his own outside of work. Warren was a talented painter, but he hesitated to sign up for a master class because he never knew what family event would come up and prevent his regular attendance. Though he was almost 30, he'd never really developed or sustained a romantic relationship. He'd been very fond of one young woman, but his sisters hated her because she had beautiful, naturally curly blond hair and no respect for Warren's obligations to his family. He was afraid of the disapproval of his three older siblings, but he also resented them terribly and never really shared with them the deeper parts of himself. He was dutiful, but sullen and somewhat bratty, continuing to play the part of the baby of the family. In therapy he commented that although he felt like he had three mothers and two fathers, otherwise he felt pretty much alone in the world. He'd learned to listen to *everybody* (except himself).

Warren's work involved setting appropriate boundaries between himself and his siblings and learning to say no. It was difficult for him, especially at first. When he learned that he would not be struck by lightning if he refused to join his sister and her family for dinner, his life and his relationships with his siblings slowly began to change. Warren then had to deal with his own fear and feelings of emptiness. He'd depended on his family to create his social life for so long that he was left having to face his lack of initiative and social skills. Once he began to discriminate and choose when to join his siblings, he was free also to appreciate them, and even miss them! He was also free to be more genuine with them. He initiated his first ever lunchtime meeting with his older brother and asked his advice about meeting women and relating successfully to them. He sought out his sister for advice on what and how to cook and disclosed more of his real self to her than he ever had. Warren was a little wide-eyed when he reported his progress in therapy. For the first time, he'd actually felt *love* for his older siblings, and realized they'd do just about anything for him. At this point, it became easier and easier (and more genuine) for Warren to say yes to his family.

Most of us do not have Warren's work to do. In these highly mobile times we are more likely to have to schedule a sibling call or visit six months in advance than to pick and choose among daily opportunities for contact. Some of the individual work to do in this context is to look and see what suits you best. If you can, be ruthlessly honest. Jo Ann shared her decision not to join the family for the second night of Passover. This may sound trivial, but it separated her from the rest of the family at first, and did not take place without some attempt at coercion to change her mind. Since she doesn't mind being a terrible sister, niece, daughter, etc., we count her out at the second Seder. You may also need to be willing to be considered a terrible traitor if and when you begin to monkey with the status quo. Again, the constructive dialectic inherent in healthy, vital sibling relationships will support the creation of new times, places, and types of interactions.

Setting the Stage

This is a reflective exploration. Take a few minutes to relax and become centered. First, connect with yourself. Acknowledge yourself for something—even for taking this time to relax and review.

Explorations 8-3   What Are We Doing Right?

What you will need:

Sibling journal; notes from past explorations; 15 minutes

Memory Lane: Allow your mind to drift through your personal history to times, places, events, and experiences you shared with your siblings.

Travel back in time, searching and remembering.

Reflections: See if you can enter into the feelings of the experiences that bring a smile to your face.

Try to reconstruct any details of these experiences.

Begin to make quick notes so that you will be able to return to these memories and add details later.

Now glance through your sibling journal or other notes from previous exercises.

Scan these notes for ideas and remembrances.

Lists and landmarks: List the events or experiences that evoke good, close feelings about your siblings.

If you have more than one sibling, you may repeat these steps for each sibling.

Notice if there are any patterns or general qualities that link these experiences together for you.

Can you generalize positive experiences into larger categories? Can you get right next to the essential quality that makes an experience one of closeness and name it?

What else comes to mind as you search for positive links from the past to the present? Note anything that interests you or draws your attention.

Is there some cumulative awareness from the process of these exercises?

What Happened

This is more a meditation than a traditional exploration. We encourage you to reflect on the overall experiences and seek out positive ones. When we look at the many ways we interact as siblings, we can tease out the strengths inherent in the relationship. Whatever truly helps us draw closer is invariably a gift we share in common.

What Draws Us Closer

Thinking about the kinds of things that help us feel closer, the authors recall simple things, such as walking and talking. Often, we do these things together, getting out on a trail or walking Forbidden Drive in Germantown, sharing the latest aspects of our lives.

One day while vacationing in Acapulco, we got to daring and teasing one another and Joel dared us to try parasailing. That's when you hook up to a parachute and a speed boat pulls you along until you're airborne, then you fly through the air for a while and hope to land in one piece somewhere near where you started. This is not the kind of behavior a normal person undertakes. It looks insane and dangerous, like bungee jumping. Well, we dared one another and the die was cast. First the oldest, then Marjory, then Joel, up in the air, flying and landing. We'd never do it again, but we still laugh about it. Among the many things we do, this spirit of the dare, and the delicious willingness we have to take it up, brings us closer together. So many wonderful opportunities have come our way. The list is almost endless.

Joel was not accustomed to talking about the issues that he's up against during the week. He's gradually changed this habit, however.

When my wife and I have a fight, or if I'm fearful of some new physical symptom or if business is not going well, I turn to my sisters. I have two insightful sisters.

They are close enough to know my history and the players but not so close that they take everything personally. Sharing with them has become enormously important to me and makes me feel closer to them.

New Conversations for Closeness

In some family situations, there is work to be done before a sense of closeness and trust can be established. That was the case with an extended therapy session a client asked Marjory to facilitate with her five sisters. Lorraine had been in individual treatment for about a year. She had been struggling, in secret, with bipolar disorder for several years and she wanted to let her sisters know the truth about her moodiness and sudden flights of fantasy and excitement. She was afraid to tell them the truth for many reasons: She feared their disapproval, was terrified that they would shun her and deny her access to their children, whom she loved, and she also feared giving up the charade she had spent her life perfecting. But she needed their help if she was to successfully negotiate the world of chronic mental illness and medication compliance and have the chance for a mostly normal life. It didn't help that her family was of the "see no evil, hear no evil, speak no evil" variety. Everything had *always* been fine, even when the oldest brother committed suicide ... but that's another story.

In any event, there we were—the six McAlly sisters and me (Marjory). We spent the better part of an afternoon together as Lorraine told her scary secret and her sisters, one by one, found a way to offer her support and encouragement. This did not take place without anger and tears, for the sisters were very hurt that Lorraine had kept such a vital piece of information to herself. The truth explained her sometimes-erratic behavior and mysterious disappearances. Maureen, the oldest of the clan, was very angry. It took most of the afternoon to help her to understand why Lorraine had kept this secret, especially from her. Maureen was twelve years older than Lorraine and had practically raised her. This was the most difficult confrontation for Lorraine, for she so desperately wanted Maureen's respect and esteem.

Lorraine reported a few weeks later that this unprecedented session had radically altered her family. Her brothers were upset that they hadn't been invited, so Lorraine and Maureen planned a gathering at Maureen's house and continued the dialogue with the whole family present, including the parents. Other issues came to the attention of the family that needed resolving, so before they went their separate ways they planned a follow-up meeting. Lorraine was practically giddy with these results. None of her fearful predictions had come true. And best of all, she felt her oldest sister's warmth and love like she hadn't felt it in years.

Now these dramatic tales from the consulting room may not look like your issues. That is a very good thing, though professional help in these matters can still be of tremendous value. There are many ways to create closeness and connection, though they may not be as extreme as the challenge Lorraine took on for herself and her family. A case in point is the story of Doris and Phoebe.

I Need Her in My Life

"I think Phoebe and I invented sibling rivalry," Doris said with her Tennessee drawl. She was commenting to our other workshop participants:

Not only were we classic fighters and competitors, but Phoebe was so cunning she lined my father up on her side. Darling Phoebe with blond curls was only sixteen months younger but she could get away with murder. Once while in the third grade, she cut school to go skinny-dipping, and when I found out, I ran home and told my father. Now, who do you think got punished?

Me, of course. When I said to my father, "You'd never let me get away with that," he nodded his head. "You're older than she is," he said. "You know better."

Phoebe and I fought out loud, and we fought in secret. We would always try to outsmart each other. Once Mom came to wake us up early. Peeking under my bed, she blurted out, "What's this mess?" And there was a pile of my dirty laundry, dolls, and toys that Phoebe had stuffed under my bed when I was out. Although I caught hell from Mom, that day Phoebe caught double hell from me.

Doris concluded that having a close relationship with Phoebe at first seemed unlikely:

She's 61; I'm turning 63. I work for a dry-cleaning establishment; Phoebe's a DJ. Would you believe she still rides a motorcycle? We're so different; if you saw us together, you'd think we were strangers. However, one day something changed. I don't know what caused it; I just made up my mind that Phoebe was all I had, and like it or not, we were going to be close. After all, she's my only sister.

As I grow older, I've come to realize how much I need family to be part of my life. There's no one else like them. So one day I went to visit her in her motor home, and I said, "Phoebe, let's face it, you're all I've got. And except for your husband Roger, I'm all you've got. Let's try to be friends." The strange thing about it was—for the first time since I've known her, she didn't contradict me.

Research undertaken by Gene Brody indicates that "sibling relationships comprised of a balance of prosocial and conflicted interactions create experiences that are most likely to nurture children's social, cognitive, and psychosocial development." (In "Sibling Relationship Quality: Its Causes and Consequences.") The experience of Doris and Phoebe is a case in point. If your sibling history looks more like a battlefield than a paradise, don't worry. The sticks and stones as well as the tender moments make for healthy, resilient adults.

Those siblings who've weathered many storms can relate to Doris's sentiments. For time has a way of radically altering relationships. Friendships change, partnerships outlive their usefulness. Perhaps because we already know our siblings' shadowy, imperfect selves, we can admit them into our hearts more readily, knowing they're unlikely to let us down. But more important, we can admit to ourselves that we have a need for closeness and allow this connection that has withstood the tests of time to flower into friendship.

Acknowledging the Simple Gifts

As a final exercise in this phase of our work, we've created an affirmation that characterizes this stage of our relationships and gives us a direction for the future. You may wish to create your own affirmation, either with your siblings or on your own.

Our Sibling Affirmation

You are a beloved friend, helper, and support. I can count on you when I need you. It's great fun to spend time with you and watch our lives unfold. I feel privileged to know you and to have you in my life. I honor and applaud the person you are and admire the person you will become.

Lest this all sound too Utopian, research by Victor Cicirelli and by Agnes Riedmann and Lynn White in *Sibling Relationships:*

Their Causes and Consequences indicates that as sibling groups reach adulthood and middle age, bonds tend to grow stronger, and rivalries tend to diminish. This holds true for siblings of any race, education level, and ethnic group. In fact, the presence of a sibling—especially a sister—enhances the quality of life for the elderly (age 68 and older) and reduces the incidence of depression. What we are suggesting, then, is a conscious and focused effort to speed this natural process and deepen it as well.

Summary
Step 8: Honor Your Strengths

- While continuing to unearth our similarities and differences, we want to understand how they define us as family.

- We want to determine how we can draw upon both our strengths and our differences to maintain our core identity and sense of togetherness.

- In *The Sibling Bond*, Stephen Bank and Michael Kahn identify optimal relationship between brothers and sisters to include a "constructive dialectic," that is, we're alike but different. This is challenging and creates opportunities for us to grow.

- In this kind of sibling relationship the growth of one member becomes incentive and inspiration to the other's growth.

- Gene Brody, in "Sibling Relationship Quality: Its Causes and Consequences," states: "Sibling relationships comprised of a balance of prosocial and conflicted interactions create experiences that are most likely to nurture children's social, cognitive, and psychosocial development."

- If your sibling history looks more like a battlefield than a paradise, don't worry. Sticks and stones as well as the tender moments make for healthy, resilient adults.

- Appreciation of each other's good points and the ability to recognize how a sibling has enriched your life strengthens everyone's participation in that relationship.

Seeds of Change

❑ As I gain perspective on our uniqueness, I am coming to see the particular warp and woof of our sibling connection—what holds us together, what draws us apart, and what molds our continuing interactions.

❑ I am now making a practice of honoring the strengths I see in each of my siblings. What's interesting to note is that the more I honor strengths, the more the strengths seem to multiply.

Grains of Hope, Pearls of Wisdom

✓ I feel more and more accepting of these strengths and differences.

✓ The shift is apparent among my siblings as well; trusting more deeply in the strength of our bond, we have become more open to experimentation, more acknowledging of one another's roles, and more insistent upon drawing deeply from our precious lifelong connection.

CHAPTER 9

Add Heart to Holidays

We are by nature a tribal species. We need each other and we need to be needed by each other. We thrive when we are loved and we are diminished in strength and vitality without love.

> Carolyn Myss, as quoted
> by Dean Ornish in *Love*
> *and Survival*

Now that you've done significant work and made headway with the eight steps, it's time to pause and take stock of where you are. Perhaps this is the moment to congratulate yourself on the strides you've taken and the opening that's available in your family for closer relationships. Whatever work has been accomplished and whatever remains, the important thing to consider is that you've truly come back to your roots. As Thich Nhat Hanh says: "A tree without roots cannot survive. A person without roots cannot survive either. You have to return to the family. You have to touch your roots."

An important part of our family life has to do with the rituals and celebrations that we experience together. These add a different dimension to our relationships. They mark time and provide continuity. In some cases they help us keep in touch. This chapter has to do with bringing consciousness to your rituals and holiday celebrations with siblings and finding ways to make them more enjoyable. We recognize that the holidays are traditionally a stressful time. With effort, creativity, and grace they can be a time of love and nurturance for the entire family.

Transforming Family Rituals and Events

Sitting at the round table were seven young adults from Williams College on a weekend retreat in upstate New York. When talk came around to family rituals, Gina, the liveliest in the group, commented on how much she liked starting out the meal with prayer:

> I was so sad to see our family tradition come to an end. We used to hold hands every evening, then speak our intentions for peace, and then say a Hail Mary and the Lord's Prayer. But then one day my older brother got too big for that kind of thing. He told my mom he wasn't into holding hands anymore. So we sat in silence, declared a brief intention, and then said the Lord's Prayer. After a while, he got so irritable, Mom just said, "We'll do one Hail Mary and eat." And that's what we wound up doing.

Important questions to ask: How can we transform a ritual or holiday from an ordeal to an enjoyable experience? How can the promise, the anticipation, and the wish for contact and intimacy be satisfied? This deserves our attention. One of the ways families make the holidays work for them is to repeat certain rituals that everyone enjoys while continually experimenting and inventing new ones. When you were growing up, remember the excitement waiting for Christmas morning to arrive, or the pleasure of drinking wine, which was normally forbidden, at Passover.

There is no question that rituals hold an important place in every family tradition. By repeating certain prayers or acts, we come to know who we are and where we belong. The very act of repetition creates a sense of ease and predictability. It's as if we would say, "We did this before. I recall this experience last year and the year before. Here we are again. Now we approach Easter; now we light the Chanukah lights. Now we face east to pray; now we fast on water."

These rituals help us mark the seasons and remind us that we're steady on course. Within chaos there is order. For beneath all the external changes, there is the feeling of changelessness—that at heart, life revolves around a timeless core; cycles repeat themselves; we come together, we move apart; and our rituals provide the means of returning to the source.

Anil and Anjani, mentioned in an earlier chapter, share their adaptation of an Indian holiday, Holi, which is family oriented and in which brothers and sisters celebrate by taking to the streets and throwing multicolored paints at one another.

"It was invented way before Americans came up with spray paint or paint guns," Anil volunteered. "It's really a friendly holiday, but you have to make sure you wear your worst clothes. And at the end of the day the tradition is that sisters honor their brothers by tying a little red string around the brother's wrist and bringing him some cake or special treat."

"But there we had to update the holiday and make it less sexist," Anjani added in.

"So I get to tie the little red string around my sister's wrist as well," Anil said with a smile.

"However," Anjani said, "I have yet to see you bake me a cake in honor of the occasion."

Though we have Mother's Day and Father's Day, we have no analogous sibling celebration. However, that shouldn't stop us from being inventive. After work has been done on the relationship, it makes perfect sense to create a ritual or get-away that informally honors our brother/sister connection.

Howard, a graphic artist, often makes collages or block-printed cards for his siblings' birthdays. His sisters, always alert to his love of "boy toys," bring him little red fire engines, model cars, and Star Wars kits to celebrate the little boy in him that never tires of having fun. And since the time they spent hiking Bryce Canyon to celebrate his fortieth birthday, the whole family has become geared to inventing retreats and rituals that are fun for everyone.

Putting Heart into Holidays

Every November and December, the media covers stories about how tough the holidays are for everyone. Between Christmas and New Year's Eve, visits to emergency rooms increase, people reporting psychological distress increases, more individuals abuse drugs and/or alcohol, and there are more incidents of domestic violence. In many families this may be the only time everyone is together.

A typical story, titled "Putting the 'Happy' Back into the Holidays," appeared at the CNN Web site on December 22, 1998, posted at: 7:21 P.M. EST by Medical Correspondent Dr. Steve Salvatore. He talks about the stress of the holidays. He quotes clinical psychologist Dr. Carol Goldberg. One of the biggest stresses at holiday time, according to Dr. Goldberg, is family. "People who don't have families tend to feel very lonely. People who do have families may have a lot of conflicts because family times bring back a lot of relationships from the past." Even those who spend their holidays with family may experience great loneliness and a sense of loss. So it seems that at holiday time you are pretty much damned if you do and damned if you don't (have family).

The best and the worst of sibling relationships can be seen during the holidays. Stress is high because people, memories, and emotionally charged rituals that have been avoided or anticipated all year can't be avoided now. In many families, alcohol consumption skyrockets.

Family Traditions Supporting the Connection

Perhaps one of the most elaborate family rituals we've ever witnessed occurred in Philadelphia at the old city Holiday Inn. While attending a conference, Marjory and Jo Ann ran into a group of African-Americans all wearing yellow T-shirts with the name of their family written across the front. Much to our amazement, we discovered that this family had been holding an annual family reunion for some twenty-seven years. Their numbers were close to three hundred and spanned six generations. Two cousins organized the gathering as their full-time jobs, producing a newsletter to keep the entire family informed of changes. The reunion itself was staged in different cities across the United States each year. The ritual was so well planned that when members of these extended families arrived, they received names and addresses of the relatives living in that particular city, a guide to local restaurants and sightseeing, and the program of activities for the two-day event at the hotel.

The annual reunion had its own set of rituals and celebrations, including special getting-to-know-you games, prizes and awards for outstanding family achievements, and a huge family tree where everyone could trace his or her connections. The highlight of the weekend was a formal banquet in the grand ballroom of the hotel. Significant life-cycle events and accomplishments were celebrated at this banquet for the entire extended clan to appreciate and admire. New babies were introduced, newly married couples, and graduations, promotions, even the loss of beloved family members were acknowledged. We watched these proceedings with fascination and envy. Our informants told us that the phenomenon of family reunions is getting bigger every year, and that there are books, magazines, and a host of other resources available to assist neophytes in creating their own reunions.

We had our own version of an extended family reunion for about ten years. Our cousin started it and kept it going. The boundaries were looser though and included his friends and neighbors. We haven't met now for about three years. In our immediate family we have a series of rituals that we've managed to preserve and accumulate through the years; some from Judaism, some from yoga, and some from personal-growth workshops we've taught or attended. Our family Chanukah party is a ritual of gift unwrapping (especially for our nephews, Andrew, Leo, and Michael) and a re-creation of the kindling of the lights as we remember the stories of our Jewish heritage.

Barbara, Joel's wife, commented that for Leo and Michael, the best traditions are the ones that stay the same each year. For example, almost every year the family attends an August family retreat at the Omega Institute that includes outdoor activities and adventures. Adults and children alike get to play. "When we alter the tradition too much, the children balk. They don't mind going away and doing something different, as long as that's what we do every year at the same time. Then they get into a routine and know what to expect."

Leo and Michael have also come to love their annual expedition to the Berkshires, where they play at Hawk Meadow Farm, ride our friend Richard's tractor, and hike October Mountain with his llamas. Although we might think it's only adults who thrive on ritual and repetition, it seems that children need that same stability to balance the newness of their continually changing life adventure.

Ashley, a student in one of Marjory's classes, described a family ritual unique to her extended family. Every year, in mid-October, she and her two sisters and two brothers, her parents, grandparents, and assorted cousins, aunts, and uncles gathered for a long weekend on a small island off the coast of Florida. At this time, they celebrated birthdays and had their Thanksgiving turkey dinner. This student found nothing unusual in celebrating Thanksgiving in October. Her family had been doing it for as long as she and her siblings could remember. The clan gathered from all over the country. There was no problem booking flights, reserving rooms in the island's small inns and hotels, and enjoying off-season prices, semideserted beaches, and so on. This annual gathering was the high point of her family calendar; an event anticipated with that same mix of longing and dread many of us experience as we approach family celebrations.

Now we turn to the rituals and activities that mark and define your family's seasons and rhythms.

Setting the Stage

Sit back, relax, and put up your feet. Begin to reflect on the things you do with your brothers and sisters every year.

Exploration 9-1 What Are My Family Rituals?

What you will need:

Sibling journal; 15 minutes

Lists and landmarks: First, create a list of events. Also list the holidays or special events that consistently bring you together.

What draws you and your brothers and sisters together? It may be visiting Mom in the nursing home, watching the new Little League pitcher in the family at a big game, or helping out weekends in your brother's new restaurant.

Now create a list of things that are "ritual behavior" though not necessarily repetitive. You may not do them in cycles, but whenever you come together, these are also part of the family pattern.

For example, in the Levitt family, when we are together, we invariably make fun of one another and lovingly dwell on our habits or weaknesses, finding ways to make jokes about them. We also tend to give gifts to one another fairly regularly, though Marjory might insist that it's not regularly enough.

Rescripting the play: Write down rituals or events that are now becoming family tradition.

For example, we have recently taken two family vacations, one in Key Largo to swim with dolphins and celebrate Marjory's fiftieth birthday, and the second at Lake Mohonk in upstate New York to work on our book and have a family holiday. This could very well turn into a new tradition for us.

Imaginary lives: Write several examples of things you wish were part of your family's tradition but are not at the moment.

For example, you really would like to spend Christmas with your brother and sister each year but owing to geography, it's too costly to bring the whole family together.

Also make note of rituals and traditions that no longer serve you and your family.

For example, the champagne toast may be inappropriate for a family with a member or members in recovery.

Reflections: Take a few minutes to review your list. See if there is any pattern or noteworthy cycle in what you see.

Remember that some of our family rituals are barely visible, buried in tradition. Now relax, and let this information simmer for a bit.

continued

As a final step, add in anything that would make this picture complete for you, and make note of anything that interests you or strikes you as important.

What Happened

How many of your friends or family take a constructive approach to the rituals they participate in? Most of the time our response shows up as a complaint. "Do we have to go to that Christmas dinner? Your uncle gets drunk and insults us. And the children hate it." In this exploration we first list the rituals we participate in and then decide which ones support and nurture us and which tend to be negative experiences. From there we're free to consider what we'll discard and what we'd like to add.

Inventing Customs That Nurture Us

As described earlier, we are born into our families and the particular set of circumstances that surround us. Without thinking, we accept preparations for first communion, confirmation, or bar/bat mitzvah, the way we celebrate (or avoid) holidays, and many more transitional events in our lives. Rarely do we consider our roles in shaping these events and the possibility of altering them to suit our changing needs. However, it is possible to adapt important life transitions and give our personal stamp to them. Much of this is natural in any family's lifecycle as the next generation steps up to keep the family traditions going. We suggest that you evaluate existing rituals and celebrations and begin to adjust and adapt them to meet your new vision of relationship.

A case in point is the way we came together to mark the transitions in our father's life. Some ten years ago he was diagnosed with Alzheimer's disease. For a good period of time he remained with the family. When his condition worsened and he began to deteriorate, we started assisting Mom to find him a nursing home.

After all the painful details were complete and Dad was transferred from the hospital, we three sat down on the third floor of Joel's house and created a ceremony from scratch. Marjory brought her tape deck and some workshop songs to play. Each of us took a turn describing our connections to Dad. I remember Joel expressing some anger that things were not complete between them. He hadn't said all he needed to say and was feeling cheated of Dad's love. Marjory expressed her disappointment that at such a critical moment of her life—stepping out into the world to receive her doctorate—Dad could not be present to witness her triumph. All of us cried when we finished the ritual sharing with the song "The Leader of the Band."

Similarly, when we received news that Dad had suffered a stroke in November 1998, the three of us joined him at the nursing home. For the last eight hours of his life, we sang his favorite songs, told him stories and jokes, and, in his final transition, prayed that he might surrender to God. There was no other ceremony we could possibly have invented to help him die. This one arose spontaneously from each of us. As much as an expression of our love for him, it also reminded us of the love and strength that we draw from our ongoing relationship with one another.

Tracy, who manages an electronics outlet and comes from a large family, shares some of their rituals and practices growing up in Iowa:

The main thing I remember hearing in our family were the words "Do unto others . . ." My father was an army chaplain who later became a manager for AT&T. Believe it or not, he and Mom put all twelve of us through college. But we were raised strictly. We always heard quotes from the Bible; we had curfews and confessions, nightly prayers and progress reports. And we all split the housekeeping. If one of us missed a chore, all twelve were grounded. So you can bet we kept on top of things. I think this type of upbringing gave us a unique kind of closeness; we learned to stick together early on. To this day Mom still organizes semiannual parties, one in December and one in June. In December we celebrate all the kids' birthdays from August through January; in June we celebrate all the birthdays from February to July. Of course the December party encompasses Christmas, and June all the weddings and graduations for that year. With twelve siblings, thirty-eight grandchildren, and seventeen great-grandchildren, that's a lot of gift-giving.

Having strengthened your sibling relationships and recognized the tour de force that you are as a family unit, you can begin to alter your responses to these key events in your lives in a conscious and purposeful way. In the following exercise, you have an opportunity to rethink some of your family rituals and gatherings, deliberate on the kind of outcome you want, and then invent the new rituals, prayers, or storytelling that suits you. An interesting side effect of this is that these retooled holidays build strength into your family. The more personal satisfaction you can design in, the more enjoyable the family gathering.

Nicole and Delores, mentioned in earlier chapters, frequently invent new rituals and celebrations. It seems that Nicole, with her flair for designing things (as an interior decorator), is always bringing the thirteen siblings together in creative ways. She recounts their millennium celebration in Georgia:

I knew we had to be together for this incredible event. So I spoke to Delores. She agreed to host the big evening party at her house, so we danced and drank and ate hors d'oeuvres under a big tent. It was incredible. We stayed up so late I was afraid no one would show up for my breakfast bash the next day. But that didn't stop anyone. At ten o'clock in the morning folks were lined up for hash browns, omelets, and Luke's famous Belgian waffles. Then later that evening all thirteen of us gathered in my living room. I asked everyone to go around, in no particular order, and pick a brother or sister. Tell them what you want them to hear. How they've changed or matured. Or what gift have they brought to your life? I was shocked when Jackie said to me, "All right, Nicole, you get to go first." I certainly hadn't planned it that way. But she said to me, "I love the way you organize us." Andrew told me how much of a mom I was to him. Holly loved the fact that I helped her design her new home. Evan said I always put us on our edge. And Roberta commented that my faith was incredible. On and on it went round the circle. Each one of us got to acknowledge and thank every brother or sister. Admittedly, sometimes I had to intervene and get them to look into each other's eyes when they were speaking. But then they made up for it by making fun of me. "Hey, teach," Andrew would say. "You gonna grade us at the end?"

The best part of all came around ten P.M. when it was Evan's turn. Evan's had problems with substance abuse for years. He's second to the youngest and the only one who's had a hard time making a living. Evan relies on Holly, Luke, or me to help him out. Luke's 48, and has made out really well; he does sportscasts and works as a TV anchor. We went all the way round the circle and he was the last one to speak.

Luke told Evan, "I won't let you stay in my house anymore because I don't trust you. We both know you've taken things from me in the past. But I'm ready to drop it at a moment's notice. All I need is evidence that you're getting your life together. You're so gifted with children; my kids adore you. And you're a bright light, like a poet or a visionary. I want you to know that I'm always here for you. There's no place else you have to go and no one who cares for you like your brothers and sisters." At that point, after so many good wishes and so much realness, Evan cried like a baby. We stayed with him for an hour, and at the end, we could all see something new in his eyes.

Not all rituals require a large number of family members to be effective. Small groups of siblings, or parents and siblings, can make up worthwhile events. Often, owing to the very nature of small families, rituals and celebrations become very important, since no one wants to lose track of one another and the events give us opportunities for coming together.

Cynthia, a friend of the family, began a new tradition when she had her own children. She was the only surviving member of her family. She worked through her husband's family, literally scattered all over the world, so that they now have brand-new holiday traditions including summertime children exchanges (her children go to Germany to spend two weeks with her brother-in-law and sister-in-law, and her niece and nephew come here). They alternate Christmas visits—one year in the United States, one year in Germany. The grandparents have happily joined in, and now both sides of this international extended family are fluent in German and in English.

Holiday Fun with the Explorations

Believe it or not, some of the explorations in this book can be used as family games during holiday visits. You can involve all generations because the youngest will appreciate having a window onto their heritage (or at least a few minutes' time-out between video games). Your parents, aunts, and uncles may also enjoy getting involved in these games. In addition, feel free to adapt or change these explorations or remove any material that might offend family members.

Setting the Stage

Many people, particularly seniors, enjoy talking about the past. These exercises can be fun for the whole family. Even school-age children can play these games with their young lives. Most of the explorations that follow are memory games about past times you shared with your siblings. Please use judgment in cases of abuse or trauma during that period (even if it was not necessarily caused by any of the siblings).

Chapter and Exploration	Short Description
1-5	First memories of each sibling.
1-7	Growing up on (your address) street.
3-1	Redo the exploration: "My Future Sibling Connection" to "The Most Fun Family Vacation" (regardless of cost).
6-1	Legends of Your Family. Ask which are the most important stories in your family.
7-1	How we're the same; how we're different.
8-2	Acknowledging each other. If the mood is right, this makes for a great Thanksgiving activity. Try a round robin and ask everyone to acknowledge someone else at the table.
9-1	What are my family rituals? Ask each person what were his or her favorite rituals/celebrations from the past and why.

Setting the Stage

Did you ever wonder where rituals came from? Some rituals, such as Christmas, reach back thousands of years. Some are only a few years old and don't have deep reasoning behind them. For example, Santa Claus used to be dressed in green in the early 1900s, but Coke advertising designers decided that red went better with their logo colors. As a result, we have a red Saint Nick.

As we have continually stressed, you have the power and the freedom to change, redesign, or make up completely new rituals. Consider a family event or transition for which you would like to create a personalized ceremony. It may be your sister's marriage, your brother's promotion, or another family member's retirement. As the examples above illustrate, you and your siblings can celebrate *anything*. Only your imagination and your desire limit you.

Exercise 9-2 Inventing a New Ritual
What you will need:

Sibling journal; an event; your calendar;
30 minutes or more if others are involved

If siblings are up for it, plan a time to meet (or gather ideas via a conference call or e-mail exchange).

You can refer to your notes from the prior exercise to give you a place to begin.

Rescripting the play: Create an outline of a new ritual and discuss what you'd each like to contribute.

If others simply rely on you to call the shots, then decide what kind of ritual might be pleasing to everyone and make a brief sketch of it.

Pow-wow: Decide what elements you'd like to include, particularly those reminiscent of your

A good singer or musician may be called upon to create a new song. The family artist may need collective experience, or those that draw upon skills and talents already in the family.

After you've gone through the initial experience, see what elements can be repeated or revived for future celebrations.

to design a special scrapbook of the event. Make sure everyone has his or her say and feels included.

Make notes in your journal and affirm the benefits you derive from this shared experience.

What Happened

Rituals that grow organically seem best. The first time you design and produce a ritual, look for people's honest additions, deletions, and modifications. As more people in the family have their say, the ritual will leave your hands and become part of the family's tradition. And after all, that's the goal!

Example

When our folks were approaching their fiftieth wedding anniversary, we three put our heads together. We wanted to celebrate them in grand tradition, and at the same time we were eager to do something different, a bit quirky (to match our quirky personalities). Rather than just the traditional big dinner party or the evening out in a restaurant, we came up with a special combination surprise: take everyone for a ride down the Delaware River on the boat *Spirit of Philadelphia*. For us this choice had special relevance because it was a longtime habit of Dad's to make corny jokes about the neighboring town "Marcus Hook." He would mix it up with Peter Pan and say to us, "Don't Mark us, Hook." At other times we'd pile into the car for a family outing, and no matter where we were actually going, Dad would say, "Okay kids, you ready for a trip to Marcus Hook?" So now on their fiftieth, Dad's two-hour cruise passed that fabled town. Mom got to have all her friends and family on board, watching snippets of Broadway shows, eating roast beef, and taking home lovely souvenirs: T-shirts with the white and blue outlines of the Philadelphia skyline, and SPIRIT OF PHILADELPHIA screened over a black background. On the backs of the T-shirts: WE SAILED TO MARCUS HOOK—May 15, 1995—HAPPY ANNIVERSARY, SEMOND AND SOPHIE LEVITT.

There was something very fulfilling about creating this particular event honoring our parents. People had a means to join in our celebration. We got to capture a moment in time that was important to us all. Besides these big-time events, there are also small gatherings and transitions that deserve your attention. Consider what changes you might make that would perk up family events. Perhaps the easiest thing is to ask yourself: "What would make it fun? What would help me feel more connected?" If you have your own children and grandchildren, you may also want to ask: "What would bring love, connection, and fun into the lives of my children?"; "What do I want them to remember about family times?"

Ben, one of our workshop participants, told us of a family event he and his twin brother, Aaron, planned to celebrate their parents' retirement and move to Israel. Knowing that they might not be able to spend much time together in the future, the twins videotaped an inventory of family thoughts, feelings, places, and memories. At a farewell dinner the twins gave for their parents, they showed this video to the assembled guests. They made copies for everyone in the family, and at regular intervals the stateside siblings update the video and send it on to their parents. Now that the twins are on-line and digital, they e-mail the latest family shots to Israel and keep in regular touch that way. The grandparents get to enjoy up-to-the-minute digital news flashes about each grandchild's growth and development.

Again, in the creation of new family rituals, let your

imagination be your guide. Engage your brothers and sisters! Invent a ritual where you gather annually to create new rituals.

You may find that your siblings are more creative than you imagined. Talk to them about inventing new games. If there are children in the picture, involve them. Also, on the next holiday or family gathering, you may want to sample our version of Sibling Picture Charades.

Sibling Picture Charades

Gather together in a small circle with paper, pen, and scorecard. One of you chooses a familiar family scene and draws it out in secret. Everyone tries to guess the scene. If you have a big family, you may decide to play this game in teams. Choose family events that everyone remembers, such as significant birthdays, holidays, or special vacations.

Releasing Outmoded Family Rituals

Every so often it becomes important to consider what tasks you perform as a family that are mechanical or meaningless. Sometimes this may be painful to acknowledge; most of us want the ritual to carry on without having to rock the boat. Perhaps the whole family drinks too much at Christmas and you're tired of dealing with the aftermath. Perhaps Thanksgiving is too much turkey and not enough camaraderie. It takes courage and care to consider changing or eliminating certain events.

Setting the Stage

Rituals bind us to the core sources of meaning in our lives. Having empty, meaningless, or toxic rituals may be worse than having none at all. Before you discard a ritual that is not working, consider transforming it into something that suits you better. One test is to imagine yourself twenty-five years in the future without that particular ritual. Did you discard it prematurely? Maybe it was the right time to let it go.

Exploration 9-3 Revise or Rule Out
What you will need:
Sibling journal; 15 minutes

Lists and landmarks: Take a few moments to consider each of your rituals or holiday traditions. Which do you find difficult, draggy, or empty of meaning?

Reflections: Take a moment to reflect on your alternatives. Write a few notes to that effect.

Is there some way that you might change or alter your participation to make the event work for you?

Rescripting the play: If you cannot create an experience of value and being present provides too much conflict or uneasiness, consider the effect of dropping out altogether.

Take a look at the ritual from the point of view of the other participants, too. How do your parents, children, relatives, and friends feel about this issue?

Lights, Camera, Action: Create a plan of action for either of these alternatives.

Consider ways to communicate your decision that will help others understand and not feel alienated from you.

Imaginary lives: In your newfound freedom, begin to think of rituals or celebrations that would have more meaning.

Return to the basics of exercise 8-2 for inspiration.

What Happened

This can be a scary exploration because, in some cases, you have to take sides or stand your ground alone. In most cases we hope you can transform the event, inject meaning, find the "good" core. However, some events are so toxic or conflicted that the best thing to do is to rule them out. In either case, the key is to communicate your intention without blame or judgment. You can reserve the right to return at a later time when this ritual becomes less toxic for you, if you choose.

Rituals for Friends and Extended Family

The same attention to detail in family rituals also applies to our friends, extended family, and those who partner with us in peer or siblinglike relationships. We need our celebrations, acknowledgments, and rituals for coming together, as well as for moving on.

Ruth, one of Jo Ann's co-workers, tells of a tradition among her friends that was unexpectedly organized by her husband fifteen years ago, as a demonstration of his love. It was early spring; their toddler was just a year old, and Ruth's husband, Ray, told her to get things in order because he was expecting a visit from his parents that weekend. Surprised but not intimidated, Ruth cleaned the house and shopped for the meals. Friday came, and much to her surprise, so did five of her friends—from all over the country.

By the time Ruth and her friends had comfortably settled in, Ray picked up their daughter and said, "Have a great weekend, ladies. Here's where you can reach me." Two days later, Ruth and her friends had had such a good time that they decided to institute a yearly get-together, traveling to one another's homes around the country. For the sake of variation, they spent one spring vacation at Disney World and one fall on a cruise to the Greek islands. (Melanie, the accountant among them, insisted on being the money collector and made up a schedule so that they could actually save for the cruise over a period of five years.) And finally, this past year, they all came together, had manicures and pedicures, spinning and step classes, and celebrated their fifteenth annual reunion at a fancy spa!

Ruth is not alone in recognizing the importance of maintaining contact and keeping up traditions with close friends. Most of us create reunions, holiday get-togethers, or special outings to come together and reinforce our connections. Consider that these events are more than placeholders in our lives. The ritual or holiday we celebrate marks the passing of time. Birthdays, weddings, confirmations, or retirement parties help us acknowledge the seasons we're passing through. It's important to keep the big picture present as we make plans. As William Bridges, author of *Transitions*, points out, rituals are important because they fill certain gaps in time:

> In native traditions the young are renewed by rituals of transition. The time-out in the non-place is their gateway to the original chaos from which the gods fashioned the world. All new form must begin in that chaos, and any gap in time or space provides access to it.
>
> Such gaps occur at the end of any cycle. At the end of a year or a season, at the end of any phase in the individual's life, in nature, or in society . . . After a time each is reborn and that is the way in which life sustains itself. It is the way of forgetting and rediscovery. It is the way of ending and beginning. In following it, the person crosses over from an old way of being to a new way of being and is renewed in the process.

Summary

- Family can be a source of stress at holiday times. Those without family feel lonely; those with family often experience the reemergence of old family conflicts.

- Building ritual and tradition into our family structure, particularly around holidays, creates a sense of predictability, ease, and belonging for all family members.

- Although we may think it's only adults who thrive on rituals and repetition, children need that same stability to balance the newness of their continually changing life adventure.

- Although we are born into our family's particular set of traditions and observances, rarely do we consider that we may have a role in changing and shaping these events.

- We suggest you evaluate existing rituals and celebrations and invent or adjust them to align with your new vision of relationship.

Seeds of Change

❑ I am taking a closer look at the observances and rituals we practice as a family.

❑ Those with little meaning are in the process of being released or transformed; new traditions are also being explored and created.

❑ This opportunity to re-create family rituals and observances is yet another means by which I get to interact and know my siblings better.

Grains of Hope, Pearls of Wisdom

✓ I am now feeling empowered to participate more fully in sibling and family life by helping shape or modify some of our rituals and celebrations.

✓ It gives me a sense of peace, joy, and belonging to recognize that what we mutually create has both a history
and a momentum carrying us forward. In other words,
these rituals and ceremonies are evidence of the legacy
we intend to provide our family of the future.

CHAPTER 10

The Sibling Template: From Family to the World

Those you have loved deeply become a part of you.
The longer you live, there will always be more people
to be loved by you and to become part of your inner
community. The wider your inner community becomes, the more easily you will recognize your own
brothers and sisters in the strangers around you. Those
who are alive within you will recognize those who are
alive around you.

Henri Nouwen,
The Inner Voice of Love

From family we move out into the world. Whatever healing
and integration comes about among brothers and sisters es-
tablishes a feeling of connection through which we begin to
sense the whole world as one family. That connection comes
out of being known and accepted by another person. It ful-
fills some of our deepest longings. In our workshops the shift
is apparent to everyone in the room. The shift and feeling of
connectedness does not depend on more visits or more contact (although that may be a logical outcome), but rather depends on a shift in thoughts and feelings. We begin to see
ourselves differently. Then we perceive our brothers and sisters in a different light. What was not possible before we can
now imagine and entertain as a new way of relating to one
another. If nothing else, we consider that worth the price of
this book.

In this final chapter we reinforce the work of the eight
steps. All that you have set in motion now takes on a life of its

own. You had a sibling template, which contributed to the dynamics between you and your brothers and sisters. Through a careful review of your past, of points of rivalry, contact, and interaction, you have in effect reshaped your sibling template so that it aligns more with who you are and what you're capable of giving and receiving in relationship. Having worked the eight steps, not only can you bring transformation to sisters and brothers, you can bring it to any relationship where you give your heartfelt attention.

Setting the Stage

What is left now is to reinforce and strengthen all you have set in motion. That involves a continual process of witnessing the strengths and achievements in one another as well as opening space for differences to show up. At last we can acknowledge that the sibling relationship has a life and momentum of its own. The most compassionate stance we can take now is to allow ourselves to witness it in all its different dimensions and open our hearts so we can be present for whatever shows up.

Exploration 10-1   Revisit Your Process

What you will need:

Sibling journal; ongoing, 10 minutes here and there

Reflection: Reflect on the changes that have taken place during the time you have been involved with this sibling process. Be specific.

Perhaps you completed only a few explorations; perhaps things have not shifted as dramatically as you wished. Take this opportunity to acknowledge yourself for whatever you did and whatever you did not do.

Take time to explore this topic fully in your sibling journal.

Has anything changed for you?

| **Lists and landmarks:** Make notes here about steps you are now ready to take or ideas that emerge for future consideration. | Gather brainstorms, whims, inspirations, and ideas here. |

What Happened

In this exploration, you took time to reflect on whatever changes you witnessed as a result of being involved in this process. It's important to be spacious and generous even with your own evaluation. You may find yourself more relaxed with your brother or more forgiving of your sister's eccentricities. What once may have appeared to be insurmountable differences between you now adds spice or provides something to laugh about over dinner.

As the youngest, Joel has had many insights about his two older sisters:

> It's a rare gift when you have people in your life who are for you. Your parents are but you rarely get to know them like a brother or sister. While I've known that my sisters are for me I somehow got it that they are *really* for me. I feel like I can talk about anything with them. In this process of writing I got to grow up a little and show them (and myself) I'm not just the baby anymore.

Whereas Marjory brought rigor and research to the work, she also brought her characteristic humor and easy interactiveness, and Jo Ann decided she didn't have to be the peacekeeper anymore. Out of these explorations came the realization that the sibling bond has a life and momentum of its own. We can watch it thrive. With time, we can also trust its sturdiness, seeing that it is capable of developing along its own lines. As Jo Ann summed up: "I'm not sure if I know my brother and sister better, or if I just feel freer to be myself.

However, my overriding feeling is one of joy and gratitude for who they each are, for who 'we are' as siblings, and for the good fortune that brought them both into my life."

An Invitation to Break New Ground

Just when you think the work is complete, it suddenly becomes clear that there's more to do. We acknowledge the extraordinary sibling work you've done. At the same time, we offer an invitation to break new ground. There are other relationships, other connections in need of your attention—some from the past, and some that will step forward from your future. Are you willing to apply the same process? You have set in motion an important template for action through the practice of the eight steps; now is the time to translate the sibling template to a broader playing field that encompasses home, community, nation, and the world at large.

Toward the New Paradigm

Now that you're ready to move toward the new paradigm, in truth it must be admitted that what we call "new" is ancient, and is simply an old paradigm of interaction reworked and brought up-to-date. In it we return to the roots of our human involvement and connection. All for one, one for all—as the saying goes. A simple story that came from the Internet elaborates this point:

A few years ago, at the Seattle Special Olympics, nine contestants, all of whom were physically or mentally disabled, assembled at the starting line for the 100-yard dash. At the gun, they all started out, not exactly in a dash, but with a relish to run the race to the finish and win. All, that is, except one little boy who stumbled on the asphalt, tumbled over a couple of times, and began to cry.

The other eight heard him cry. They slowed down

and looked back at the boy. Then simultaneously they all turned around and went back. A girl with Down's syndrome bent down and kissed him, saying, "This will make it better." Then all nine linked arms and walked together to the finish line. Everyone in the stadium stood up and cheered for several minutes nonstop.

People who were there are still telling the story. Why? Because deep down we know this one thing: What matters in life more than winning for ourselves is helping others win, even if it means slowing down and changing our course.

(From an e-mail from LORRAINE KAY 2/16/00)

Stories such as this remind us of our essential relatedness. For a brief moment we pierce the veil of separation and remember that we really live life in common with others. In fact, the terms *community* and *communication* acknowledge within their roots that what we share we share in common.

Hopefully, the era of rugged individualism has run its course. We have diversified and individuated. And following the mergers, acquisitions, agribusiness, and e-commerce that marked the passing of the twentieth century, we come back to a humanizing center. For as we once de-emphasized personal relationships in favor of virtual reality, in all its various guises, we now stand poised on the edge of an interrelatedness of dramatic proportions.

Gradually it dawns on us how much we need our tribes, our families, and our communities to befriend and support us. And we need our relationships to have the kind of sturdiness and reliability that will offset the stresses and demands of our lives. In many ways our communities serve as blood ties; our friends and co-workers as siblings. For no matter how far we expand the boundaries of our electronic world, we can never stray far from our tribal roots.

That brings us full circle. Back to our families, back to our siblings. In a sense, our sibling relationships provide an important template for the future. Just as our relationship to authority develops out of the seeds of the parental paradigm, so our relationship to peers assumes the qualities of our original sibling connection. And relationship to peers is the all-important playing field where we now gather.

This is an invitation to break new ground. We can choose to go back to the original sibling relationship and revive and revitalize its inner workings, and at the same time feel the strengthening within our families of origin that will carry us forward to society at large. Conversely we can observe how our relationships to siblings have influenced friends and co-workers, and use that as a starting point for transforming our other adult connections. Either way, we participate in a new dimension of relatedness.

The New Paradigm

As we have observed through the workings of this book and our accumulated research, we are now moving toward a different organization of society than we've experienced in the past. Undoubtedly we are on our way to a paradigm of relatedness, conceived in the twentieth century but fleshed out and brought vitally alive in the twenty-first. More than the zeitgeist of peer relationships as described in Robert Bly's *The Sibling Society*, we can identify the prevailing mood as one of friendship in the spirit of true brother- and sister-hood.

This paradigm evolves from the changes in family structure, decentralization of the nuclear family, reconsideration of the values of traditional family and romantic love, and the leveling of the hierarchical playing field. All of these changes bring us expressions of affection, loyalty, and community that are best characterized by sibling partnerships, devoid of the intensity and attachment of romantic love, and more egalitarian than the parent-child connection.

So the zeitgeist leans toward enduring friendships. Once upon a time forged in blood, our new relationships lengthen beyond blood ties. What that means for us as siblings is that it is no longer in our interests to see our relationships as necessary or obligatory but rather as a privilege that family life bestowed upon us and as a process that helps us develop deeper ties. Through a conscious and deliberate approach, we transform our ties, yielding even greater fulfillment and relatedness.

A final forecast: We're on the eve of reproducing the sibling template with others. This relationship, which was born out of necessity, can now be fashioned into a deeper bond, into an experience of communal friendship and mutual respect and caring that sustains and supports us through all of life's changes. Not only can we count on our brothers and sisters as a source of strength within the family, they now help us define our relationships outside the family. How we love and care for them is the model through which we come to view the whole world as family.

Thank you,
Jo Ann, Marjory, and Joel

Bibliography

Alpert, Barbara. *No Friend Like A Sister*. New York: Berkley Books, 1996.

Altus, William D. "Birth Order and Its Sequelae." In Urie Bronfenbrenner (ed.). *Influences on Human Development*. Hinsdale, IL: Dryden Press, 1972: 600—611.

Alvarez, Julia. *How the Garcia Girls Lost Their Accents*. Chapel Hill, NC: Algonquin Books, 1991.

Bank, Stephen P., and Michael D. Kahn. *The Sibling Bond*. New York: Basic Books, 1982/1997.

Barks, Coleman, and John Moyne (ed/trans). *The Essential Rumi*. San Francisco: HarperCollins, 1996.

Barovick, Harriet. "Reluctant Referees." *Time*. March 22, 1999: 91.

Bean, Orson. *Too Much Is Not Enough*. Secaucus, NJ: Lyle Stuart, Inc., 1988.

Becker, Selwyn B., Melvin J. Lerner and Jean Carrol. "Conformity As a Function of Birth Order and Type of Group Pressure: A Verification." In Urie Bronfenbrenner (ed.). *Influences on Human Development*. Hinsdale, IL: Dryden Press, 1972.

Biro, David. "Silent Bond." *New York Times Magazine*. October 11, 1998: 94.

Bly, Robert. *The Sibling Society*. New York: Vintage/Random House, 1996.

Borysenko, Joan, Ph.D. *Pocketful of Miracles*. New York: Warner Books, 1994.

Bowlby, John. *Loss: Sadness and Depression*. New York: Basic Books, 1980.

Breunlin, Douglas C. "The Sibling Connection." *Family Therapy Networker*. Jan./Feb., 1994: 25.

Bridges, William. *Transitions: Making Sense of Life's Changes*. Reading, MA: Perseus Books, 1998.

Brody, Gene H. (ed.) *Sibling Relationships: Their Causes and Consequences*. Norwood, NJ: Ablex Publishing Co., 1996.

Brody, Gene H. "Sibling Relationship Quality: Its Causes and Consequences." *Annual Review of Psychology* 49, no. 1 (1998): 1–24.

Brown, Dennis. "Fair Shares and Mutual Concern: The Role of Sibling Relationships." *Group Analysis: Journal of Group Analytic Psychotherapy* 31, no. 3 (September 1998): 315–26. London: Sage.

Brunori, Luisa. "Siblings." *Group Analysis: Journal of Group Analytic Psychotherapy*. 31, no. 3 (September 1998): 307–14. London: Sage.

Carlson, Randy. *The Cain and Abel Syndrome*. Nashville,TN: Thomas Nelson, 1994.

Carter, B., and M. McGoldrick. (eds.). *The Changing Family Life Cycle: A Framework for Family Therapy*. (2nd ed.). NY: Gardner Press, 1998.

Castañeda, Carlos. *The Wheel of Time*. Los Angeles: LA Eidolona Press, 1998.

Cicirelli, Victor G. "Sibling Relationships in Middle and Old Age." In Gene H. Brody (ed.). *Sibling Relationships: Their Causes and Consequences*. Norwood, NJ: Ablex Publishing Co., 1996: 47–74.

Colapinto, Jorge. "Structural Family Therapy." In A. S. Gurman and D. P. Kniskern (eds.). *Handbook of Family Therapy*, II. New York: Brunner/Mazel, 1991.

Cummings, e.e. In *ee cummings: Complete Poems 1904–1962*. (ed. George Firmage) New York: Liveright Publishing, 1991.

Curtis, Natalie (ed.). *The Indian's Book*. Avenel, NJ: Portland House, 1987.

Dornstein, Ken. "Where My Brother Fell to Earth." *The New Yorker*. December 21, 1998: 42–46.

Eacott, Madeline J. "Memory for the Events of Early Childhood." *Current Directions in Psychological Science* 8, no. 2 (April 1999): 46–49. *Journal of the American Psychological Society*. Malden, MA: Blackwell Pubs. 1999: 46–49.

Ellwood, Robert. "A New Look at the Three Objects: Universal Brotherhood." *The Quest. Journal of the Theosophical Society*. July/August 1999: 140–43.

Erikson, Erik H. *Identity, Youth, and Crisis*. New York: W. W. Norton, 1968.

Esquivel, Laura. *Like Water for Chocolate*. New York: Anchor/Doubleday, 1989/1992.

Fishel, Elizabeth. *Sisters: Shared Histories, Lifelong Ties*. Berkeley, CA.: Conari Press, 1979/1994.

Franks, Lucinda. "Annals of Childhood: Miracle Kid." *The New Yorker*. May 17, 1999: 68–77.

Frazer, James George. *The Golden Bough*. New York: Collier/McMillan, 1922/1950.

Freud, Anna, and Sophie Dann. "An Experiment in Group Upbringing." In Urie Bronfenbrenner (ed.). *Influences on Human Development*. Hinsdale, IL.: Dreyden Press, 1972: 449–73.

Freud, Sigmund. *Group Psychology and the Analysis of the Ego* (ed./tr. James Strachey). New York: W. W. Norton, 1959.

Gallagher, Nora. "Things Seen and Unseen." *Doubletake*. Fall 1998: 24–26.

Ginsberg, Herbert, and Sylvia Opper. *Piaget's Theory of Intellectual Development*. Englewood Cliffs, NJ: Prentice-Hall, 1969.

Gladis, Mariah F. *Exact Moments of Healing*. Unpublished manuscript. 1999.

Gladwell, Malcolm. "Annals of Behavior: Do Parents Matter?" *The New Yorker*. August 17, 1998: 54.

Hanh, Thich Nhat. *The Sun, My Heart*. Berkeley, CA: Parallax Press, 1988.

———*Going Home*. New York: Riverhead Books, Penguin Putnam, 1999.

Harding, M. E. *Women's Mysteries: Ancient and Modern*. New York: G. P. Putnam's Sons, 1971.

Harrison, Jim. "First Person Female." *New York Times Magazine*, May 16, 1999: 98–101.

Helligar, Jeremy, Danielle Morton, and Sue Miller. "Family Matters." *People Magazine*. March 1, 1999: 93–100.

Helligar, Jeremy, Natasha Stoynoff, Jennifer Longley, Beverly Keel, Julie Jordan, Helena Bachman, and Josie Ballenger. "Against All Odds." *People Magazine*. June 14, 1999: 108–116.

Hochman, Gloria. "No Fault Parenting." *Philadelphia Inquirer Magazine*. December 1, 1996: 12.

Hoyt, Carolyn. "She's a Stupid Little Brat!" *Good Housekeeping Magazine*. October 1999: 86–87.

Kahn, Michael D., and Karen G. Lewis. *Siblings in Therapy*. New York: W. W. Norton, 1988.

Kerr, Michael E. "Family Systems Theory and Therapy." In A. S. Gurman and D. D. Kniskern (eds.). *Handbook of Family Therapy* vol. I. 1981: 226–64.

Klagsbrun, Francine. *Mixed Feelings: Love, Hate, Rivalry and Reconciliation Among Brothers and Sisters*. New York: Bantam, 1992.

Kurosawa, Akira (director). 1950. *Rashomon* (video), available from Embassy Home Entertainment, 1901 Ave. of the Stars, Los Angeles, CA 90067.

Leder, Jane Mersky. *Brothers and Sisters: How They Shape Our Lives*. New York: Ballantine Books, 1991.

Lederer, Richard. "On Language: Playing with a Full Deck." *New York Times Magazine*. August 27, 1998: 22.

Lee, Li Young. *Rose*. Rochester, NY: BOA Editions, 1986.

Levine, Stephen. *Healing into Life and Death*. Garden City, NY: Anchor Press/Doubleday, 1987.

Levine, Stephen and Ondrea. *Embracing the Beloved: Relationship As a Path of Awakening*. New York: Anchor Press/Doubleday, 1996.

Levitt, Joel. *Internet Guide for Maintenance Management*. New York: Industrial Press, 1998.

Lozoff, Bo. *Deep and Simple: A Spiritual Path for Modern Times*. Durham, NC: Human Kindness Foundation, 1999.

Mann, Susan. "Surviving the Fault Line." *Hope Magazine*. Spring 1999: 52–55.

Maratos, Jason. "Siblings in Ancient Greek Mythology." *Group Analysis* 31, no. 3 (1998): 341–50.

Markowitz, Laura R. "Shared Passages." *Family Therapy Networker*. Jan/Feb. 1994: 18–29, 66–69.

Max, D. T. "House of Cards." *New York Times Magazine*. March 28, 1999: 34–39.

McGoldrick, Monica. "Women and the Family Life Cycle." In B. Carter and M. McGoldrick (eds.). *The Changing Family Life Cycle*. New York: Garden Press, 1988: 29–68.

McInerney, Jay. "The Grape Rush: How Mondavi Uncorked California." *The New Yorker*. September 28, 1998: 96–100.

McKibben, Bill. "What Only-Child Syndrome?" *New York Times Magazine*. May 3, 1998: 48.

McQuaid, Peter. "Four Brothers Walking on Air." *New York Times Magazine*. March 21, 1999: 31.

Mead, Margaret. *Male and Female*. New York: William Morrow, 1949.

Merkin, Daphne. "Smart Alecks: Chilling with the Coen Brothers." *The New Yorker*. March 23, 1998: 98–99.

Merrell, Susan Scarf. *The Accidental Bond: How Sibling Connections Influence Adult Relationships*. New York: Fawcett/Columbine, 1995.

Moorman, Margaret. "My Sister's Keeper." *Family Therapy Networker*. Jan/Feb. 1994: 41–47.

Myles, Eileen. "Mothers and Daughters." *Civilization*. Dec./Jan. 1998/1999: 92.

Myss, Carolyn A., and C. Norman Shealy. *The Creation of Health*. Walpole, NH: Stillpoint Publishing, 1993.

Nelson, Antonya. "Party of One." *The New Yorker*. (Fiction Issue.) June 1999: 140–49.

Nouwen, Henri. *The Inner Voice of Love*. New York: Image Books/Doubleday, 1998: p. 59.

Novick, Sheldon M. "The Temptation of the Sublime." *Doubletake*. Winter 2000: 17–21.

Opler, Morris E. *An Apache Life Way*. New York: Cooper Square, 1965.

Ornish, Dean, M.D. *Love and Survival*. New York: HarperCollins, 1998.

Paterson, Andy, and Nicholas Kent (producers). 1998. *Hilary and Jackie* (video), October Films, Film Four, and Intermedia Films, 1998. Distributed by Polygram Video, New York, NY.

Paulhus, Delroy L., Paul D. Trapnell, and David Chen. "Birth Order Effects on Personality and Achievement Within Families." *Psychological Science*. 10 no. 6 (1999): 482–88. *Journal of the American Psychological Society*. Malden, MA: Blackwell Pubs.

Peterson, Brenda. *Sister Stories: Taking the Journey Together*. New York: Penguin, 1996.

Quindlen, Anna. "Siblings: Life's Most Complex Relationship." *Philadelphia Inquirer Magazine*. November 1, 1998: 11–19.

Reiner, Carl (director). 1990. *Sibling Revelry* (video), available through Castle Rock Entertainment in association with Nelson Entertainment, 335 N. Maple Drive, Beverly Hills, CA 90210.

Riedmann, Agnes, and Lynn White. "Adult Sibling Relationships: Racial and Ethnic Comparisons." In Gene H. Brody (ed.) *Sibling Relationships: Their Causes and Consequences*. Norwood, NJ: Ablex Publishing Co., 1996: 105–26.

Rothbart, Mary K. "Birth Order and Mother-Child Interaction in an Achievement Situation." In Urie Bronfenbrenner (ed.). *Influences on Human Development*. Hinsdale, IL: Dryden Press, 1972.

Safer, Jeanne. "Must You Forgive?" *Psychology Today*. July/August, 1999: 30–33, 70–73.

Saline, Carol, and Sharon J. Wohlmuth. *Sisters*. Philadelphia, PA: Running Press, 1994.

Sandmaier, Marian. *Original Kin: The Search for Connection Among Adult Sisters and Brothers*. New York: Dutton, 1994.

Satir, Virginia. *Peoplemaking*. Palo Alto, CA: Science & Behavior Books, 1972.

Seuss, Dr. (Theodore and Audrey Geisel). *I Had Trouble in Getting to Solla Sollew*, New York: Random House, 1965.

Sleek, Scott. "Blame Your Peers, Not Your Parents, Author Says." *APA Monitor*. October 1998: 9. American Psychological Association.

St. Michel, Carrie. "Genetic Tricks and Treats." *Good Housekeeping Magazine*. October 1999: 242.

Stewart, Robert, Andrea Kozak, Lynn Tingley, Jean Goddard, Wendy Cassel, and Elissa Blake. "Adult Sibling Relationships: A Comparison Across the Late Adolescence to Late Adulthood Years." Presentation: Conference on Human Development. Birmingham, AL: April 1996. Available at http://www.oakland.edu/~stewart/agetype.html

Stewart, Robert, Jean Goddard, Renee Rumsley, Andrea Kozak, and Lynn Tingley. "Siblings, Best Friends, and Significant Others: A

Comparison of Interpersonal Relationships from Adolescence to Late Adulthood." Presentation at the Biennial Meeting of the Society for Research in Child Development, Washington, D.C., April 1997. Available at http://www.oakland.edu/~stewart/sibbfso.html

Stewart, Robert, Lynn Tingley, Andrea Kozak, and Jean Goddard. "An Analysis of Sibling Association Across the Lifespan and Between Different Types of Sibling Relationships." Manuscript in progress 1997. Available at http://www.oakland.edu/~stewart/sibcontact.html

Strauss, Alix. "The Joy of Funerals." *New York Times Magazine.* November 29, 1998: 148.

Sutton-Smith, Brian, and B. G. Rosenberg. *The Sibling.* New York: Holt, Rinehart and Winston, 1970.

Taibbi, Robert. "Notes From an Only Child." *Family Therapy Networker.* Jan/Feb. 1994: 39.

Tessler, Nancy. "The Other Part of Me." *Family Therapy Networker.* Jan/Feb. 1994: 45.

Toman, Walter. *Family Constellation* (3rd edition). New York: Springer, 1976.

————*Family Therapy and Sibling Position.* Northvale, NJ: Jason Aronson, Inc., 1993.

Von Ziegesar, Peter. "Brothers." *Doubletake.* Winter 2000: 14–16.

Wagner, Karen Dineen. 1999. "Siblings: For Better or Worse." *Psychiatric Times.* May 1999: 34.

Walsh, Froma. "Promoting Healthy Functioning in Divorced and Remarried Families." In A. S. Gurman and D. P. Kniskern (eds.). *Handbook of Family Therapy* vol. II. 525–45. New York: Brunner/Mazel.

Waskow, Howard and Arthur. "Becoming Brothers." *Family Therapy Networker.* Jan/Feb. 30–38.

Wilke, Gerhard. "Oedipal and Sibling Dynamics in Organizations." *Group Analysis* 31, no. 3: 269–82. London: Sage, 1998.

Wooster, E. Gerald. 1998. "The Resolution of Envy Through Jealousy." *Group Analysis* 31, no. 3: 327–40. London: Sage, 1998.

More Depth in the Explorations

Centering Exercises, Meditations, and Relaxation Exercises

Introduction

At this time there are literally hundreds of resources available for those who want to learn more about relaxation, meditation, and centering. Calming the mind and body through some disciplined practice or technique is helpful in every area of life. Ample research demonstrates that taking the time to focus within and consciously cultivate relaxation skills enhances overall health and well-being. As a prelude to or preparation for the exercises in this book, a brief period of deliberate relaxation or meditation is highly recommended. We offer the following as suggestions, especially for those who have little or no experience with meditation/relaxation techniques.

No one technique works for all people. If you try one thing and it doesn't work, try another. Add your personal variations to the suggestions we offer, or invent something of your own. If you have a practice that already works for you, use that. Some of our workshop participants and volunteers substituted a time of prayer, a vigorous jog, a bubble bath, or an aerobics class as prelude to working on the exercises. Jo Ann enjoys seated meditation,

Marjory swims laps, Joel enjoys a long walk. Exploring your preferences will help you to arrive at a practice that suits you.

Any conscious practice designed to help you focus, center, and relax will have the following components:

* A particular time and place, free from distraction.

* A clear intention to shift your state of awareness.

* Comfortable clothing and footwear, or at the very least, loosen tight clothing and slip off your shoes.

* An environment comfortable enough to allow for relaxation (i.e., not too hot, not too cold).

A–1. Essential Relaxation/Centering Exercise

Find a comfortable place and position either sitting or lying down.

* Sit upright with your legs crossed, arms relaxed, hands resting lightly, palms up, on each thigh.

* Sit upright in a chair, your feet planted firmly on the floor, arms relaxed, hands resting lightly, palms up, on each thigh.

* Lie on your back on a mat, rug, or other firm surface, arms relaxed at your sides, hands resting on the floor, palms up.

Allow your eyes to close and begin to focus on your breath. Just notice the rhythm of your breathing, without trying to change anything. Observe your breath. Feel each breath as it enters through your nose and exits through your nose. Can you feel the movement of air at the tip of your nose as your breath enters and exits?

As you observe, allow your breath to deepen and slow down. Continue to pay attention to the rhythm and feeling of your breathing. If thoughts begin to intrude, simply note them, and gently bring your attention back to your breath.

* Include a mantra, prayer, or special word and repeat it, silently, as you continue to breathe, observe your breath, and

bring your attention back to the breath whenever a thought intrudes.

* Include an image of a peaceful scene, a sacred or special figure, a loved one, and see this image as you inhale, exhale.

* Include specific commands to relax your body, part by part, organ by organ, muscle by muscle.

* Include gentle, nondistracting music in the background.

* Remember—this is *not* a nap!

By setting a timer or allowing yourself to emerge naturally from this time of relaxation, slowly bring yourself back to the present. Open your eyes. You may feel like stretching, moving around. Allow yourself to do so, then turn your attention to the next exercise.

A–2   *Variations on Essential Relaxation Exercise*

* Walking Meditation: Focus on your breath, as above, while consciously and slowly walking in a protected environment, indoors or out. Keep your gaze soft and focused on each footstep. Put all of your attention and energy into your stepping. Feel your heel touch the ground, then the ball of your foot. Last, feel your toes push against the earth to lift your foot and prepare for the next step.

* Movement Meditations: Any movement that pleases you can be used meditatively, as above, with walking. You can turn any activity into a movement meditation by slowing down, turning your full attention to the movement, and remaining in contact with your body throughout the entire movement. Focus on the breath, and gently return to your focus if and when your mind wanders.

* Vigorous Movement As Meditation: Certain traditions have perfected this, such as the Sufis and followers of Rajneesh. Vigorous, repetitive movement is undertaken with the focus

of attention on the inner experience. Be sure to practice
these in a safe place and to avoid strain to the muscles.

* Drawing Meditation: Using a soft pencil and large pieces of
  blank paper, soften your focus, center on your breathing, and
  allow your arm to move, pencil in hand, on the surface of
  the paper. Your goal is to enter into the movement and sen-
  sation of drawing. You may substitute tempera, watercolor,
  or other medium of your choice.

If you are interested in more-detailed training in relaxation and
meditation, we've prepared a list of resources for you. There are
many, many others. The books and cassettes below are a few that
we have found useful, inspiring, or both!

Resources

Boorstein, Sylvia. *Don't Just Do Something. Sit There*. NY: Harper-
Collins, 1996.

Brother Charles. *Synchronicity: Genesis*. Cassette recording. Faber,
VA: M.S.H. Association, 1987.

Goldstein, Joseph. *The Experience of Insight*. Boulder, CO: Shambala, 1983.

Kabat-Zinn, Jon. *Wherever You Go, There You Are*. NY: Hyperion,
1984.

Kornfeld, Jack. *A Path with Heart*. NY: Bantam, 1998.

LeShan, Lawrence. *How to Meditate*. Boston: Little, Brown &
Co., 1999.

Rosenberg, Larry. *Breath by Breath: The Liberating Practice of Insight
Meditation*. Boston: Shambala, 1999.

Additional Resources for Stretching and Relaxation.

The following audio- and videotapes are available through shop
or mail order at Kripalu Center, Box 793, Lenox, MA 01240.

Audiotapes:

Art of Relaxation, Jonathan Foust (Sudhir)

Deep Relaxation, Nischala Joy Devi

Dynamic Stillness, Nischala Joy Devi

Healing Meditations, Sandra Scherer (Dayashakti) and Carolyn Lundeen (Sudha)

Meditations for Overcoming Depression, Joan Borysenko, Ph.D.

Morning and Evening Meditations and Prayers, Joan Borysenko, Ph.D.

The Gentle Series (led yoga), with Rudy Peirce

Touch of Grace (CD and audio), Jonathan Foust (Sudhir)

Yoga of Grace and Light, Grace in Motion, Nancy Foust (Megha)

New You Yoga: Two Guided Experiences, Todd Norian

Yoga for Beginners, Nancy Foust (Megha)

Yoga Breaks for the Person on the Go, Genie Austin (Deva)

Videotapes:

Discovering Kripalu Yoga, led by Nancy Foust (Megha): Two 30-minute experiences for beginners

Transformation! Advanced Yoga Sadhana, led by Todd Norian. (guidance through the five stages of Kripalu Yoga using press points and focused awareness)

Two 30-Minute Yoga Experiences, led by Don Stapleton, Ph.D. (explores the potential of Hatha Yoga to increase vitality and balance in your life)

Kripalu Yoga Gentle, led by Carolyn Lundeen (Sudha) (an excellent series of postures for beginning yoga students)

Kripalu Yoga Dynamic, led by Stephen Cope (Kaviraj) (an excellent series of advanced postures and yoga practices)

APPENDIX B:

Internet Resources

The Internet is an easy and quick place to find resources about any topic including sibling issues. Please note that the Internet changes every day. Old sites go away and change addresses and new ones replace them. Do not be surprised if some of these links are gone by the time you try them.

Some Internet Sites of Interest

There is an excellent site for Americans of African descent. It covers many issues relevant to all families. This link leads to an article on dealing with adult sibling rivalry. "Take small steps to ease adult sibling rivalry."
http://blackfamilies.com/living/family_relationships/adult_rivalry.html

Ohio State University has been sponsoring some in-depth looks at adult sibling relationships. The article "Adult Sibling Relationships," FLM-FS-6-99, by Joyce A. Shriner, Extension Agent, Family and Consumer Sciences, Ohio State University Extension, Hocking County, might be of interest.
http://www.ag.ohio-state.edu/~ohioline/flm99/fs06.html

An interesting site for and by women has different experts answering questions. There are also discussion groups, ads targeted at women, and interesting stories. This story was printed in the "Ask the Psychologist" column. "My sister and I fought as kids, and I'm still jealous and resentful toward her. How can I get past these feelings?" First published in *Chatelaine*'s September 1998 issue. © Catherine Gildiner.
http://www.chatelaine.com/index.html

Oakland University has some interesting material on the adult sibling relationship. The article "Adult Sibling Relationships: A

Comparison Across the Late Adolescence to Late Adulthood Years" was a paper originally presented at the Conference on Human Development, Birmingham, Alabama, April 1996, by Robert B. Stewart, Andrea L. Kozak, Lynn M. Tingley, Jean M. Goddard, Elissa M. Blake, and Wendy A. Cassel.

Contents: Introduction, A Comparison Across Four Stages of Life, The Impact of Birth Order on the Nature of Sibling Relationships, Unraveling the Typologies of Adult Sibling Relationships.
http://www.oakland.edu/~stewart/agetype.html

The resource Web page "Adult Sibling Relationships in Middle Adulthood" was created by Julie Hill, University of Missouri-Columbia, as part of an interactive workshop for undergraduate students in Human Development and Family Studies.
http://web.missouri.edu/~c668934/adult sibling relationships.htm

An interesting article appeared in the University of Queensland *Family Center Journal*, December 1999, "Communication Within Adult Sibling Relationships," by Nicole Doherty. For more information or to participate in her study, please contact Nicole Doherty at the School of Psychology, University of Queensland, on: (W) 3365 7428 or e-mail nicoled@psy.uq.edu.au

The article can be found at:
http://www2.psy.uq.edu.au/~family/Dec99%20words.html

A researcher at the University of Indiana has some interesting projects going on and a great list of articles. The chief investigator is Victoria Hilkevitch Bedford, Ph.D. E-mail bedford@uindy.edu Rank: Associate Professor Specialization: Developmental Psychology. Clinical and Research Interests: Adult Sibling Relationships, Affect and Personal Relationships, Attachment in Adulthood, Family and Aging, Intergenerational Relationships, Social Support, Personal Networks, and Well-Being.
http://psych.uindy.edu/bedford.html

The religious world has a lot to contribute to the discussion of how we treat one another, especially family members. As we discussed, the Bible has several important stories about siblings. The article is titled "How Good and Pleasant It Is When Brothers Live Together in Unity!" Most of us survived a "brutal training" in our preparation for adulthood: living with siblings! Many of us have children in the midst of this "training" right now. God has placed these people in our lives. How can we minister to our siblings and learn from them? How can we help our children benefit from this special relationship?

This site is from the Fields of Ministry: Your Family III [Siblings] Adult Devotions.

http://www.northlandcc.org/salt_light/week_15/week15a.htm

Another religious resource is the Jewish Learning Connection. In the link below, the rabbis discuss the story of Joseph, one of the most difficult sibling stories in the Bible. *Jewish Learning Connection's Weekly Fax Newsletter* 3, issue 9.

* Week of December 19, 1997 / 20 Kislev, 5758

http://www.cleffent.com/vayaishev5758.html

The Oxygen site is a woman-to-woman site with newsgroups, forums, and information of interest to women. They look deeply at all relationship issues and could be a great resource.

http://momsonline.com/asafamily/

One of the saddest moments in life is the burying of a sister or brother. Volunteers have put together an international organization to give comfort to survivors. Compassionate Friends is for people who have lost a brother or sister (or a child).

http://www.inetworld.net/geondebi/tcf.html

For an example of a memorial, visit:

http://www.inetworld.net/geondebi/dee.html

Permissions